Application of Zakat
From Classical and
Contemporary Perspective

Application of Zakat
From Classical and Contemporary Perspective

M Kabir Hassan
University of New Orleans, USA

Magda Ismail Abdel Mohsin
INCEIF University, Malaysia

Aishath Muneeza
INCEIF University, Malaysia

NEW JERSEY · LONDON · SINGAPORE · BEIJING · SHANGHAI · HONG KONG · TAIPEI · CHENNAI · TOKYO

Published by

World Scientific Publishing Co. Pte. Ltd.
5 Toh Tuck Link, Singapore 596224
USA office: 27 Warren Street, Suite 401-402, Hackensack, NJ 07601
UK office: 57 Shelton Street, Covent Garden, London WC2H 9HE

Library of Congress Cataloging-in-Publication Data
Names: Hassan, Kabir, author. | Mohsin, Magda Ismail Abdel, author. | Aishath Muneeza, author.
Title: Application of zakat : from classical and contemporary perspective /
  M. Kabir Hassan, University of New Orleans, USA, Magda Ismail Abdel Mohsin,
  INCEIF University, Malaysia, and Aishath Muneeza, INCEIF University, Malaysia.
Description: USA : World scientific, 2024. | Includes bibliographical references and index.
Identifiers: LCCN 2023027653 | ISBN 9789811276149 (hardcover) |
  ISBN 9789811276156 (ebook) | ISBN 9789811276163 (ebook other)
Subjects: LCSH: Zakat. | Zakat--History. | Islam--Economic aspects.
Classification: LCC BP180 .H373 2024 | DDC 297.5/4--dc23/eng/20230705
LC record available at https://lccn.loc.gov/2023027653

British Library Cataloguing-in-Publication Data
A catalogue record for this book is available from the British Library.

Copyright © 2024 by World Scientific Publishing Co. Pte. Ltd.

All rights reserved. This book, or parts thereof, may not be reproduced in any form or by any means, electronic or mechanical, including photocopying, recording or any information storage and retrieval system now known or to be invented, without written permission from the publisher.

For photocopying of material in this volume, please pay a copying fee through the Copyright Clearance Center, Inc., 222 Rosewood Drive, Danvers, MA 01923, USA. In this case permission to photocopy is not required from the publisher.

For any available supplementary material, please visit
https://www.worldscientific.com/worldscibooks/10.1142/13406#t=suppl

Desk Editors: Balasubramanian Shanmugam/Claire Lum/Yulin Jiang

Typeset by Stallion Press
Email: enquiries@stallionpress.com

We dedicate this book to all our students.

Foreword by Prof. Azmi Omar

Zakat is not only a worship activity for Muslims, but it also provides socio-economic benefits to societies. However, today, we are unable to fully unlock the potentials of the zakat, although it was successfully implemented during the early Islamic period. Over the years, we have witnessed the evolution of zakat administration from community-based to state-based. To ensure zakat is implemented effectively in societies, it is imperative to create awareness about it and to ensure that the human capital required for the purpose is created. Hence, this book is indeed timely.

Through zakat, we can redistribute wealth equitably in our societies. The Islamic economic system encourages those who are wealthy to take care of those who are poor and needy, thereby reducing the gap between the rich and poor. Zakat is one of the important pillars of the Muslim faith, and today, innovative mechanisms with technology are being used in societies to create efficient mechanisms to enhance zakat's role.

This book covers not only the classical rules and application of zakat from a classical perspective, but it also extensively discusses zakat's contemporary applications. I have no hesitation to state that this book will be an important source of information and reference to students, researchers, and practitioners who would like to know about zakat. The simple language used in this book with review questions included at the end of each chapter gives an opportunity for readers to increase their level of understanding about zakat independently.

I take this opportunity to congratulate and thank the authors of this book for initiating and completing this landmark project. I have full confidence that through the knowledge gained from this book, Muslim

Ummah will benefit and, in due course, we will be able to untap the full potentials of zakat. May Allah (SW) give us the strength and the ability to learn from this book and implement what we understand.

Prof. Dato' Dr. Azmi Omar
President and CEO
INCEIF University, Malaysia

Foreword by Prof. Habib Ahmed

With the onslaught of the COVID-19 pandemic, there was a realization that the governments alone are not able to deal with the multiple crises due to the lack of resources. An alternative source of financial resources in Muslim societies is Islamic social finance that has great potential in resolving some of the social welfare problems. However, these social finance sources are not being used optimally. Given that the world faces increased risks that can worsen the economic situation for many, there is a need to activate modes of Islamic social finance in an efficient and effective manner to enhance overall welfare and alleviate poverty.

Islamic teachings have instituted specific social finance instruments that can help to promote equitable distribution of income and enhance social welfare. A key distributive instrument is zakat which is obligatory for all Muslims who have wealth above a threshold level. Based on the worldview that Allah (SW) is the ultimate owner of all resources, zakat is considered as a right of the poor on the wealth owned by people. Being a pillar of Islam, every wealthy Muslim has a religious obligation to give compulsory alms or zakat to eight legal recipients stated in Quran that includes the poor and needy. Zakat is a wealth tax that is levied annually and can be considered as an important tool of socio-economic justice in societies while preserving the integrity of property rights of all individuals.

Today, at a time when activation of Islamic social finance instruments is in the limelight, having a book published focusing on the application of zakat is a timely contribution made by the authors. Therefore, I commend the efforts of all the authors of this book who have made it easy for the readers to understand the significance of zakat by shedding light on the classical and contemporary application of it. Importantly, the authors discuss how modern tools and approaches can be used to enhance the impact of zakat in this digital age. I have confidence that through this book, the readers will be able to obtain useful information about the concept of zakat and its application during contemporary times.

The information provided in this book is not limited to the Shariah rules applicable to zakat, but it also covers various aspects of zakat from a practical perspective by highlighting the key issues and presenting relevant case studies. This book also provides some review questions at the end of each chapter. Though many books have been written on zakat, so far, there are few that can be used as textbooks. This book fills the gap and can be used in academic institutions to teach the subject matter. Since zakat is a timeless concept, I believe that this book will provide endless benefits to Muslim communities in understanding and applying zakat.

Prof. Habib Ahmed
Durham University Business School
2022 IsDB Prize Winner in Islamic Economics

Foreword by Prof. Zainulbahar Noor

Zakat is one of the Islamic social finance instruments that is required to be taught in academic institutions to ensure that the talent pool required to implement it is produced. One of the most critical challenges which are faced today in terms of using zakat effectively in communities is lack of human talent pool with competency and capacity to do so. As such, to unlock the full potential of zakat, it is imperative to assist academic institutes to teach students about zakat in a manner that the students not only understand zakat as an 'ibadat activity for its giver, but they also comprehend the socio-economic impact created by it in societies.

Up until today, we do not have a centralized database established to collect information about zakat collection and zakat disbursement at a global level to understand the real impact it creates. But what we know is that the full potential of zakat is not exploited in the world and we have to work toward it. For instance, it has been reported that in Indonesia, a Muslim-majority country, IDR 327 trillion (USD 20.97 billion) per year needs to be collected as zakat and one could imagine how much poverty can be eradicated via zakat if Muslims collectively in the world holistically disburse zakat to its deserved legal recipients.

Today, zakat is not taught in academic institutions as a subject on its own. However, I strongly believe this is the right time for us to introduce zakat as a subject on its own in academic institutions as this book on zakat alone is sufficient to make this case. If a book can be written exclusively on zakat, then definitely zakat can be taught as a single subject in academic institutions where the students will have the opportunity to learn it in depth enabling them to understand the significance of Islamic finance and economics.

I congratulate the authors of this book for their unabated effort in completing this book successfully. I have no doubt that the readers, researchers, policymakers, and practitioners will benefit from the information provided in this book. May Allah (SW) make this book a source via which reliable information about zakat could be obtained.

Prof. (HC) Dr. Zainulbahar Noor, MEc
Secretary General of the World Zakat and Waqf Forum (WZWF)
Jakarta, Indonesia

Preface

Zakat is the third pillar of Islam. Though zakat is a worship activity fulfilled by the giver, it helps alleviate poverty among the societies by assisting those living in poverty to become financially independent. It is true that the principles of zakat derived from Shariah would remain static irrespective of the time. However, to achieve efficiency in zakat administration, within the parameters of Shariah, even innovation and technology can be used. For students and researchers studying Islamic economics and zakat, it is hard to obtain the contemporary application of zakat from one single book as the books available in the market focus on elaborating the fiqh or jurisprudence of zakat. As such, the objective of this book is to provide the opportunity to learn the basics of zakat and its contemporary application by highlighting innovative practices of it with issues and challenges.

In writing this book, we have given paramount consideration to use simple explanations and to provide opportunities for the readers to do self-evaluation by providing review questions at the end of each chapter. Chapter 1 covers the overview of the institution of zakat, Chapter 2 focuses on the role of zakat in transforming the Muslim societies by shedding light on the developments that have taken place in the past and relating to the contemporary developments as well, Chapter 3 discusses the similarities and the differences between zakat, tax, *sadaqat*, and *waqf*, Chapter 4 provides the types of zakat and zakatable wealth, Chapter 5 discusses the conditions to give zakat, Chapter 6 zooms into the economic impact of zakat, Chapter 7 discusses the calculation of zakat, Chapter 8 focuses on zakat administration, Chapter 9 is on the role of zakat in achieving sustainable development goals, Chapter 10 discusses the use of technology in enhancement of zakat administration, Chapter 11 looks at the zakat development programs, and Chapter 12 discusses the issues and challenges in zakat administration.

It is hoped that this book will be an important source of reference to all those who want to know about zakat and through this book zakat administration will be strengthened in the world. May Allah (SW) increase our knowledge through this book. We also take this opportunity to thank all those who assisted us in completing this project.

About the Authors

M. Kabir Hassan is Professor of Finance in the Department of Economics and Finance at the University of New Orleans. He currently holds three endowed titles: Chairs-Hibernia Professor of Economics and Finance, Hancock Whitney Chair Professor in Business, and Bank One Professor in Business at the University of New Orleans. Professor Hassan is the winner of the 2016 Islamic Development Bank (IDB) Prize in Islamic Banking and Finance. Professor Hassan received his B.A. in Economics and Mathematics from Gustavus Adolphus College, Minnesota, USA, and M.A. in Economics and Ph.D. in Finance from the University of Nebraska-Lincoln, USA, respectively. Dr. Hassan stood first in the combined merit list in the Secondary School Certificate (SSC, equivalent to O level) in 1978 from Comilla Zilla School, Comilla, Bangladesh, in 1978 and Higher Secondary Certificate (HSC, equivalent to A level) in 1980 from Comilla Victoria Government College, Comilla, Bangladesh, in 1980, respectively. Professor Hassan has been selected as a Senior Fulbright Scholar for 2022–2023. He is a financial economist with consulting, research, and teaching experiences in development finance, money and capital markets, Islamic finance, corporate finance, investments, monetary economics, macroeconomics, Islamic banking and finance, and international trade and finance. Professor Hassan has done consulting work for the World Bank, International Monetary Fund, African Development Bank, Transparency International-Bangladesh (TIB), Islamic Development Bank, United Nations Development Program (UNDP), the Bangladesh Bank, the Saudi Arabian Monetary Authority (SAMA), Government of Turkey, and many private organizations. Professor Hassan has been elected as a Board Member of Ethics and Governance Committee and Education Board of the Accounting and Auditing Organization for the Islamic Financial Institutions (AAOIFI). Professor Hassan has recently been appointed as the Distinguished Visiting Professor at the National University of Malaysia (UKM). Dr. Hassan has recently been elected to the Advisory Council of the World Zakat Forum (WZF), 2021–2023. Professor has also been selected to be a member of Oxford University Said Business School faith-based investing initiative advisory board Member in 2021. He has also been selected to be a member of Christian Michelson Institute (CMI) in 2021.

Magda Ismail Abdel Mohsin is currently at INCEIF University, Malaysia, which is known as the global University of Islamic Finance. She obtained her doctorate in Islamic Civilization/Islamic Economy from the International Institute of Islamic Thought and Civilization (ISTAC)/ the International Islamic University Malaysia (IIUM) in 2003. Prior to joining INCEIF in 2007, she taught many subjects in Islamic economics and Islamic finance at the International Islamic College IIC, besides she was appointed as the Head of Economic Department for two years and as Deputy Chief Executive Academic for two years in the same college. She presented many papers at national and international levels held in different countries, such as Washington DC, the UK, Singapore, Maldives, India, Indonesia, Turkey, the UAE, Kuwait, Qatar, Algeria, Tunis, and Sudan besides local conferences in Malaysia. Moreover, she conducted many training sessions on *waqf* and zakat locally and internationally: locally with Redmoney, the International Centre for Waqf Research ICWR, and the International Federation of Red Cross and Red Crescent IFRC, and internationally with IRTI and the National Awqaf Foundation of South Africa in South Africa, the Singapore Institute of Management (SIM) in Singapore, Le Centre Nationale de la Recherche Scientifique in Algeria, BAZNAS in Indonesia, and Bilim Ve Sanat Vakfi in Turkey. With reference to the research, she is the author of the two books on *waqf* entitle: *Cash Waqf: A New Financial Product* and *Corporate Waqf: From Principle to Practice* both published by Pearson Malaysia Sdn. Bhd. 2009 and 2014, respectively. She is also the editor of the latest book on *waqf* entitled *Financing the Development of old Waqf Properties: Classical Principles and Innovative Practices around the World*, Palgrave Macmillan, 2016. Moreover, she has published many articles on *waqf*, zakat, Islamic microfinance, and Islamic economics more recently on fintech and blockchain. Furthermore, she is the recipient of two awards on *waqf* publications: Best/outstanding paper award for the paper "Financing through cash-*waqf*: A new innovation for the 21st Century" and Emerald Group 2013 and Best book *Corporate Waqf: From Principle to Practice* which had been translated into Arabic by Imam Muhammad ibn Saud Islamic University Riyadh, Saudi Arabia, Sheikh Rashid bin Dail Research Chair for Endowments Studies 2015. In 2016, she also received the Outstanding Women Achiever for contribution and achievement in the field of Islamic Economics and Finance, given under the seal of Venus International Foundation, India. In 2018 and 2019, she has been recognized by Cambridge Analytica IF as one of the top 30 most influential women in Islamic finance.

Aishath Muneeza is Professor and Associate Dean for students and internationalization at INCEIF University in Malaysia which is known as the global University of Islamic Finance. She has served as the first female Deputy Minister of Ministry of Islamic Affairs in Maldives, Deputy Minister of Ministry of Finance and Treasury in Maldives, Head of Islamic Finance of Capital Market Development Authority of Maldives, member of Islamic Fiqh Academy (National Fatawa Council of Maldives), first chairman of Hajj pilgrimage fund, Maldives Hajj Corporation Limited, and chairman of Maldives Center for Islamic Finance Limited which was set by the government of Maldives to strategize Maldives as the hub of Islamic finance in South Asia. From 2011 to 2022, she was the chairman of apex Shariah Advisory Council of Capital Market Development Authority of Maldives. She is an elected executive committee member of Bar Council of Maldives.

Contents

Foreword by Prof. Azmi Omar — vii
Foreword by Prof. Habib Ahmed — ix
Foreword by Prof. Zainulbahar Noor — xi
Preface — xiii
About the Authors — xv
List of Figures — xxvii
List of Tables — xxix

1. **Overview of the Institution of Zakat** — 1
   1.1 An Overview on Zakat — 1
     1.1.1 Definition of zakat — 1
     1.1.2 Conditions for zakat givers — 2
     1.1.3 Conditions for zakat recipients — 2
     1.1.4 Restrictions on giving zakat — 2
   1.2 Muslim Scholars' Views on Zakat — 2
   1.3 Objectives of Zakat in Quran — 6
     1.3.1 Objectives of zakat share to its recipients — 6
     1.3.2 Objectives of state to administer zakat — 8
     1.3.3 Objectives of zakat on its givers — 9
     1.3.4 Objectives of zakat on its recipients — 10
     1.3.5 Objectives of zakat in Muslim society — 10
     1.3.6 Objective of zakat as an alternative to *riba* — 10

    1.4 Objectives of Zakat in Sunnah   11
    1.5 Zakat in Religions Prior to Islam   13
    Self-Assessment Quiz (MCQs)   16
    Self-Assessment/Recall Questions   18
    Answers to Self-Assessment Quiz (MCQs)   20

2. **Role of Zakat in Alleviating Poverty in Muslim Societies: Past and Present**   **21**
    2.1 Zakat: A Religious and Social Obligation   21
    2.2 Zakat Socio-financial Products for Alleviating Poverty   22
        2.2.1 Zakat socio-financial product for assisting the Faqir/poor   22
        2.2.2 Zakat socio-financial product for empowering the Miskeen/needy   23
        2.2.3 Zakat socio-financial product for supporting *Amil*/zakat manager   23
        2.2.4 Zakat socio-financial product for supporting Al-Muallafah Qulubuhm   24
        2.2.5 Zakat socio-financial product for liberating fi ar-Riqab/the captives   24
        2.2.6 Zakat socio-financial product for financing Al-Gharimin/debtor   24
        2.2.7 Socio-financial product for assisting fisabilillah causes/for the sake of Allah   25
        2.2.8 Socio-financial product for supporting Ibnus Sabil/stranded during a journey   25
    2.3 Classical Cases in Alleviating Poverty in Muslim's Society via Zakat   25
    2.4 Contemporary Cases in Alleviating Poverty in Selected Muslim Countries   26
        2.4.1 Current role of zakat in Malaysia   27
            2.4.1.1 Meeting the basic needs via zakat   27
            2.4.1.2 Providing healthcare via zakat   27
            2.4.1.3 Supporting education via zakat   28
            2.4.1.4 Providing affordable housing via zakat   29
        2.4.2 Current role of zakat in Indonesia   30
            2.4.2.1 Meeting the basic needs via zakat   30
            2.4.2.2 Settling debtors' loan online via zakat   30
            2.4.2.3 Providing healthcare via zakat   30

		2.4.2.4 Economic program via zakat	32
		2.4.2.5 Reducing poverty via zakat	32
		2.4.2.6 Supporting education via zakat	34
		2.4.2.7 Livestock breeding via zakat	35
		2.4.2.8 Enhancing agriculture via zakat	37
	2.4.3	Current role of zakat in selected countries in Africa	38
		2.4.3.1 Meeting the basic needs via zakat	38
		2.4.3.2 Enhancing agriculture via zakat	38
		2.4.3.3 Humanitarian assistance via zakat	38
		2.4.3.4 Building cities via zakat	39
2.5	Role of Zakat in Eliminating *Riba*		39
	2.5.1	Current situation of compound interest in Muslim countries	39
	2.5.2	Case of zakat through salary deduction scheme	41
Self-Assessment Quiz (MCQs)			43
Self-Assessment/Recall Questions			46
Answers to Self-Assessment Quiz (MCQs)			48

3. Similarities and Differences between Zakat, Tax, *Sadaqat*, and *Waqf* — 49

3.1 Similarities and Differences between Zakat and Taxes		49
3.1.1 Similarities of zakat and taxes		49
3.1.2 Differences between zakat and tax		51
3.1.3 Impact of tax and zakat on Prices		53
3.2 Similarities and Differences between Zakat and *Sadaqat*		55
3.2.1 Similarities between zakat and *sadaqat*		55
3.2.2 Differences between zakat and *sadaqah*		57
3.3 Similarities and Differences between Zakat and *Waqf*		58
3.3.1 Similarities of zakat and *waqf*		58
3.3.2 Differences between zakat and *waqf*		59
Self-Assessment Quiz (MCQs)		61
Self-Assessment/Recall Questions		64
Answers to Self-Assessment Quiz (MCQs)		66

4. Types of Zakat and Zakatable Wealth — 67

4.1 Types of Zakat	67
4.2 Zakat Al-Fitr and Its Objective	68
4.3 Zakat on Wealth	71
4.3.1 Zakat on gold and silver	73

4.3.2 Zakat on agriculture products	74
4.3.3 Zakat on honey	75
4.3.4 Zakat on livestock	75
4.3.5 Zakat on animal products	78
4.3.6 Zakat on fishing	78
4.3.7 Zakat on minerals, buried treasures, and rikaz	78
4.3.8 Zakat on commercial/business inventory	79
4.3.9 Zakat on rented buildings	80
4.3.10 Zakat on fixed capital	80
4.4 Contemporary Issues on Zakatable Assets	80
4.4.1 Zakat on monthly salary	80
4.4.2 Current practices on zakat on monthly salaries	81
4.4.3 Zakat on earning of laborers or professionals	82
4.4.4 Zakat on bonds and shares	83
4.4.5 Zakat on cryptocurrencies	84
4.5 Disregarding Zakatable Wealth in Muslim Countries Today	86
4.5.1 Lack of statistical data on zakat funds	88
4.5.2 Lack of statistical data on zakat collection	88
Self-Assessment Quiz (MCQs)	92
Self-Assessment/Recall Questions	94
Answers to Self-Assessment Quiz (MCQs)	96
5. Conditions to Give Zakat	**97**
5.1 Conditions to Give Zakat	97
5.2 The Procedure to Give Zakat	100
5.3 Zakat Is an Act of Worship to the Giver	103
5.4 Zakat Given to *Amil* of Zakat	106
Self-Assessment Quiz (MCQs)	110
Self-Assessment/Recall Questions	112
Answers to Self-Assessment Quiz (MCQs)	114
6. Zakat Socio-financial Products for Its Recipients and Their Economic Impact	**115**
6.1 Zakat Socio-financial Products via Zakat Recipients	115
6.1.1 Zakat socio-financial products for fuqara and its economic impact	116
6.1.2 Zakat socio-financial products for masakin and its economic impact	118

		6.1.3 Zakat socio-financial products for amilin and its economic impact	119
		6.1.4 Zakat socio-financial products for Muallaf and its economic impact	120
		6.1.5 Zakat socio-financial products for riqab and its economic impact	122
		6.1.6 Zakat socio-financial products for gharimin and its economic impact	123
		6.1.7 Zakat socio-financial products for fisabilillah and its economic impact	125
		6.1.8 Zakat socio-financial products for Ibnu Sabil and its economic impact	125
	6.2	Those Who Are Not Eligible to Receive Zakat	126
		6.2.1 The Prophet's family	126
		6.2.2 Rich people	127
		6.2.3 Relatives of zakat giver	127
		6.2.4 Atheist and Kafir Harbi	128
	Self-Assessment Quiz (MCQs)		129
	Self-Assessment/Recall Questions		132
	Answers to Self-Assessment Quiz (MCQs)		134
7.	**Calculation of Zakat**		**135**
	7.1	Standards Guiding Zakat Calculation	135
	7.2	Approaches in Zakat Calculation	136
		7.2.1 Calculating zakat of business including cash, receivables, and precious metals	136
		7.2.2 Calculating zakat of agricultural produce	137
		7.2.2.1 Standards and guiding principles governing zakat calculation	139
		7.2.2.2 Approaches in calculation of zakat	142
	7.3	Issues in Zakat Calculation	144
	7.4	Innovative Ways to Assist Zakat Calculation	146
	Self-Assessment Quiz (MCQs)		148
	Self-Assessment/Recall Questions		150
	Answers to Self-Assessment Quiz (MCQs)		152
8.	**Administration of Zakat**		**153**
	8.1	Zakat Administration	153
		8.1.1 Approaches in zakat administration	154
		8.1.1.1 Centralized approach to zakat administration	155

           8.1.1.2 Decentralized approach to zakat
                    administration   155
           8.1.1.3 Distributed approach to zakat administration   156
           8.1.1.4 Delegated approach to zakat administration   156
           8.1.1.5 Isolated (unsupervised) approach to zakat
                    administration   157
      8.1.2 History of zakat administration   157
      8.1.3 Governance and accounting requirements for zakat
            organizations   159
      8.1.4 Issues in zakat administration   162
      8.1.5 Case Study: Federal Territory Islamic Religious
            Council (Majlis Agama Islam Wilayah Persekutuan
            [MAIWP]) Malaysia   164
   Self-Assessment Quiz (MCQs)   166
   Self-Assessment/Recall Questions   168
   Answers to Self-Assessment Quiz (MCQs)   170

9. **Role of Zakat in Achieving Sustainable Development
   Goals**   **171**
   9.1 The Sustainable Development Goals [SDGs]   171
       9.1.1 Untapped potential of zakat   172
       9.1.2 Use of zakat in achieving sustainable
             development goals   173
       9.1.3 Challenges in using zakat in achieving sustainable
             development goals   175
       9.1.4 Selected case studies   176
             9.1.4.1 UNHCR zakat for refugees   176
             9.1.4.2 BAZNAS and UNDP zakat for COVID-19
                     support/recovery   177
   Self-Assessment Quiz (MCQs)   179
   Self-Assessment/Recall Questions   181
   Answers to Self-Assessment Quiz (MCQs)   182

10. **Use of Technology to Enhance Zakat Administration**   **183**
    10.1 Technology and Zakat Administration   183
         10.1.1 Types of technologies used to enhance zakat
                administration   184
                10.1.1.1 Blockchain (digital/distributed ledger)   184
                10.1.1.2 Web-based applications   186

		10.1.1.3 Mobile USSD/WAP/apps/digital wallets	186
		10.1.1.4 Internet-of-Things (IoT)	187
		10.1.1.5 Robo officer/Chatbot	188
	10.1.2	How technology has been used to enhance zakat administration	188
	10.1.3	Challenges in employing technology to enhance zakat administration	190
	10.1.4	Selected case studies	192
		10.1.4.1 Blockchain use case: Crypto zakat	192
	Self-Assessment Quiz (MCQs)		195
	Self-Assessment/Recall Questions		197
	Answers to Self-Assessment Quiz (MCQs)		198

11. Zakat Management Programs — 199

11.1 Zakat Management Programs: What and Why — 199
11.2 Practice of Zakat Management Programs Across the World — 201
11.3 Impact of Zakat Management Programs on Asnaf — 203
11.4 Factors to Consider in Formulating Zakat Management Programs — 205
11.5 Selected Case Studies — 207
    11.5.1 Selangor State' Asnaf Entrepreneurial Program (Malaysia) — 207
    11.5.2 International Federation of Red Cross and Red Crescent Societies [IFRC] and Perlis Islamic Religious Council and Malay Customs (Majlis Agama Islam dan Adat Istiadat Melayu Perlis [MAIPS]) Zakat Program (Kenya) — 209
    11.5.3 UNHCR Refugee Zakat Fund [zakat fund] — 212
Self-Assessment Quiz (MCQs) — 215
Self-Assessment/Recall Questions — 217
Answers to Self-Assessment Quiz (MCQs) — 218

12. Contemporary Issues and Challenges in Zakat Administration — 219

12.1 Issues and Challenges in Collecting Zakat — 220
    12.1.1 Lack of credible zakat-collecting institutions — 220

	12.1.2 Absence of institutional governance framework for zakat collection	221
	12.1.3 Inability to identify zakat payers	221
12.2	Issues and Challenges in Managing Zakat Fund	222
	12.2.1 Lack of transparency in administering zakat funds	222
	12.2.2 Corruption, misappropriation, and embezzlement	223
	12.2.3 Imprudent zakat program affects zakat funds	223
12.3	Issues and Challenges in Disbursement	224
	12.3.1 Insufficient data on asnaf leads to their exclusion in zakat disbursement	224
	12.3.2 Poor disbursement organization leading to tragedies	225
	12.3.3 Strict localization of zakat disbursement	225
12.4	Selected Case Studies	226
	12.4.1 Death of asnaf from zakat disbursement uproar, Bangladesh	226
	12.4.2 Alleged corruption scandal in Zakat Pulau Penang (ZPP), Malaysia	226
	12.4.3 Alleged mismanagement of zakat funds, Singapore	227
	12.4.4 Poor zakat management wanes confidence and raises doubts, Brunei	228
Self-Assessment Quiz (MCQs)		229
Self-Assessment/Recall Questions		231
Answers to Self-Assessment Quiz (MCQs)		232

Index 233

List of Figures

Figure 3.1.	Determination of equilibrium price and quantity	53
Figure 3.2.	Effect of taxes on prices	54
Figure 3.3.	Effect of zakat on prices	54
Figure 4.1.	List of zakatable wealth	74
Figure 5.1.	Zakat virtual assistant	101
Figure 5.2.	Zakat metaverse	102
Figure 5.3.	Paying zakat through *Amil*	108

List of Tables

Table 2.1.	Zakat on basic needs during COVID-19	28
Table 2.2.	Previous studies about poverty reduction via zakat	33
Table 2.3.	The impact of zakat on the BAZNAS stockbreeding program 2020–2022	36
Table 2.4.	Total lending by World Bank between 1970 and 2020 for poverty alleviation programs	40
Table 2.5.	Zakat collection from salary	42
Table 4.1.	*Nisab* and zakat on camels	76
Table 4.2.	*Nisab* and zakat on cows	77
Table 4.3.	*Nisab* and zakat on sheep and goats	77
Table 4.4.	Current administration of zakat in Muslim countries	87
Table 4.5.	Zakat collection and distribution in US dollars	89
Table 4.6.	Lack of statistical data on zakat collection from all types of zakatable wealth	90
Table 5.1.	Zakat calculator	100
Table 7.1.	Zakatable wealth, *nisab*, and rate for zakat calculation.	140

Chapter 1

Overview of the Institution of Zakat

Learning Outcomes

At the end of this chapter, students must be able to

- understand an overview on zakat,
- acknowledge the views of Muslim scholars on zakat,
- deduce the objectives of zakat from Quran and Sunnah,
- realize the existence of zakat prior to Islam.

1.1 An Overview on Zakat

1.1.1 *Definition of zakat*

The Arabic root word of zakat is *zaka* which means "purification", "increase," "growth", "blessings", and "betterment".[1] Linguistically, zakat is defined as purity and increment, meaning that zakat purifies and increases the wealth as it cleanses its owner from any selfishness and greed for wealth and it purifies its recipients' hearts from any envy and jealousy. Zakat is an obligation imposed by Allah (SW) on Muslims' wealth justifying the right of the poor over the wealth of the rich for a healthy Muslim society as mentioned in many Quranic verses. Moreover, zakat is the third pillar of Islam; hence, it is obligatory upon all Muslims to give part of their wealth to its specified recipients.

---
[1] Al-Qardawi, Y. *Fiqh Al Zakat: A Comparative Study* (Vol. 1).

1.1.2 Conditions for zakat givers

All Muslims whose wealth possesses the *nisab* (a minimum amount of wealth held for a year) must pay zakat. Nevertheless, there are several conditions that must be fulfilled before giving the zakat, such as zakat giver must be an adult Muslim who has attained the age of puberty, he must be free, i.e., not be a slave, and he must have full ownership of the wealth and that wealth has been earned from *halal*/lawful means.[2] Moreover, that wealth must reach *al-nisab* after holding for a *haul*/a completion of one full Hijri year.

1.1.3 Conditions for zakat recipients

Zakat recipients are not like any other type of charity or donation; its recipients are specified clearly in Quran (Surah al-Tauba 9:60) into only eight categories of people: *fuqara*/poor, *miskins*/needy, *'amileen 'alihah*/zakat managers, *muallafat-ul-qulub*/reverting to Islam, *fi ar-riqab*/liberating slaves/captives, *al-gharimin*/debtors, *fi sabillillah*/for the sake of allah, and *ibn-us-sabil*/the wayfarer.

1.1.4 Restrictions on giving zakat

There are some restrictions on giving zakat such as a person who qualifies to pay zakat is not eligible to receive it. It is also not permissible to give zakat to the husband, wife, parents, grandparents, and children and grandchildren. Moreover, zakat fund is not permissible to be used to build a mosque. It is recommended to give zakat to the poor and needy within the community or within the same country until enriching them. Furthermore, the collected zakat fund must be spent during the same year not only to satisfy its recipients until it enriched them but also to assist them to become active members in their societies and becoming zakat givers the following years.

1.2 Muslim Scholars' Views on Zakat

Al-Nawawi viewed zakat as one of the five inseparable practices and identities in Islam.[3] Zayas added that it is an annual premium upon one's

---

[2] *Ibid.*
[3] Nawawi, A. (1976). *Forty Hadith.* Damascus: The Holy Koran Publication House.

accumulated wealth that surpasses the minimum threshold amount (*nisab*) and dedicated to the eight classes of recipient or *mustahiq*.[4] Al-Qaradawi deduced that the root word of zakat is from the word zaka that means to grow or to increase. When it relates to things, zaka means to increase, but when it relates to a person it becomes to grow or a betterment of a person — righteousness such as *tazkiyah* process. Another meaning of zakat in Arabic words is cleanliness or purity from dirt. Hence, zakat can be comprehended as the purification process along with the growth of wealth.[5] Majeed added that zakat could serve as "the causal link" between spiritual belief and economic well-being. The injunction of zakat is, therefore, designed in a way that takes care of the welfare of all members in the community and creates a more prosperous and peaceful culture.[6]

Zaman shows that zakat endogenously aligns with Islamic moral economy which aims at creating a just environment whereby the less fortunate can be elevated and has a space to grow as *ihsani* behavioral norms suggest.[7] Kahf believes that zakat is a right of the poor people of the society and that it is an obligatory financial duty of the rich people in the society.[8] Shariff insisted that there is no other scheme in this world except Islam where it is clearly stated that the right of poor people is a duty of both individual and government through zakat.[9]

With reference to Hudaefi, he stated that zakat is an Islamic obligation which represents the third of the five pillars of Islam. It obliges a 2.5% payment of yearly tax on the productive wealth of Muslim individuals and

---

[4] de Zayas, F. G. (1960). *The Law and Philosophy of Zakat*. Damaskus: Al-Jadidah Printing Press.
[5] Al-Qaradawi, Y. (1999). *Fiqh Al-Zakah: A Comprehensive Study of Zakah Regulations and Philosophy in the Light of the Qur'an and Sunna*. London: Dar Al Taqwa.
[6] Majeed, M. T. (2019). Real wellbeing of the ummah and economic performance: Islamic perspectives and empirical evidence. *Pakistan Journal of Applied Economics*, Vol. 29, No. 1, pp. 1–31. Available at: http://www.aerc.edu.pk/wp-content/uploads/2019/06/Paper-752-TARIQ-MAJEED-I-1.pdf.
[7] Zaman, N. & Asutay, M. (2009). Divergence between aspirations and realities of Islamic economics: A political economy approach to bridging the divide. *IIUM Journal of Economics and Management*, Vol. 17, No. 1, pp. 73–96.
[8] Kahf, M. (2013). Potential effects of zakat on government budget. *International Journal of Economics, Management and Accounting*, Vol. 5, No. 1. Available at: https://journals.iium.edu.my/enmjournal/index.php/enmj/article/view/31
[9] Shariff, A. M. *et al.* (2011). A robust zakah system: Towards a progressive socio-economic development in Malaysia. *Middle-East Journal of Scientific Research*, Vol. 7, No. 4, pp. 550–554.

commercial firms that have reached the *nisab* (full ownership) and haul (one lunar year) of owning the wealth.[10]

Sābiq agreed with Bin-Nashwan that zakat is that portion of a man's wealth which is designated for the poor,[11] hence it is a significant mechanism of wealth redistribution and social service provision. It orders well-to-do people to share 2.5% of their productive wealth and dispenses it among the less privileged with lower income in society.[12] Hamid stated that zakat is payable on business revenues and assets, gold and silver, and savings at the basic rate of 2.5%.[13] Hossain believes that zakat is a form of worship which involves wealth. When a Muslim person's earnings reach a prescribed amount (*nisab*) in excess of his needs, that person is required to pay a portion (on monetary wealth and on gold and silver, it is 2.5% or the 40th part of the wealth) of his earnings to the poor and needy.[14] Hudaefi, Caraka, and Wahid stated that zakat in the Islamic jurisprudence is charged in agricultural products. A 10% zakat is required for agricultural products irrigated with rainwater and a 5% zakat is charged other than that. Islam also requires zakat al-fitr or fitrah that requires one sha' compulsory levy or an equivalent of 2.5 kg of rice, wheat, dates, sago, or other staple food. Zakat al-fitr must be paid before 'Eid al-Fitr (Islamic holy day).[15] Mohammed believed that Islam requires its followers to pay zakat so that the money collected can be of help for the poor to have basic

---

[10] Hudaefi, F. A., Caraka, R. E., & Wahid, H. (2022). Zakat administration in times of COVID-19 pandemic in Indonesia: A knowledge discovery via text mining. *International Journal of Islamic and Middle Eastern Finance and Management*, Vol. 15, No. 2, pp. 271–286. DOI: 10.1108/IMEFM-05-2020-0250.

[11] Sābiq, A.-S. *et al.* (1991). *Fiqh-us-Sunnah: Az-Zakah and as-Siyam*. Washington, DC: American Trust Publications.

[12] Bin-Nashwan, S.A., Abdul-Jabbar, H., Aziz, S.A., & Haladu, A. (2020). Zakah compliance behavior among entrepreneurs: Economic factors approach. *International Journal of Ethics and Systems*, Vol. 36, No. 2, pp. 285–302. DOI: 10.1108/IJOES-09-2019-0145.

[13] Hamid, S., Craig, R., & Clarke, F. (1993). Religion: A confounding cultural element in the international harmonization of accounting? *Abacus*, Vol. 29, No. 2, pp. 131–148. DOI: 10.1111/j.1467-6281.1993.tb00427.x.

[14] Hossain, M. Z. (2012). Zakat in Islam: A powerful poverty alleviating instrument for Islamic countries. *International Journal of Economic Development Research and Investment*, Vol. 3, No. 1, pp. 1–11.

[15] Hudaefi, F. A. & Beik, I. S. (2021). Digital zakāh campaign in time of Covid-19 pandemic in Indonesia: A netnographic study. *Journal of Islamic Marketing*, Vol. 12, No. 3, pp. 498–517. DOI: 10.1108/JIMA-09-2020-0299.

requirements in life.[16] This is supported by Norulazidah who supported that zakat is not just a pillar of Islam for worshiping Allah (SW) but is a right of the poor people of the society.[17]

Raimi further added that zakat is compulsory alms as well as the third pillar of Islam which entails giving out annually 2.5% of an individual's net monetary income or wealth to eight disadvantaged groups in the society.[18]

Farah Aida referred to the historical evidence and show that through sincere adherence and effective implementation of the zakat system, poverty was almost completely wiped out and, thus, achieved socio-economic and spiritual advancement and wider well-being of all those under his rule.[19] Moreover, Chapra explains that the existence of unique Islamic economic practices such as the prohibition of *riba* or the injunction to observe zakat could serve as the causal links between theological belief and economic performance.[20]

Gambling and Karim differentiate between the conventional tax and zakat and show that zakat is viewed by Muslims as a means of "purifications" and not just an obligation and that morally, zakat promotes sharing of wealth and eliminates greediness, while socially, it helps reduce poverty within the community.[21] Al-Mamun added that zakat is an Islamic religious "tax" charged to the rich and well-to-do members of the society

---

[16] Mohammed, J. A. (2007). *Corporate Social Responsibility in Islam*. Auckland University of Technology Doctoral Thesis. DOI: 10.2139/ssrn.2593945.

[17] Norulazidah, D. H., Omar Ali, & Myles, G. D. (2010). The consequences of zakat for capital accumulation. *Journal of Public Economic Theory*, Vol. 12, No. 4, pp. 837–856. DOI: 10.1111/j.1467-9779.2010.01476.x.

[18] Raimi, L., Patel, A., & Adelopo, I. (2014). Corporate social responsibility, *waqf* system and zakat system as faith-based model for poverty reduction. *World Journal of Entrepreneurship, Management and Sustainable Development*, Vol. 10, No. 3, pp. 228–242. DOI: 10.1108/WJEMSD-09-2013-0052.

[19] Farah Aida, A. N., Rashidah, A. R., & Normah, O. (2012). Zakat and poverty alleviation: Roles of zakat institutions in Malaysia. *International Journal of Arts and Commerce*, Vol. 1, No. 7, pp. 61–72.

[20] Chapra, M. U. (2008). Ibn Khaldun's theory of development: Does it help explain the low performance of the present-day Muslim world? *Journal of Socio-Economics*, Vol. 37, No. 2, pp. 836–863. DOI: 10.1016/j.socec.2006.12.051.

[21] Gambling, T. E. & Karim, R. A. A. (1986). Islam and "social accounting". *Journal of Business Finance & Accounting*, Vol. 13, No. 1, pp. 39–50. DOI: 10.1111/j.1468-5957.1986.tb01171.x.

for distribution to the poor and the needy and other recipients based on certain customary benchmarks according to the Quran.[22]

1.3 Objectives of Zakat in Quran

The word "zakat" is mentioned 30 times in Quran, and 28 times it is linked with prayer hence showing its importance similar to the prayer since both prayer and zakat are among the second and third pillars of Islam. Hence, this shows the importance of zakat in line with the importance of prayer.

With reference to *sadaqah* (singular) and *sadaqaat* (plural), it has been mentioned 16 times in Quran: five of them mentioned as *sadaqah* and eleven of them mentioned as *sadaqaat*. As mentioned above, zakat is different from *sadaqah* since zakat is obligatory, and it must be given to only eight recipients from a specified amount of wealth once reached *nisab* on annual basis. Nevertheless, there are two Quranic verses which carry the essence of zakat via *sadaqaat* and *sadaqah*. In Surah al-Tauba, verse 60, the term "sadaqaat" is mentioned, referring to the obligatory zakat and indicating that it is to be given to eight specific recipients. Similarly, verse 103 of the same chapter highlights the role of the state in managing zakat to purify, increase, and bring blessings to the Muslim society.[23]

1.3.1 *Objectives of zakat share to its recipients*

Zakat recipients are specific and fixed and that it must be given to eight categories of recipients as mentioned in the following Quranic verse:

إِنَّمَا ٱلصَّدَقَٰتُ لِلْفُقَرَآءِ وَٱلْمَسَٰكِينِ وَٱلْعَٰمِلِينَ عَلَيْهَا وَٱلْمُؤَلَّفَةِ قُلُوبُهُمْ وَفِى ٱلرِّقَابِ وَٱلْغَٰرِمِينَ وَفِى سَبِيلِ ٱللَّهِ وَٱبْنِ ٱلسَّبِيلِ ۖ فَرِيضَةً مِّنَ ٱللَّهِ ۗ وَٱللَّهُ عَلِيمٌ حَكِيمٌ

> *Alms-tax is only for the poor and the needy, for those employed to administer it, for those whose hearts are attracted 'to the faith', for*

---

[22] Al-Mamun, A., Haque, A., & Jan, M. T. (2019). Measuring perceptions of Muslim consumers toward income tax rebate over zakat on income in Malaysia. *Journal of Islamic Marketing*, Vol. 11, No. 2, pp. 368–383. DOI: 10.1108/JIMA-12-2016-0104.
[23] Al-Qardawi, *op. cit.* (Vol. 2).

'freeing' slaves, for those in debt, for Allah's cause, and for 'needy' travellers. 'This is' an obligation from Allah. And Allah is All-Knowing, All-Wise. (Surah al-Tauba 9:60)

Hence, those who are entitled to receive the zakat are: *fuqara*/poor, *miskins*/needy, *'amileen 'alihah*/zakat managers, *muallafat-ul-qulub*/ reverting to Islam, *fi ar-Riqab*/liberating slaves/captives, *al-gharimin*/ debtors, *fi sabillillah*/for the sake of Allah, and *ibn-us-sabil*/the wayfarer. Let's define each one and show their objectives in Muslim society.

1. ***Fuqara*/Poor:** These are people who live below the minimum requirements of livelihood and material possessions. They are the ones who live in an insecure condition but do not ask for help. The main objective of this share is not only to provide them with their basic needs but also to provide them with the means to work and be active members in the society as long as they are fit and healthy to work and earn their living.
2. ***Miskins*/Needy:** These are people who just have the minimum requirements of livelihood and material possession and they ask for help. Similar to the *fuqara*, the main objective of this share is not only to provide them with their basic needs but also to provide them with the means to work and be active members in the society as long as they are fit and healthy. *Miskins* may take less time compared to the *fuqara* in becoming active members in the society.
3. ***'Amileen 'Alihah*/Zakat Managers:** These are the officials' managers for collecting zakat from all eligible Muslims and distributing it to its eight recipients. The main objective of this share is to motivate zakat managers to increase their shares through collecting zakat from all eligible Muslims and at the same time ensure continuous employment through the efficient distribution of zakat to its recipients. Hence, just redistribution of wealth will be realized in Muslim society.
4. ***Muallafat-ul-Qulub*/Reverting to Islam:** These are people who are inclined to enter or have already reverted to Islam. The main objective of this share is to strengthen them in Islam and to win their hearts and spread the words of Allah to their communities.
5. ***Fi ar-Riqab*/Liberating Slaves/Captives:** Historically speaking, these are the people who want to buy their freedom, so through paying

their masters money from zakat share, they get their freedom. Recently prisoners of war, criminal prisoners, and families of prisoners had been included in this category of zakat recipients. The main objective of this share is to support prisoners' families and assist in financing their children's education.
6. **Al-Gharimin/Debtors:** These are the people who are in debt and who do not have the means to settle their personal debt for social responsibilities. The main objective of this share is to help in settling this debt which was meant to meet their crucial needs.
7. **Fi Sabillillah/for the sake of Allah:** This share is meant to help people who are struggling for the love of Allah in any form of serving Islam, such as the propagation of Islam and Jihad including education.
8. **Ibn-us-Sabil/the Wayfarer:** These are the travelers who are stranded during their journey and lost their money or their belongings. The main objective of this share is to assist those travelers and at the same time to encourage more traveling to explore and gain new knowledge from other civilizations that can benefit the Muslim ummah at large.

1.3.2 Objectives of state to administer zakat

The administration of zakat must be handled and managed by the state/government as highlighted in the above-mentioned Surah al-Taubah (9:103). In this verse, Allah (SW) asked his Messenger (PBUH) as he was the head and leader of the Islamic state at that time to collect zakat from Muslims and distribute it according to the mentioned eight zakat recipients. This practice was followed at the time of the Prophet (PBUH) where the collection and the distribution of zakat were directly placed under the state. This was then followed during the time of the first Caliph Abu Bakr al-Siddiq (RA) who said that he will fight against those who refused to pay their zakat. The same was practiced by all Caliphs; after Abu Bakr al-Siddiq (RA), they used to appoint agents to collect the zakat money from all eligible Muslims and from all Muslim countries and place it in the Baitulmaal to be distributed to the recipients of zakat.[24]

The institution of zakat is a national and an in-house financial scheme to lift up the spirit of human beings beyond the love of material

---

[24] Namazi, Mahmood. Bayt al-Mal and the distribution of zakah (unpublished paper).

achievement. It has many objectives which had been highlighted in both the Quran and the Hadith. Some of the objectives are highlighted in the following Quranic verse:

خُذْ مِنْ أَمْوَالِهِمْ صَدَقَةً تُطَهِّرُهُمْ وَتُزَكِّيهِم بِهَا وَصَلِّ عَلَيْهِمْ إِنَّ صَلَاتَكَ سَكَنٌ لَهُمْ وَاللَّهُ سَمِيعٌ عَلِيمٌ

Of their goods (wealth), take alms, that so thou mightest purify and sanctify them; and pray on their behalf. Verily thy prayers are a source of security for them: And Allah is One Who heareth and knoweth. (Surah al-Taubah 9:103)

As mentioned in the above Quranic verse, it increases the wealth of zakat givers and purifies not only their wealth but also all bad behavior which might arise among individuals on a regular basis. According to Al-Qardawi (Al Qardawi vol. II), zakat has three impacts; on the zakat payers, zakat receivers and on Muslim society.

1.3.3 *Objectives of zakat on its givers*

The objectives of collecting zakat from zakat payers are many, for example, *zakat* purifies the soul from miserliness when paid out of submission to the command of Allah. In this case, it purifies the soul of a Muslim from greed and miserliness and hence acts as a purifier that trains the Muslims to give and spend selflessly. It also liberates their souls from the stinking love of wealth, slavery, material gains, and acquisitions. Moreover, zakat is a means of training Muslims on the virtues of generosity and a means of purification from greed. Being paid on a regular basis, year after year, this act will train zakat payers to give and spend for charitable purposes. In addition, zakat circulates the wealth from the have to the have not, hence fulfilling the right of zakat recipients in a just way. In this case, zakat improves the ties of mutual love since it links the rich and the poor together with ties of brotherhood and love. Furthermore, zakat brings growth to wealth even though zakat seems to tax the principal of the wealthy; it is a cause of blessing and growth to Muslims' wealth, a blessing from Allah that brings prosperity, and an increase in demand for consumption goods caused by the distribution of zakat which brings vitality to business.

1.3.4 Objectives of zakat on its recipients

The objectives of zakat on its recipients are also many. For example, zakat frees the receiver from any humiliation of needs and assists in satisfying the basic needs for a decent living. Moreover, zakat liberates its recipients from material needs in terms of living a good and prosperous life which is Islam's objectives for all human beings. In addition, it purifies the souls of zakat recipients from all sort of envy and hatred toward the rich as long as their right has been transferred to them in an ethical manner.

1.3.5 Objectives of zakat in Muslim society

The objectives of zakat in Muslim society can be seen in the achievement of the above-mentioned impacts where, a healthy and an ethical society will be established in which the relationship between the rich and the poor will be based on strong bonds of care, fraternity, and solidarity, hence purifying the whole Muslim society from all sort of corruptions. Moreover, zakat giving increases and purifies the wealth of Muslim (payers), hence reducing the gap between the rich and the poor and eradicating poverty. Achieving this, government will not be forced to external borrowing for the eradication of poverty hence eliminating dealing with *riba*/interest.

1.3.6 Objective of zakat as an alternative to riba

Since *riba* has been prohibited in Islam and has been replaced with different alternative financial tools in Islam, zakat also is one of these tools as mentioned in Surat al-Rum:

وَمَا آتَيْتُم مِّن رِّبًا لِّيَرْبُوَ فِي أَمْوَالِ النَّاسِ فَلَا يَرْبُو عِندَ اللَّهِ ۖ وَمَا آتَيْتُم مِّن زَكَاةٍ تُرِيدُونَ وَجْهَ اللَّهِ فَأُولَٰئِكَ هُمُ الْمُضْعِفُونَ

And whatever you give for interest to increase within the wealth of people will not increase with Allah. But what you give in zakah, desiring the countenance of Allah — those are the multipliers. (Surat al-Rum 30:39)

Hence, one may ask how zakat is one of the alternative financial institutions that help eliminate *riba* from the Muslim society. The answer to this is very simple; if the management of zakat is handled by the state, this will give the responsibility to the state to establish eight financial institutions, each according to the recipients of zakat. This in turn will help in eliminating *riba* and eradicating poverty from Muslim societies at the micro and macro levels.

At the micro level, by giving the due zakat to the eight recipients of zakat, the disposable income of the poor and needy classes will be enhanced, and it will stop them from borrowing with *riba* to meet their essential needs. It is also supposed to help default debtors settle their debts besides many other positive effects. Consequently, at the macro level, state will not resort to external borrowing with *riba* to finance their anti-poverty programs, or at least minimize this borrowing to the lowest level possible, because the state will use the funds collected from zakat (besides other public revenues) to finance its anti-poverty programs and development plans, especially for the poor and needy people. Moreover, distributing zakat among those who really need money enhances aggregate consumption (demand) and thus impacts positively on economic growth, especially when the marginal propensity to consume among poor people is much higher than middle- or high-income classes, which means a higher increase in gross domestic product (GDP).

1.4 Objectives of Zakat in Sunnah

Zakat in sunnah has been highlighted in many *ahadith* of the Prophet (PBUH) such as on the authority of Ibn Omar, may Allah be pleased with them, he said: The Messenger of Allah, may Allah's prayers and peace be upon him, said: *Islam has been built on five pillars: testifying that there is no god but Allah and that Muhammad is the Messenger of Allah, performing the prayers, paying the zakat, performing hajj/pilgrimage, and fasting the month of Ramadan* (Narrated by Al-Bukhari & Muslim). Hence, this shows that among the five pillars of Islam giving, zakat is the third pillar of Islam after prayer and which shows the great importance of zakat in Islam.

Moreover, the administration of zakat to be managed by the state is also mentioned in the following hadith[25]:

> Anas narrates that "a man asked the Messenger of Allah (PBUH), If I give *zakah* to the person you send, would I be fulfilling it as far as Allah and His Messenger are concerned?' The Prophet answered, 'Yes, if you give it to my messenger, you are freed from that obligation as far as Allah and His Messenger are concerned. You deserve its reward, and if it is tampered with later, the sin is on whoever changes it."

This practice was followed at the time of the Prophet (PBUH) where the collection and the distribution of zakat were directly placed under the state. This was then followed during the time of the first Caliph Abu Bakr al-Siddiq (RA) who said that he will fight against those who refused to pay their zakat. The same was practiced by all Caliphs; after Abu Bakr al-Siddiq (RA), they used to appoint agents to collect the zakat money from all eligible Muslims and from all Muslim countries and place it in the Baitulmaal to be distributed to the recipients of zakat.[26]

Moreover, zakat has to be managed by the state/government in terms of its collection from all eligible Muslims on all types of zakatable wealth for distribution it to the eight recipients of zakat as in the above-mentioned Quranic verse. The reasons for the state to handle the management of zakat are many: Some of these reasons are for the benefit of the recipients of zakat while others are for the benefit of the giver of zakat, in addition to its benefit for the whole Muslim society in general.[27]

For example, the reasons for the state to handle the management of zakat for the benefit of the recipients of zakat are by receiving zakat directly from the state and not from the rich, Muslims will preserve their dignity from any direct humiliation. Moreover, some Muslims may have no concern in paying their obligation if left to them, so in this case, the rights of the recipients of zakat will be lost resulting in expanding their poverty. In addition, giving zakat to its recipients will help them satisfy their basic needs within the same year and will motivate them to work harder to be zakat payers in the following years.

---

[25] Al-Qardawi, *op. cit.*
[26] Namazi, Mahmood, *op. cit.*
[27] Al-Qardawi, *op. cit.*

The reasons for the state to manage zakat for the benefit of zakat givers are that it will encourage the Muslims to fulfill their obligation toward giving the compulsory zakat through the right channels. Moreover, in case some Muslims own the assets but do not know where to pay their due zakat, or if they even do not know if they are eligible to pay the zakat. The zakat collector will assist them to fulfill such obligation. In addition, in case some Muslims dislike such payment because of greed or stinginess, through regular payments of zakat, this will help them behave according to the Islamic teaching.

For the reasons of the state managing zakat for the benefit of the whole Muslim society, through collecting zakat from all eligible Muslims and redistributing it in a just and fair way to all its recipients, this will help in reducing poverty, creating a just and ethical society free from *riba*.

1.5 Zakat in Religions Prior to Islam

Even though zakat has been imposed on Muslims during the time of the Prophet (PBUH), this does not mean that zakat was not known prior to Islam. As we know, Allah (SW) sent many messengers and prophets to guide people to the true path and to worship Allah (SW) alone and to comply with all His commands. Zakat is one of the acts of worship that Allah (SW) granted all His messengers and prophets to encourage their people to give it. Hence, all messengers of Allah (SW) called their people to perform the duty of zakat and to take out the right of the poor from the wealth of the rich. However, the portion of how much of zakat to be given to the poor was not mentioned and it was left to the mercy and kindness of the rich. But with the advent of Islam, zakat portion for zakat al-fitr and zakat on wealth is determined very clearly in the Sunnah of the Prophet (PBUH) as will be discussed in Chapter 4.

The following are some of the Quranic verses which show that Allah (SW) ordered all His Prophets to perform the duty of zakat:

In Surat Al-Baiyinah, Allah (SW) ordered the people of the book to practice regular charity which is the zakat:

وَمَا أُمِرُوا إِلَّا لِيَعْبُدُوا اللَّـهَ مُخْلِصِينَ لَهُ الدِّينَ حُنَفَاءَ وَيُقِيمُوا الصَّلَاةَ وَيُؤْتُوا الزَّكَاةَ وَذَلِكَ دِينُ الْقَيِّمَةِ

And they have been commanded no more than this: To worship Allah, offering Him sincere devotion, being true (in faith); to establish regular prayer; and to practise regular charity; and that is the Religion Right and Straight. (Surat al-Baiyinah 98:5)

With reference to Surat al-Anbyiya, the message was directed to both Prophet Ibrahim and Prophet Lut as Allah (SW) ordered them to give zakat.:

وَجَعَلْنَاهُمْ أَئِمَّةً يَهْدُونَ بِأَمْرِنَا وَأَوْحَيْنَا إِلَيْهِمْ فِعْلَ ٱلْخَيْرَٰتِ وَإِقَامَ ٱلصَّلَوٰةِ وَإِيتَآءَ ٱلزَّكَوٰةِ ۖ وَكَانُوا۟ لَنَا عَٰبِدِينَ

And We made them leaders guiding by Our command. And We inspired to them the doing of good deeds, establishment of prayer, and giving of zakāh; and they were worshippers of Us. (Surat al-Anbiya, 21:73)

Similarly, in Surah Maryam, Allah (SW) also mentioned His Prophet Ismail, peace be upon him, and praised him, as he commanded his family to establish prayer and pay zakat:

وَكَانَ يَأْمُرُ أَهْلَهُ بِٱلصَّلَوٰةِ وَٱلزَّكَوٰةِ وَكَانَ عِندَ رَبِّهِۦ مَرْضِيًّا

He used to command his people to offer prayer and give zakat, and was liked by His Lord. (Surah Maryam 19:55)

Likewise, in Surah Maryam, Prophet Jesus, peace be upon him, also highlighted that Allah (SW) ordered him to give zakat:

وَجَعَلَنِى مُبَارَكًا أَيْنَ مَا كُنتُ وَأَوْصَٰنِى بِٱلصَّلَوٰةِ وَٱلزَّكَوٰةِ مَا دُمْتُ حَيًّا

He has made me a blessing wherever I go, and bid me to establish prayer and give zakat as long as I live (Surah Maryam verse 19:31)

Moreover, in Al-Baqarah, Allah (SW) also ordered the people of Israel to give zakat:

وَإِذْ أَخَذْنَا مِيثَٰقَ بَنِىٓ إِسْرَٰٓءِيلَ لَا تَعْبُدُونَ إِلَّا ٱللَّهَ وَبِٱلْوَٰلِدَيْنِ إِحْسَانًا وَذِى ٱلْقُرْبَىٰ وَٱلْيَتَٰمَىٰ وَٱلْمَسَٰكِينِ وَقُولُوا۟ لِلنَّاسِ حُسْنًا وَأَقِيمُوا۟ ٱلصَّلَوٰةَ وَءَاتُوا۟ ٱلزَّكَوٰةَ ثُمَّ تَوَلَّيْتُمْ إِلَّا قَلِيلًا مِّنكُمْ وَأَنتُم مُّعْرِضُونَ

We made a covenant with the Children of Israel: "Worship none but Allah. And be good to parents, and relatives, and orphans, and the

needy. And speak nicely to people, and pray regularly, and give zakat." Then you turned away, except for a few of you, backsliding. (Al-Baqarah 2:83)

Even though, the above Quranic verses show that the obligation of giving zakat is known to all prophets prior to Prophet Muhammad (PBUH), with the advance of Islam, zakat becomes obligatory and one of the five pillars of Islam. Moreover, a detailed explanation of zakat is given in Quran and the Sunnah of the Prophet (PBUH).

Self-Assessment Quiz (MCQs)

Question 1: Zakat literally means
(a) Decrease
(b) Assist
(c) Purify
(d) None Of these

Question 2: Zakat is the ____ pillars of Islam
(a) 1st
(b) 2nd
(c) 3rd
(d) 4th

Question 3: Zakat was made compulsory in the ____ century of Hijrah
(a) 1st
(b) 2nd
(c) 3rd
(d) 4th

Question 4: Who said that there was no difference between Salat and Zakat?
(a) Hazrat Ali (R.A)
(b) Hazrat Umer (R.A)
(c) Hazrat Abu Bakar (R.A)
(d) Hazrat Usman Ghani (R.A)

Question 5: How many times the word Zakat is mentioned in al-Quran?
(a) 42
(b) 32
(c) 22
(d) 42

Question 6: Zakat is meant for the people of
(a) Prophet Ibrahim and Ismail
(b) Prophet Musa
(c) Prophet Mohammed
(d) To all Prophets

Question 7: One of the zakat recipients is for the
(a) Husband or wife
(b) Grandparents
(c) Debtor
(d) Children

Question 8: Zakat objectives are many with the exception of
(a) Financing the poor and the needy
(b) Freeing its receiver from any humiliation
(c) Satisfying the basic needs of the poor and needy
(d) Providing a decent living for the poor and needy

Question 9: The following is not the reason for the state to manage zakat:
(a) Encouraging the Muslims to fulfill their obligation toward zakat
(b) Assisting its givers in calculating their zakat
(c) Excluding the greedy people from paying zakat
(d) Collecting zakat from all eligible Muslims

Question 10: The following is not a condition for zakat givers:
(a) Muslims whose wealth had reached *al-nisab*
(b) Muslims whose wealth is from unlawful means
(c) Muslims who have attained the age of puberty
(d) Muslims who have full ownership of the wealth

Self-Assessment/Recall Questions

Question 1: What do you understand by zakat?
Question 2: Discuss the conditions for zakat givers and zakat recipients.
Question 3: Highlight the objectives of zakat as mentioned in both al-Quran and al-Sunnah.
Question 4: Based on the specified zakat recipients as mentioned in Surah al-Tauba (9:60), justify who should be included under these categories today and why? Provide examples.
Question 5: Discuss why zakat has to be managed by the state? And why during the time of Caliph Abu Bakr al-Siddiq he wanted to fight those who refused to pay him their zakat?

Answers to Self-Assessment Quiz (MCQs)

1. c
2. c
3. b
4. c
5. b
6. d
7. c
8. a
9. c
10. b

Chapter 2

Role of Zakat in Alleviating Poverty in Muslim Societies: Past and Present

Learning Outcomes

At the end of this chapter, students must be able to

- understand how zakat can fulfill its religious and social obligations,
- establish eight socio-financial tools for transforming Muslim societies,
- present the role of zakat in eradicating poverty,
- show how zakat can eliminate *riba*/interest from Muslim societies,
- appreciate the classical and the contemporary cases in alleviating poverty in Muslim societies via zakat.

2.1 Zakat: A Religious and Social Obligation

Zakat has spiritual, material, and economical obligations toward its givers, recipients, and the whole Muslim society:

- spiritual and material purification of its giver, specifically zakat does not only purify the wealth of a Muslim but also purifies his heart from selfishness and greed for wealth,
- spiritual purification of its recipient, as it purifies his heart from envy and jealousy, from hatred and uneasiness, and it fosters in his heart, instead, goodwill, and warm wishes for the giver,

- spiritual purification of the society at large from class warfare and suspicion, from ill feelings and distrusts, from corruption and disintegration, and from all such evils,
- economically, zakat will circulate the wealth from the rich to the poor resulting in a just distribution and redistribution of wealth and a healthy society.

2.2 Zakat Socio-financial Products for Alleviating Poverty

As explained clearly in Chapter 1, zakat management must be handled by the government in terms of its collection and distribution. Its collection must be from all eligible Muslims whose wealth reached *al-nisab* and from the 14 types of zakatable wealth to be distributed to its eight recipients on annual basis.

A quick glance at its zakatable wealth (which includes livestock, gold, silver currency and jewelry, commercial assets, agriculture, honey and animal products, mining, fishing, rented buildings, plants, and fixed capital, and lately zakat includes salary, wages, bonuses, grants, gift, and dividend income)[1] shows that huge amount of zakat fund will be collected on annual basis not only to support its zakat recipients but also in assisting the government in developing Muslim societies according to the teaching of Islam. For example, through the huge amount of zakat funds that will be collected on annual basis, this will provide the fund needed for establishing anti-poverty programs rather than resorting to external borrowing hence, eliminating *riba*/interest from Muslim society. Similarly, through its zakat recipients, eight social-financial products can be established to empower its recipients, hence alleviating their poverty.[2]

2.2.1 *Zakat socio-financial product for assisting the Faqir/poor*

This financial institution is meant to help the poor individuals who are without any means of livelihood and material possessions and who will

---

[1] Al-Qardawi, Y. *Fiqh Al Zakat: A Comparative Study* (Vol. 1).
[2] Mohsin, M. A. (2013). Potential of zakat in eliminating *riba* and eradicating poverty in Muslim countries. European Journal of Business and Management, Vol. 5, No. 11, pp. 114–126.

be forced to borrow with *riba* to provide for them. Therefore, by financing this category of zakat recipients and providing them with the basic needs and with the jobs they need, their situation will improve and they will be active members in the society, and hence the following years, they will be zakat givers rather than being zakat recipients. This act will help stop this category of poor from borrowing with *riba* to meet their basic needs.

2.2.2 *Zakat socio-financial product for empowering the Miskeen/needy*

This financial institution is meant to finance the needy individuals according to their basic necessities either in cash or in kind or both. They may have a job but their income is below the minimum requirement. So, in this case, financing this category of people can be in terms of providing them with skills and means to find better jobs not only to meet their basic necessities but also to improve their overall situation. This category may take lesser years than the above-mentioned category in terms of being zakat givers. Similar to the above, through this financial institution, this category of zakat recipient will not be forced to borrow with *riba* to meet their needs.

2.2.3 *Zakat socio-financial product for supporting 'Amil/zakat manager*

This financial institution is meant to finance the appointed zakat managers in terms of collecting, keeping records, gathering information, and distributing to the mentioned zakat recipients. For efficient management of zakat, the state must appoint its staff based on the dignity of each individual in terms of his ethics, honesty, and responsibilities toward himself and his society at large. Consequently, this efficient management will result not only in earning lawful earnings and gaining good reputation but also in increasing their earnings through collecting the zakat from all eligible Muslim and hence their portion of earnings will increase. Furthermore, the efficient management of this institution will help eliminate borrowing with *riba* among the rest of the zakat recipients.

2.2.4 Zakat socio-financial product for supporting Al-Muallafah Qulubuhm

This financial institution is meant to finance people who are inclined to enter or have already converted to Islam. Besides, it also helps in financing *da'wah*/spreading the words of Allah globally to reach all individuals living in this world. Moreover, using this share in spreading the knowledge of the prohibition of *riba* globally, e.g., through a global channel, this can help people to stop dealing with *riba*.

2.2.5 Zakat socio-financial product for liberating fi ar-Riqab/the captives

Historically speaking, this financial institution is meant to finance those who need the money to pay their master to buy their freedom. Recently, prisoners of war, criminal prisoners, and families of prisoners had been included in this category of zakat recipients. Therefore, financing them can take the form of liberating prisoners of war or educating criminal prisoners and providing them with the skills to find jobs once they are out of prison or financing their families while they are in prison. This share will also stop this category of recipient from borrowing with *riba*.

2.2.6 Zakat socio-financial product for financing Al-Gharimin/debtor

This group includes all who do not own *nisab* above what is needed to pay their debts, those whose debts are for personal use, and those whose debts are caused by their social and political responsibilities. Therefore, this financial institution for *al-gharimin* can finance those who have financial difficulties in repaying their borrowed loan to meet their crucial needs and also to assist them in finding an extra job to meet their needs in the future.

2.2.7 Socio-financial product for assisting fisabilillah causes/for the sake of Allah

This financial institution is meant to finance any form of struggle or work for the love of Allah. Therefore, it can finance the fighters and the border guards, buy weapons and military ships, build barracks, etc. without depending on any external borrowing with *riba* to finance this category.

2.2.8 *Socio-financial product for supporting Ibnus Sabil/ stranded during a journey*

This financial institution is meant to help the travelers who face difficulties in continuing their journey due to reasons such as loss of their money or their belongings. Hence, the presence of this financial institution in Muslim countries is more recommended to encourage more travelers to travel in order to explore, share, and gain latest knowledge that can benefit the Muslim Ummah at large.

2.3 Classical Cases in Alleviating Poverty in Muslim's Society via Zakat

One may ask the following question: Can zakat eradicate poverty from Muslim society?[3] Historically speaking, there were two incidents which confirmed that zakat managed to eradicate poverty during the time of S. Umar ibn al Khattab (13–22H) and during the time of S. Umar bin Abdul Aziz (99–101H).

Abu Ubaid reports from Amr bin Shuayb that Muadh ibn Jabal continued as a governor in Yemen from the time of the Prophet (PBUH) until the time of Caliph Umar ibn al Khattab. During the time of Caliph Umar ibn al-Khattab, Muadh ibn Jabal sent the balance of zakat, after disturbing it to the eight recipients of zakat in Yemen, to Madinah. However, Caliph Umar ibn al Khattab rejected this act and informed him to take from the rich people in Yemen to be given to the poor among them. Then, Muadh clarified that he already did so, and this is the balance which no one wants to take from him. The same happened for three consecutive years.

The second incident happened during the time of S. Umar ibn Abdul Aziz when the governor of Egypt wrote to him asking what to do with the proceeds of zakat as he didn't find deserving poor or needy all over the country. Caliph Umar ibn Abdul Aziz replied to him to do the following:

---
[3] Hassan, M. K. (2010). An integrated poverty alleviation model combining zakah, awqaf and micro-finance. Unpublished Paper Presented at the Seventh International Conference – The Tawhid/Epistemology Zakah and Waqf, Bangi.

to buy slaves and set them free, to build rest areas on the highways, to help young men and women get married, to repay borrowers' debts, and to give orphans and needy until they are all enriched.[4]

From these two incidents, we realized that if zakat is distributed to its recipients until it enriched them and on annual basis, this will help empower them and make them zakat givers rather than zakat recipients hence eradicating their poverty. Once this is achieved, then the balance of zakat can be channeled to other needy within the society to satisfy their needs and can also be transferred to other states or to other Muslim countries that still need to eradicate their poverty.

2.4 Contemporary Cases in Alleviating Poverty in Selected Muslim Countries

At the present time, the collection of zakat is regulated by the state or religious body in almost all Muslim countries while contributions are made on voluntary basis since its collection was left for the Muslims to give either directly to the recipients or to the zakat agent. Therefore, contribution of zakat cannot be realized in today's Muslim economy since its amount is negligible. In order to activate its objective, it is believed that its administration must be centralized and its collection must be made compulsory upon all eligible Muslims on all its zakatable wealth. Nevertheless, the recent revival of zakat in some Muslim countries shows an optimistic approach in achieving its objective.

Today, zakat funds are distributed through two approaches: consumptive and productive programs. Through consumptive programs, zakat is given to fulfill the basic needs of its recipients, such as food, shelter, and clothing. While through productive programs, zakat is given to improve the quality of life of its recipients through various economic programs. Such approaches have been carried out successfully in various countries, such as Malaysia, Indonesia, and some selected countries in Africa.

2.4.1 Current role of zakat in Malaysia

In Malaysia, zakat matters are administered by the State Islamic Religious Councils (SIRCs). Even though it is a state centralized body, its collection

---

[4] Ahmed, Habib (2004). Role of zakah and awqaf in poverty alleviation, IRTI 2004, Occasional Paper No. 8, p. 31.

is voluntary. Nevertheless, it has been acknowledged that its current zakat system managed to enhance its zakat recipients through the following:

2.4.1.1 Meeting the basic needs via zakat

Recently, the Federal Islamic Religious Council (MAIWP) has encouraged a variety of zakat programs to meet the basic needs of the poor and needy in the different states of Malaysia. For meeting the basic needs, MAIWP identified 10 programs which are Eid al-Fitr assistance, takaful *asnaf* assistance, debt settlement assistance, house rent deposit assistance, monthly house rent, home repair assistance, vehicle purchase assistance, emergency assistance, disaster assistance, and marriage assistance.[5]

Moreover, MAIWP also opens up opportunities for additional assistance for any other needy or productive programs which do not only cover the basic needs. For example, during the current pandemic, MAIWP provided various types of assistance, such as RM21.84 million was given to provide the basic needs in addition to others, as shown in Table 2.1.

2.4.1.2 Providing healthcare via zakat

Similarly, during this pandemic, the poor people faced many difficulties to access good healthcare service that leads to lower their quality of life.[6] Again, health program was provided through zakat to help the underprivileged overcome these problems.[7] For example, MAIWP managed to distribute RM3.27 million from zakat fund to provide respiratory assistance to seven hospitals in Malaysia.[8]

Furthermore, a study which was conducted in 2017 using crosstab analysis of 60 respondents in three regions, namely Penang, Kelantan, and

---

[5] Zakat Assistance Schemes. https://www.maiwp.gov.my/i/index.php/en/skim-bantuan.

[6] Kefeli, Z. et al. (2017). Factors affecting quality of life of medical assistance recipients of zakat fund in Malaysia. *International Journal of Economics, Management and Accounting*, Vol. 25, No. 1, pp. 125–140.

[7] Ali, A. F. M., Ibrahim, M. F., & Ab Aziz, M. R. (2019). Missing items in zakat distribution: A case in Kelantan, Malaysia. *International Journal of Zakat*, Vol. 4, No. 1, pp. 1–24. https://doi.org/10.37706/ijaz.v4i1.117.

[8] MAIWP. Homemakumat Bantuan Kecemasan, Musaadahcovid19 MaiwpSunday August 28, 2022 Makumat Bantuan Kecemasan, MUSAADAHCOVID19 MAIWP. https://www.maiwp.gov.my/ (same like No. 5).

Table 2.1. Zakat on basic needs during COVID-19.

No	Programs	Beneficiaries	Amounts (RM)
1	Monthly financial assistance	24.196 *Asnaf*	9,67 million
2	Additional special zakat assistance	24.196 *Asnaf*	12,1 million
3	Daily food assistance throughout the Movement Control Order (MCO)	678 box	0.05 million
4	Pillow and mattress assistance for special homeless center		0.02 million
	Total		21.84 million

Source: MAIWP (2020). The Role of Zakat Institution in Facing COVID-19: A Case Study of the Federal Territory Islamic Council (MAIWP) of Malaysia Hambari, Arif Ali Arif, Muntaha Artalim Zaim KIRKHS, International Islamic University Malaysia (IIUM) Paper to be Presented at the 4th International Conference of Zakat (ICONZ) 7–8 October 2020, Surabaya, Indonesia. https://www.iconzbaznas.com/submission/index.php/proceedings/article/view/225.

Negeri Sembilan, and multiple regression analysis shows a positive impact of zakat on health. The findings show two important facts: first that the medical assistance from zakat fund has increased the beneficiaries' quality of life. Second, while comparing health, income, and education, health becomes the significant factor to increase the quality of life.[9]

2.4.1.3 Supporting education via zakat

According to the majority of Muslim scholars, increasing the level of education is regarded as one of the objectives of *maqasid shariah* in the preservation of the '*aql*, which is very important.[10] Hence, with reference to zakat, supporting education was placed under the category of *fii sabilillah* as recommended by many Muslim scholars. In Malaysia, there are several zakat programs on education.

For example, Lembaga Zakat Negeri Kedah (LZNK) managed to distribute zakat funds to Universiti Utara Malaysia (UUM) to assist its beneficiaries in the university. To make it easier, UUM uses an e-wallet application to disburse the fund to the beneficiaries. Most of the

---

[9] Kefeli *et al. Op. cit.*
[10] Bandar Baru Nilai (2022). Empowering education among asnaf through. Vol. 3, No. 1, pp. 20–31.

beneficiaries are university students and they use the fund to fulfill their needs, such as food, books, and clothing during the study.[11]

Moreover, through zakat institution, zakat funds are provided for education programs in Universiti Teknologi Malaysia (UTM) as a partner of Johor Islamic Religious Council (MAIJ). In this university, zakat fund is distributed to the *al-gharim, fisabilillah, al-fakir, al-miskin,* and *al-amil.* In the case of UTM, it was realized that most of the beneficiaries are undergraduate students (87.9%) who used zakat funds for food and drinks (49.9%) followed by daily needs (36%) besides helping another family member (9.9%).[12]

2.4.1.4 *Providing affordable housing via zakat*

One of the most innovative ways in providing affordable housing is through *Asnaf* Personal Financing-i facility scheme which was initiated by Bank Islam Malaysia Berhad in July 2020 to provide affordable housing for salaried *Asnaf* through a joint venture of Bank Islam and State Zakat authority in Malaysia. In this scheme, the first half of financing this project is from Bank Islam and the second half from zakat funds. This scheme is meant for those who earn below RM 1500 per month in order to own a house or to build a house on an identified land. Recently, Bank Islam with Kedah State of Zakat Authority (LZNK) managed to build and handed two affordable housing to selected salaried *asnaf* in 2021. The success of this scheme encouraged Bank Islam to build another 30 houses for eligible salaried *asnaf* in 2022 or early next year and are further planning to expand the scheme nationwide in the future.[13]

2.4.2 *Current role of zakat in Indonesia*

In Indonesia, the management of zakat is carried out by the National Amil Zakat Agency known as BAZNAS and which is established by

---

[11] Noor, M. M. B. M., Rahim, A. K. B. A., & Hussain, M. N. B. M. (2020). Bantuan Zakat Kepada Asnaf Pelajar Menerusi Aplikasi E-Wallet (Kiplepay): Analisis Di Universiti Utara Malaysia. *Azka International Journal of Zakat & Social Finance*, Vol. 1, No. 1, pp. 102–115.

[12] Hamzah, N. B. *et al.* (2021). Vol. 1, No. 2, pp. 187–209. DOI: 10.51377/Azjaf. Vol1no2.37.

[13] The Malaysian Reserve, Wednesday, October 12, 2022. https://themalaysianreserve.com/2021/05/10/bank-islam-to-hand-over-30-houses-to-asnaf/.

the government. Similar to Malaysia, the collection of zakat is yet to be compulsory by BAZNAS. Nevertheless, BAZNAS manage to achieve many objectives via the collection of zakat at the present time through the following sections.

2.4.2.1 *Meeting the basic needs via zakat*

The most popular zakat program is the one for distributing the zakat to meet the basic needs such as clothing, food, and housing for the poor and the needy. Many programs like this are carried out by zakat managers to help in meeting the basic needs of these categories in Indonesia.

2.4.2.2 *Settling debtors' loan online via zakat*

As one of the basic needs, BAZNAS plays a great role in establishing its online loan repayment program which is designed to help *asnaf gharimin*. Before providing such assistance, BAZNAS ensures that the *mustahik/ zakat deserver* does borrow money through online loans to meet their basic needs and not for any conspicuous consumption. Hence, in this case, zakat funds help in giving financial assistance to settle the debt.[14]

2.4.2.3 *Providing healthcare via zakat*

Through zakat funds, BAZNAS managed to establish a health program which is known as Rumah Sehat BAZNAS (RSB). This health program has the vision to become a model for health services and empowerment, especially for the poor with national standards. The target of this program is the poor, from children to the elderly. Currently, RSB has spread in six locations, namely DKI Jakarta, Bangka Belitung, Yogyakarta Special Region, South Sulawesi, East Java, and Central Sulawesi.

Broadly speaking, RSB has two types of services, namely in-building services and out-of-building services. The first type of service includes Emergency Unit (ER), laboratory, inpatient, dental and oral clinic, psychological consultation, general clinic, and so on. Meanwhile, services

---

[14] Saputra, M.I., Adhiningsih, S.M., Hudaefi, F.A., & Zaenal. M.H. (2020). Mustahik Terjerat *Riba* Fintech: Apa Peran Zakat? *Policy Brief Pusat Kajian Strategis BAZNAS*, pp. 1–9. https://drive.google.com/file/d/1xbChqfArCZTAzBA3lhtMa_LBA1c_-Ed5/view.

outside the RSB building include BAZNAS Mobile Health Unit (UKK), elderly center, nutrition center, Healthy School Children Program (PASS), Underprivileged Health Partners (MKPS), health community development, and ASI-MPASI Fighters (PAM).[15]

Similarly, Rumah Sehat Terpadu Dompet Dhuafa was established in 2012 and has the purpose of providing services to *mustahik* with an integrated and easy system. This hospital is expected to be the answer to the health problems experienced by *mustahik* but with easy services and not confusing them. The location of Rumah Sehat Terpadu Dompet Dhuafa is in Bogor Regency and occupies an area of 7.6 hectares. Some of the facilities owned by this healthy house are specialist doctors, polyclinics, operating rooms, Emergency Units (ER), pharmacies, and so on.

In addition to Bogor Regency, integrated health homes, hospitals, and clinics owned by Dompet Dhuafa have also been spread in various locations in Indonesia. There are two integrated hospitals, namely the Rumah Sehat Terpadu Dompet Dhuafa and Rumah Sehat Terpadu Dompet Dhuafa dan Qatar Charity Dompet Dhuafa, both of which are located in Bogor. Meanwhile, there are also AKA Medika Sribhawono Hospital in Lampung, Ahmad Wardi Eye Hospital in Serang, Sayyidah Mother and Child Hospital in East Jakarta, Lancang Kuning Hospital in Riau, Kartika Pulomas Hospital in Jakarta, Griya Medika Hospital in Lampung, and Naura Clinic in Depok.[16]

2.4.2.4 *Economic program via zakat*

Through zakat funds, BAZNAS managed to come up with a scheme known as *ZChicken BAZNAS* in 2022. The main objective of this scheme is to produce 1,000 ZChicken sellers in Java, Indonesia.[17] ZChicken is an economic program in the form of selling ready-to-eat chicken. This program includes three things, namely a chicken farm, a marinated chicken production house, and a distribution center (Republika 2022). *Mustahik* are also provided with assistance so that their business can run smoothly.[18]

---

[15] "BAZNAS". Accessed August 29, 2022. https://baznas.go.id/rsb.
[16] "RS Rumah Sehat Terpadu Dompet Dhuafa". Accessed August 29, 2022. https://www.rumahsehatterpadu.or.id/.
[17] Republika (2022). Baznas Luncurkan Program Usaha ZChicken Di Semarang. *Republika*.
[18] BAZNAS (2022). www.baznas.go.id.

The potential profit from selling this chicken can reach IDR4–5 million per month.[19]

2.4.2.5 Reducing poverty via zakat

Some studies have been conducted recently on productive zakat which shows its direct impact on the economic growth and purchasing power and reduces Indonesia's poverty level effectively.[20] The funds from zakat lead to the national income per capita, especially for *al-mustahiq*. Zakat also contributes positively to raising the purchasing power household consumption expenditure of society, particularly for poor people.[21]

Similarly, some studies revealed that zakat disbursement in the form of consumption-based or productive-based programs could reduce poverty significantly. For example, in Central Java, a productive-based zakat fund program improves *mustahik* households' income.[22] Using the CIBEST model, which involves material and spiritual aspects to calculate welfare and prosperity, the program successfully brings the *mustahik* out of poverty. On average, *mustahik* households' income increases by 147.14% after participating in the program. Their income increases from Rp 874,000.00/month to Rp 2,160,000.00/month.[23] The program also successfully decreases material, spiritual, and absolute poverty indices by 49.6%, 1.6%, and 12.3%, respectively.[24] Meanwhile, the welfare index increased by 63.7%.[25] Some previous studies about poverty reduction as the impact of zakat disbursement programs are summarized in Table 2.2.

---

[19] *Ibid.*
[20] Sulaeman, S., Majid, R., & Widiastuti, T. (2021). The impact of zakat on socio-economic welfare before COVID-19 pandemic in Indonesia: A quantitative study. *International Journal of Zakat*, Vol. 6, No. 2, pp. 75–90. https://doi.org/https://doi.org/10.37706/ijaz.v6i2.301.
[21] *Ibid.*
[22] Beik, I. S. & Pratama, C. (2017). Zakat impact on poverty and welfare of mustahik: A CIBEST model approach. *AFEBI Islamic Finance and Economic Review*, Vol. 1, No. 01, p. 1. https://doi.org/10.47312/aifer.v1i01.16.
[23] *Ibid.*
[24] *Ibid.*
[25] *Ibid.*

Table 2.2. Previous studies about poverty reduction via zakat.

Author(s)	Year	Subject	Poverty reduction (%)
Beik and Pratama	2017	Productive Zakat Fund Programs by *Dompet Dhuafa* in the Province of Central Java	49.6% (material poverty) 1.6% (spiritual poverty) 12.3% (absolute poverty)
Beik and Arsyianti	2016	Productive-based zakat programs of BAZNAS BAZIS DKI Jakarta and *Dompet Dhuafa* in Greater Jakarta	30.15 (material poverty) 91.30 (absolute poverty)
Beik and Tsani	2015	Zakat distribution and utilization programs in South Lampung regency	18.60
Beik	2013	Productive-based zakat programs of BAZNAS BAZIS DKI Jakarta and *Dompet Dhuafa* in Greater Jakarta	16.79
Purnamasari	2010	Zakat distribution and utilization programs in Garut regency	21.40
Anriani	2010	Zakat distribution and utilization programs in Bogor city	8.77

Source: Processed data BAZNAS, www.baznas.go.id (2022).

Another study was conducted in 2016 regarding the impact of zakat on human development index at the household level of zakat productive recipients. Using two periods of observation, the study shows that the level of human development index of households receiving productive-based zakat is significantly higher than in the first period. The study also concluded that zakat, particularly productivity-based zakat, can play an essential role in improving the welfare of poor households.[26]

The distribution of zakat is also carried out in rural areas. For example, in a 2016 study, zakat's impact on two villages, Tamiang Village and Sindangsari Village, was conducted using the zakat impact index.

---

[26] Mohammad, S. N. (2016). "Special feature" new waves in Islamic economics: Renovation of the traditional economic institutions (*waqf* and zakat) and reconsidering early generations, *Kyoto Bulletin of Islamic Area Studies*, Vol. 9, pp. 1–3. https://repository.kulib.kyoto-u.ac.jp/dspace/bitstream/2433/210347/1/I.A.S_009_042.pdf.

The results of this study indicate that the impact of zakat given to the two villages has a reasonably positive impact on *mustahik*.[27]

2.4.2.6 Supporting education via zakat

In Indonesia, there are so many children who cannot continue their education to college because of financial constraints. To find a job vacancy with a high school diploma is also quite difficult. Due to these problems, many zakat institutions pay attention to educational programs, such as in the case of Mandiri Entrepreneur Center (MEC) and the integrated scholarship and learning support supported by Amil Zakat al-Ihsan Central Java.

With reference to the first one, Yatim Mandiri Amil Zakat Institution offers an educational program in the form of the MEC. This program is free of charge and the object is to help children who come from low-income families (Dhuafa) and have completed high school education.[28] In the program, these children will be given informal education about entrepreneurship which consists of three remarkable programs: digital business, digital publishers, and social media marketers.[29] The output of this program is that these children can open their businesses or get jobs according to their abilities. The guidance carried out by MEC is to increase not only entrepreneurial capacity but also academic and Islamic knowledge. So, it is hoped that after graduating from this program, they can carry out worship well, improve the family economy, and have broad insight.

The MEC program has been carried out in several places, one of which is in Bogor, West Java. Graduates from this program are proven to be able to compete in entrepreneurship.[30] The program participants also feel an increase in the spirit of independence, academic understanding, and spiritual aspects that make them even better.[31]

With reference to the second program, the integrated scholarship and learning support supported by Amil Zakat al-Ihsan Central Java, this

---

[27] Nashir, S. A. & Nurzaman, M. S. (2019). The impact of zakat empowerment program on village. *ICEBESS 2018*, Vol. 305, pp. 124–27. https://doi.org/10.2991/icebess-18.2019.22.
[28] Haura, S. *et al.* (2021). Proses Pemberdayaan Anak Yatim Melalui Program Mandiri Entrepreneur Center (MEC), Vol. 2, No. 2.
[29] Center (2022).
[30] Haura, S. *et al. Op. cit.*
[31] *Ibid.*

program is carried out into two programs. First is the integrated scholarship program aimed at elementary, junior high, and high school students accompanied by mentoring to improve their character, spirituality, and independence. Second is the learning assistance program to facilitate community learning communities, especially for underprivileged children, densely populated areas, and prone to faith.[32] In general, the forms of coaching applied at the Amil Zakat Al-Ihsan Central Java are more focused on mental and moral development.[33]

2.4.2.7 Livestock breeding via zakat

Zakat on livestock is also a program that is quite popular in Indonesia. The majority of poor people in Indonesia who live in rural areas make this program suitable for development. On a macro level, animal husbandry is one of the sectors that supports food availability with a variety of animal protein source products it produces, starting from milk, eggs, and meat.[34]

One of the *amil* zakat institutions that has a main focus on animal husbandry is Nurul Hayat in Surabaya. To ensure the program runs smoothly, Nurul Hayat carries out three main processes, namely screening, production, and market.[35] Nurul Hayat's livestock program has succeeded in increasing *mustahik's* income, raising awareness of giving alms to *mustahik*, and also making *mustahik* more independent.[36]

In 2022, the number of breeders fostered by Nurul Hayat reached 68 breeders spread across 10 regions in Indonesia with a total of 568 sheep and generated income for farmers of Rp 227,903,400.[37] The alms produced by these farmers reached Rp 10,520,500 and were given to 103 beneficiaries.[38] This program has proven to help *mustahik* to remain empowered even though they are still in the midst of the COVID-19 pandemic.

---

[32] Lazisjateng (2022).
[33] Tho'in (2017).
[34] Maghfirlana & Widiastuti (2019).
[35] *Ibid.*
[36] *Ibid.*
[37] Nurul Hayat (n.d.). Program Ternak Desa Sejahtera. https://nurulhayat.org/program-ternak-desa-sejahtera/.
[38] *Ibid.*

Another livestock program that is also interesting to highlight is the cattle, goat, and sheep farming program by BAZNAS. There are four main activities in this program, namely the Center for Livestock Cultivation, Center for Product Processing, Center for By-product Processing, and Center for Animal Feed. To ensure that livestock can be managed properly by *mustahik*, BAZNAS also provides infrastructure assistance, such as production equipment and cages.

Local assistants are also prepared by BAZNAS to help farmers improve their knowledge and skills in raising livestock, such as basic knowledge about handling sick animals, the mating process, and giving birth, to marketing. In addition, local facilitators are also expected to help increase the sense of ownership and solidarity among farmer groups.

Currently, several livestock center programs produce not only raw meat but also other processed products, such as compost, leather crackers, leather crafts, and so on. Several other livestock centers have also carried out a more advanced process by processing raw meat into ready-to-eat food. This will certainly increase the value added of the livestock center and the income of farmers.

Table 2.3 shows the result of a study which determines the impact of the BAZNAS livestock program using two measuring tools. First is the BAZNAS Welfare Index (BWI) which measures the condition of *mustahik* from three aspects, namely spiritual-economic, independent, and health-educational. The second measuring tool is the poverty index which measures how many *mustahik* are out of the poverty line. From Table 2.3, it can be seen that the value of BWI is increasing every year which reflects the success of the program. In addition, the number of *mustahik* who are lifted from poverty also increases every year, namely 0.51% in 2020, 0.65% in 2021 to reach 81% in 2022.

Two other studies were also conducted to measure the impact of livestock programs. Using Sustainable Livelihood Impact Assessment, the livestock empowerment center in Magelang has improved by 1.40 from

Table 2.3. The impact of zakat on the BAZNAS stockbreeding program 2020–2022.

BAZNAS Welfare Index (BWI)			Poverty Index ($\Delta P0$)		
2020	2021	2022	2020	2021	2022
0.71 (Good)	0.77 (Good)	0.78 (Good)	0.51	0.65	0.81

Source: Processed data BAZNAS, www.baznas.go.id (2022).

Role of Zakat in Alleviating Poverty in Muslim Societies: Past and Present   37

the inception of the program. The program has improved the livelihood of the participants and the social asset in the community through the infrastructure provided, training, and assistantship.[39] In addition, research on the impact of a similar program in Tanah Datar, West Sumatra, also produced a positive impact. Overall, the program of livestock center in Tanah Datar District has been upgrading the local people who are assisted, providing them with hands-on training to improve their knowledge and skills in sheep/goat rearing and to solidify kinship among the farmers.[40]

2.4.2.8 Enhancing agriculture via zakat

Zakat also managed to enhance the agriculture sector in Indonesia through a program known as Salam Tani. In this program, the distribution of zakat in agriculture is carried out by Nurul Hayat Bojonegoro which was created in 2018. In this case, products from farmers are purchased using a salam contract with the aim that farmers can be more prosperous because the harvest is purchased at a reasonable price. Not only from the economic aspect, but this program also helps improve the spiritual aspect felt by the farmers.[41]

2.4.3 Current role of zakat in selected countries in Africa

2.4.3.1 Meeting the basic needs via zakat

There is a hunger crisis in the Horn of Africa consisting of Somalia, Ethiopia, Eritrea, and Djibouti. It is caused by the drought in years which leads to insufficient harvest and crops and furthermore, malnutrition. To fulfill the basic needs of those people, Zakat Foundation of America established programs to distribute food to the needy.[42]

---

[39] Pusat Kajian Strategies BAZNAS (2019). The poverty among farmers in Indonesia and zakat empowerment program. www.puskasbaznas.com.
[40] Pusat Kajian Stategis BAZNAS (2019). The impact of zakat for mustahik: Case of livestock center in Tanah Datar.
[41] Mukminin, A. Y. *et al.* (2022). Efektivitas Program Salam Tani Menggunakan Metode Analisis Indonesia Magnificence Of Zakat pada LAZ Nurul Hayat Bojonegoro.
[42] Zakatorg (n.d.). The hunger crisis in the Horn of Africa. zakat.org.

Another example of zakat on basic needs is from UNHCR's Refugee Zakat. The zakat fund collected by the UNHCR is distributed to refugees from Nigeria, Ethiopia, and Somalia. The programs include cash assistance, livelihoods support, and emergency relief.[43]

2.4.3.2 Enhancing agriculture via zakat

Zakat on agriculture in Ghana is supported by Zakat Foundation of America. The beneficiaries of this program are 10 women in Jamam Ghana Village. The plant chosen is cassava since it plays a crucial role for underprivileged people in Ghana. Given its characteristics, cassava is regarded as a valuable source of carbohydrates that is also relatively simple to cultivate. As a result, the program can help the beneficiaries to move out of poverty. Before the zakat program, people in Ghana bought cassava from the seller and produced a staple food called gari. But now, since they have their cassava land, they can minimize the cost and make more profit.[44]

2.4.3.3 Humanitarian assistance via zakat

In 2017, the International Federation of Red Cross and Red Crescent Societies (IFRC) and the Kenya Red Cross joined other aid groups in launching international emergency appeals. Their goals are to provide people with access to water, food, and healthcare before helping them to recover and rebuild their lives. Recognizing the growing difficulties involved in raising emergency funds to assist the droughts in Kenya, IFRC approached Zakat Council of the Malaysian State of Perlis (Majlis Agama Islam Perlis MAIPS) for assistance. In response, MAIPS contributed zakat for funding the drought assistance program in Kenya. With such funding, Malaysia was able to help one million people in rural Kenya in meeting their basic needs.[45]

---

[43] UNHCR. (n.d.). https://zakat.unhcr.org/africa/.
[44] Zakatorg (n.d.). Zakat foundation of America supported Cassava cooperative in Ghana. https://www.zakat.org/planting-better-futures-zf-supported-cassava-cooperative-ghana.
[45] Beyond Charity: The transformative power of zakat in humanitarian crises. https://www.alnap.org/system/files/content/resource/files/main/Kenya_case_study_2018_003.pdf.

2.4.3.4 *Building cities via zakat*

In 2016, the Zakat House of Kuwait managed to finance Al-Rahma City in Somaliland through zakat funds. This city includes schools for boys, workshops, an administrative building, a dispensary, girls' schools, a craft institute, service buildings, a masjid, a hospital, a bakery, a restaurant, residential apartments for the medical doctors, a sports area, an event hall, and an orphanage.[46]

2.5 Role of Zakat in Eliminating *Riba*

Riba/interest is one of the key factors in the spread of poverty in Muslim countries. It is effortless profit in which its interest money goes from the poor countries to the rich countries as well as from the poor individuals to the rich people which make them even richer, whereas in Islam, the rich are supposed to give money to the poor. As such, *riba* has been prohibited in Islam and has been replaced with alternative financial and socio-financial tools such as zakat as mentioned in Surat al-Rum (30:39):

> *And whatever you give for interest to increase within the wealth of people will not increase with Allah. But what you give in zakah, desiring the countenance of Allah — those are the multipliers.* (Surat al-Rum 30:39)

2.5.1 *Current situation of compound interest in Muslim countries*

Currently, majority of Muslim countries are borrowing with *riba* for the economic development or for anti-poverty programs. Unfortunately, all these countries today are suffering from compound interest. For example, according to Mr. Obasanjo, the ex-President of Nigeria during the G8 meeting, regarding the external borrowing for the sake of developing his country and eradicating poverty, said the following:

> *All that we had borrowed up to 1985 or 1986 was around $5 billion and we have paid about $16 billion yet we are still being told that we owe*

---

[46] https://www.alraimedia.com/article/607526/م-الأولى-المرحلة-انتهاء-الزكاة-بيت/محليات الصومال-في-الكويت-مجمع-ن.

about $28 billion. That $28 billion came about because of the injustice in the foreign creditors' interest rates. If you ask me of what is the worst thing in the world, I will say it is compound interest.[47]

Nigeria is not the only country; other Muslim countries fall under the same trap of borrowing for the sake of development and hence end up repaying more than what they borrowed.

Table 2.4 shows the total lending by World Bank between 1970 and 2020 for some selected Muslim countries for poverty alleviation programs. The main objective of such borrowing is to reduce poverty through anti-poverty programs and SME projects. However, this does not happen since the majority of these Muslim countries find themselves caught in

Table 2.4. Total lending by World Bank between 1970 and 2020 for poverty alleviation programs.

Country	Total lending (USD millions)	Interest rate (%)
Bangladesh	54	9.7
Chad	39	–
Egypt	20,390	18.3
Indonesia	54,913	10.5
Jordan	6,568	8.7
Malaysia	3,915	4.9
Morocco	18,669	–
Nigeria	6,687	16.9
Pakistan	10,583	8.5
Senegal	155	5.1
Sudan	32	16.2
Syria	579	–
Tunisia	10,473	–
Turkey	42,006	–

Source: World Bank Group Finances (2020) and World Bank (2019).

---

[47] Mohsin, M. A. (2020). A fresh view on zakah as a socio-financial tool to promote ethics, eliminate *riba* and reduce poverty. *International Journal of Management and Applied Research*, Vol. 7, No. 1 (see also youtube: http://www.youtube.com/watch?v=SaeRum-GJMY).

poverty due to the amount of interest paid on loans which they will likely continue to pay for generations to come.[48]

The question that may arise is as follows: Can zakat replace *riba*/interest in playing its role as an anti-poverty program? The following section will answer this question.

2.5.2 *Case of zakat through salary deduction scheme*

A study conducted by Magda Abdel Mohsin[49] shows that a huge amount of zakat can be collected only through salary deduction scheme, which is currently practiced successfully in Malaysia and which will collect more that the amount borrowed by all these countries to meet their objective in reducing poverty.

For example, if we assume the Muslim population in a given country is 23 million, out of which three million are rich people, 10 million are middle-class people, and the rest of the population are unproductive members of the society (young, poor, and old age). Assuming that the collection of zakat becomes compulsory, this means on average the rich can give $1000/year and the middle class can give $100/year as zakat. Therefore, a total of $4 billion/year can be collected as zakat as in the said country.

Rich people	3 million × $1000 = $ 3.00 billion
Middle class people	10 million × $ 100 = $ 1.00 billion
Total	$4.00 billion

Following the same example, let us estimate how much zakat fund can be collected from these countries to meet their objective without resorting to the external borrowing with *riba*/interest which is prohibited in Islam. Similarly, let us assume that the rich people in each of these countries will give $1000/year as zakat and the middle-class people will give $100/year zakat, hence, a huge amount of zakat fund will be collected compared to the borrowed amount as seen in Table 2.4.

Table 2.5 shows the Muslim population in these countries, percentage of the poverty, the assumption of the population of the rich and middle class, and the amount collected of zakat through salary deduction scheme.

---
[48] *Ibid.*
[49] *Ibid.*

Table 2.5. Zakat collection from salary.

Country	Muslim population (mil)	Upper class (mil)	Middle class (mil)	Upper class giving USD1000 zakat per year (bil)	Middle class giving USD100 zakat per year (bil)	Total zakat collection from salary in USD (bil)
Bahrain	0.91	0.2	0.5	0.2	0.05	0.25
Bangladesh	135.1	27	73	27	7.3	34.3
Egypt	77.7	15.5	42.6	15.5	4.26	19.76
Indonesia	218	43.6	150	43.6	15	58.6
Iran	77.1	15.4	47	15.4	4.7	20.1
Iraq	33	6.6	20	6.6	2.0	8.2
Jordan	4.4	0.9	2.9	0.9	0.29	1.19
Malaysia	18.3	3.7	14.3	3.7	1.43	5.13
Morocco	32	6.4	25.5	6.4	2.55	8.95
Nigeria	83	16.6	28	16.6	2.8	19.4
Oman	3.2	0.6	2.2	0.6	0.22	0.82
Pakistan	172	34.4	99	34.4	9.9	44.3
Sudan	29.9	5.8	10	5.8	1	6.8
Tunisia	10.8	2.2	7	2.2	0.7	2.9
Turkey	73.9	14.8	56	14.8	5.6	20.4

Source: Mohsin, M. A. *Op. cit.*

Table 2.5 shows that the collection of zakat fund from salary deduction scheme alone amounts to billions of USD compared to the external debts in millions of USD in which Muslim countries were forced to the external borrowing to eradicate their poverty. Hence, through efficient collection of zakat through salary deduction scheme, this will prevent the Muslim countries to borrow and hence will eliminate *riba* from Muslim society with special reference when dealing with poverty eradication.[50]

---

[50] *Ibid.*

Self-Assessment Quiz (MCQs)

Question 1:
1. Providing shelter to mustahik
2. To fulfill the basic needs
3. Capital assistance for mustahik
4. To improve the quality of life of mustahik through economic programs

From the statements above, which are the characteristics of zakat consumptive?
(a) 1 and 2
(b) 1 and 3
(c) 1 and 4
(d) 2 and 3
(e) 3 and 4

Question 2:
1. Providing shelter to mustahik
2. To fulfill the basic needs
3. Capital assistance for mustahik
4. To improve the quality of life of mustahik through economic programs

From the statements above, which are the characteristics of zakat productive?
(a) 1 and 2
(b) 1 and 3
(c) 1 and 4
(d) 2 and 3
(e) 3 and 4

Question 3:
1. Free hospital service
2. Pay off student loans
3. Scholarship
4. Livestock breeding program

From the statements above, which are the programs of zakat on education?
(a) 1 and 2
(b) 1 and 3

(c) 1 and 4
(d) 2 and 3
(e) 3 and 4

Question 4: Somalia, Ethiopia, Eritrea, and Djibouti are facing a serious hunger crisis. Which following zakat institution already has a distribution food program to help those people overcome the situation?
(a) BAZNAS
(b) Zakat Foundation of America
(c) The Federal Islamic Religious Council
(d) Muslim Charity
(e) Brotherhood Muslim Union

Question 5:
1. Zakat productive such as agriculture programs can help people to increase their quality of life
2. Indonesia and Malaysia have several health programs
3. Some studies indicate that zakat productive can reduce the poverty level
4. Zakat can be used to fulfill the basic needs of mustahik
   From the statements above, which are true?
   (a) 1, 2, 3, and 4
   (b) 1, 2, and 3
   (c) 1, 2, and 4
   (d) 1, 3, and 4
   (e) 1 and 2

Question 6: Which of the following statement is not correct?
(a) Zakat has spiritual, material, and economical obligations toward its givers
(b) Zakat purifies the heart of its recipients from selfishness and greed for wealth
(c) Zakat purifies the heart of its recipients from envy and jealousy
(d) Zakat circulates the wealth from the have to the have not

Question 7: The balance of the collected zakat within a year can be channeled to
(a) Buying slaves and freeing them
(b) Helping young men and women get married
(c) Assisting orphans and needy until they are all enriched
(d) Transferring the balance of the collected zakat to the following year to assist the poor and needy

Question 8: The transformative power of zakat in Malaysia is not realized in
(a) Meeting the basic need of the poor and needy
(b) Providing healthcare for the poor and needy
(c) Cultivating agricultural land to feed the poor and needy
(d) Providing affordable housing for asnaf

Question 9: The transformative power of zakat in Indonesia is not realized in
(a) Providing affordable housing for asnaf
(b) Meeting the basic needs of the poor and needy
(c) Settling debtors' loan online
(d) Reducing poverty

Question 10: The transformative power of zakat in selected countries in Africa is not realized in
(a) Enhancing agriculture
(b) Providing humanitarian assistance
(c) Building cities
(d) Building hospitals

Self-Assessment/Recall Questions

Question 1: Discuss how zakat can fulfill its religious and social obligations.

Question 2: Elaborate on the role of zakat in achieving its eight objectives.

Question 3: Explain how zakat can eradicate poverty. Provide past and present examples.

Question 4: Justify how zakat can eliminate *riba*/interest from Muslim societies.

Question 5: Discuss the contemporary transformative power of zakat in Muslim societies.

Answers to Self-Assessment Quiz (MCQs)

1. a
2. e
3. d
4. b
5. d
6. b
7. d
8. c
9. a
10. d

Chapter 3

Similarities and Differences between Zakat, Tax, *Sadaqat*, and *Waqf*

Learning Outcomes

At the end of this chapter, students must be able to understand the similarities and differences between

- zakat and tax,
- zakat and *sadaqat*,
- zakat and *waqf*.

3.1. Similarities and Differences between Zakat and Taxes

3.1.1 *Similarities of zakat and taxes*

Zakat and tax seem to be similar to each other at a glance in terms of payment of a certain amount of money or wealth to both recipients. However, while defining both terms, zakat is one concept and tax is another. Nevertheless, similarities can be deduced as presented in the following points:

- Zakat is a compulsory due on Muslim's wealth. Tax is also a mandatory payment imposed by a government or nation on its citizens without any contractual exchange.[1] Hence, both zakat and tax are compulsory and mandatory in nature for those who are in capacity or eligible to pay it.

- Zakat is levied from Muslim's wealth that reached a minimum amount that is subject to obligation which is known as *al-nisab*. Such giving is without any direct exchange by Muslims to the Islamic state, regardless of the benefits that the *zakat* payer may get from the state. Tax is also levied based on the payers' ability, regardless of the benefits derived from the services provided by the public authority using tax proceeds. Hence, both zakat and tax are not commercial exchanges between payers and recipients. There is no reciprocity between the money collected and the services the payer receives in the case of tax. As a member of society, the payer is obligated to pay tax. Zakat is also paid by every Muslim, without any direct transaction, regardless of the benefits received from the state.
- Zakat management is handled by the state and also tax is managed by the state.
- Zakat is a specified right on Muslims' wealth as a socio-financial tool in redistributing the wealth for the benefit of the whole society.[2] Tax is also revenue for the government to achieve economic, social, political, and other goals. Hence, both zakat and tax can help in contributing to the community development and its empowerment without compromising the original poverty alleviation programs.[3] In modern philosophy, zakat and taxes have social, economic, and political goals in addition to financial goals. The zakat system assures equitable wealth distribution and broadly impacts the entire social structure. If zakat becomes an institution, it will form a communal social security program for mutual aid/sympathy, and the resources will be available for further social development.[4] Similarly, the tax system can influence the growth of the

---

[1] Al-Dalimy. *Constitutional and Legal Restrictions in Implementing the General State Budget Revenues* الضوابط الدستورية والقانونية للرقابة على تنفيذ الموازنة العامة للدولة من باب الإيرادات.
[2] Al-Qardawi. *Fiqh Al Zakat: A Comparative Study* (Vol. 2).
[3] Adachi, M. Discourses of institutionalization of zakat management system in contemporary Indonesia: Effect of the revitalization of Islamic economics.
[4] Abdullah, M., & Suhaib, A. Q. The impact of zakat on social life of Muslim society.

economy by influencing physical capital, human capital, and total factor productivity.[5]
- Zakat helps the government to eradicate poverty by providing the basic needs for all in terms of food, shelter, healthcare, and education, while taxation also allows a government to purchase services and social insurance schemes, including health, education, physical security, or social solidarity infrastructure.[6]

3.1.2 *Differences between zakat and tax*

Regardless of the above points of similarities, the followings are some divergences between zakat and taxes:

- The most important difference between zakat and tax can be seen from the theoretical foundation in which both instruments are levied. From a legal perspective, taxes are imposed based on contractual theory. It is the relationship between the state and its citizens whereby taxes are paid in exchange for services the state provides, such as security and other public services.[7] Many criticized this theory as it is flawed in the foundation. There is no way to achieve justice in any exchange between taxes and benefits received by the taxpayer because it is impossible to estimate the exact benefit each citizen receives from government spending on security, law enforcement, the judiciary system, education, and national defense. The second theory to levy taxes is that of state sovereignty. This theory explains taxes through the authority of the state as the sovereign entity with the right to divide the tax burden based on the solidarity of all members of society, independent of any benefits they receive from the state's services. Taxation appears to be an intrinsic right or entitlement associated with sovereign existence. Furthermore, others believe that because taxation is so important to sovereignty, autonomy in establishing the tax system is more important than autonomy in other regulatory areas.[8] On the other hand, zakat is levied on Muslim's wealth in accordance with the theory of obligation

---

[5] Stoilova, D. & Patonov, N. Tourism & management studies an empirical evidence for the impact of taxation on economy growth in the European Union.
[6] Brooks, N. & Hwong, T. *The Social Benefits and Economic Costs of Taxation.*
[7] Al-Qardawi. *Op. cit.*
[8] Christians, A. Sovereignty, taxation and social contract.

and *khilafah*/viceregency. From the theory of obligation, Allah (SW), the Greater and Provider, has the authority to impose a responsibility on His workers in gratitude to Him, as well as to test them in order to identify the wrongdoer from the doer of good. Allah (SW) requires the payment of zakat as a kind of financial worship, in which humanity spend their valuable assets in thanksgiving to Allah (SW) and in search of His pleasure.[9] Meanwhile, the theory of viceregency implies that all creatures belong to Allah. What a human possesses is not belong to him/her in essence, as a result, it is not surprising that humans, the vicegerents, should spend these conferred goods (including zakat payment) for Allah's (SW) purposes and to elevate Allah's (SW) message. This is the simplest way to express thanks and thankfulness.

- In terms of terminology, the word zakat indicates purity, growth, and blessing. Meanwhile, tax implies imposition, estimation, and charge. As a result, a tax is regarded as both a charge and a liability. On the other hand, zakat stimulates purity, holiness, and progress. It is implied that hoarding wealth without cleaning it by giving the right that Allah (SW) imposes on the poor turn's wealth into a source of sin and evil, but giving zakat causes the growth. Furthermore, zakat creates a sense of purification not just for the assets given for zakat but also for the payment and the recipient since it purifies them from vanity, hatred, and selfishness and extends a kind hand to the destitute.[10]
- By default, zakat is a form of worship of Muslims in thankfulness and gratitude toward Allah, while tax is just an official form of the obligation imposed on the citizen of the country regardless of their religion.
- Regarding the ratios or minimum amount of payment, zakat as a form of worship, the objects of zakat and their payment ratios cannot be adjusted or amended by man. Hence, it will remain constant whatever the circumstances and ages. Zakat on wealth would be only 2.5% over the total zakatable assets once it exceeds the *nisab* (minimum amount that is subject to obligation) and there is no space for negotiation. Meanwhile, taxes can alter by the regulation of a particular country. It

---

[9] Al-Qardawi. *Op. cit.*
[10] *Ibid.*

is enacted by people and is always subject to change and redeterminations.
- Zakat recipients are eight beneficiaries and cannot be changed while tax beneficiaries are not specific and government can change from time to time.
- Zakat has spiritual and ethical goals in addition to its socio-economic goals, whereas taxes do not. The Prophet (PBUH) used to pray for the blessings of zakat payers and instructed his companions to do so since it is mandatory. Taxes are separated from such spiritual and ethical goals.[11]

3.1.3 *Impact of tax and zakat on Prices*

From an economic point of view, the determination of equilibrium price and quantity will be through the intersection of demand D1 and supply S1 curves. In a competitive market, price will function to equalize the quantity demanded by consumers and the quantity supplied by producers, resulting in an economic equilibrium of price and quantity at P_E and Q_E as highlighted in Figure 3.1.

Hence, without a tax, the equilibrium price will be at P_E and the equilibrium quantity will be at Q_E. However, after a tax is imposed, the price consumers pay will shift to P_c and the price producers receive will shift to P_p. The consumers' price will be equal to the producers' price plus the cost of the tax. Since the consumers will buy less at the higher consumer

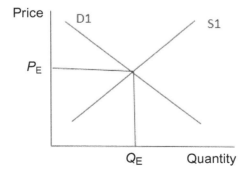

Figure 3.1. Determination of equilibrium price and quantity.

---

[11] Al-Qardawi. *Op. cit.*

54   Application of Zakat: From Classical and Contemporary Perspective

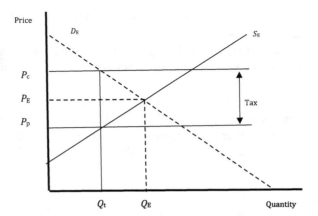

Figure 3.2.   Effect of taxes on prices.

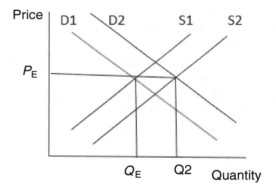

Figure 3.3.   Effect of zakat on prices.

price P_c and producers will sell less at a lower producer price P_p, the quantity sold will fall from Q_E to Q_t as shown in Figure 3.2.

Hence, this will prevent many people from buying such a product, especially if it essential good and services.

On the contrary, being guided by Islamic ethics, all eligible Muslims give their zakat. This in turn increases demand for goods and services and will shift the demand curves from D1 to D2. Similarly, the supply of goods and services will increase to meet the new demand, hence shifting the supply curves from S1 to S2 without changing the price. Therefore, the effect of zakat will create more jobs to meet the demand in the market hence resulting in a sustainable price which is affordable by all categories of people, i.e., price will not change as shown in Figure 3.3.

3.2 Similarities and Differences between Zakat and *Sadaqat*

3.2.1 *Similarities between zakat and sadaqat*

As the primary source of shariah, Quran has been mentioning the words of zakat (زكاة) and its derivations more than 25 times and *sadaqah* (صدقة : singular) or *sadaqaat* (صدقات : plural) more than 10 times.[12] The following are some Quranic verses talking about zakat:

وَأَقِيمُوا الصَّلَوٰةَ وَءَاتُوا الزَّكَوٰةَ وَارْكَعُوا مَعَ الرَّٰكِعِينَ

establish prayer and give zakat and bow with those who bow [in worship and obedience. (Al-Baqarah 2:43)

إِنَّمَا وَلِيُّكُمُ اللَّهُ وَرَسُولُهُ وَالَّذِينَ ءَامَنُوا الَّذِينَ يُقِيمُونَ الصَّلَوٰةَ وَيُؤْتُونَ الزَّكَوٰةَ وَهُمْ رَٰكِعُونَ

ally is none but Allah and [therefore] His Messenger and those who have believed — those who establish prayer and give zakat, and they bow [in worship]. (Al-Ma'idah 5:55)

الَّذِينَ إِن مَّكَّنَّٰهُمْ فِي الْأَرْضِ أَقَامُوا الصَّلَوٰةَ وَءَاتَوُا الزَّكَوٰةَ وَأَمَرُوا بِالْمَعْرُوفِ وَنَهَوْا عَنِ الْمُنكَرِ ۗ وَلِلَّهِ عَٰقِبَةُ الْأُمُورِ

[And they are] those who, if We give them authority in the land, establish prayer and give zakat and enjoin what is right and forbid what is wrong. And to Allah belongs the outcome of [all] matters. (Al-Hajj 22:41)

While the following are some Quranic verses talking about *sadaqah*:

قَوْلٌ مَّعْرُوفٌ وَمَغْفِرَةٌ خَيْرٌ مِّن صَدَقَةٍ يَتْبَعُهَا أَذًى ۗ وَاللَّهُ غَنِيٌّ حَلِيمٌ

---

[12] Kaltsum & Muqsit. *Tafsir Ayat-Ayat Ahkam*.

speech and forgiveness are better than charity followed by injury. And Allah is Free of need and Forbearing. (Al-Baqarah 2:263)

خُذْ مِنْ أَمْوَالِهِمْ صَدَقَةً تُطَهِّرُهُمْ وَتُزَكِّيهِم بِهَا وَصَلِّ عَلَيْهِمْ ۖ إِنَّ صَلَاتَكَ سَكَنٌ لَّهُمْ ۗ وَاللَّهُ سَمِيعٌ عَلِيمٌ

[O, Muhammad], from their wealth a charity by which you purify them and cause them increase, and invoke [Allah's blessings] upon them. Indeed, your invocations are reassurance for them. And Allah is Hearing and Knowing. (At-Taubah 9:103)

إِن تُبْدُوا الصَّدَقَاتِ فَنِعِمَّا هِيَ

you disclose your charitable expenditures, they are good. (Al-Baqarah 2:271)

يَمْحَقُ اللَّهُ الرِّبَا وَيُرْبِي الصَّدَقَاتِ ۗ وَاللَّهُ لَا يُحِبُّ كُلَّ كَفَّارٍ أَثِيمٍ

destroys interest and gives increase for charities. And Allah does not like every sinning disbeliever. (Al-Baqarah 2:276)

From the above Quranic verses, the following similarities can be presented:

- Zakat and *sadaqah* are interchangeably used to maintain compulsory meaning and sometimes voluntary meaning. Some verses use the word zakat as the subsequent word to solat "wa aqamus solata wa atawu zakat" to enhance the most obligatory nature that Muslims are required to fulfill. Hence, it can be concluded that the word *sadaqah* is a general term to represent the meaning of *al-infaaq*/spending which includes zakat.
- Zakat and *sadaqah* would not reduce wealth of their payer. Instead, spending in the way of Allah causes an increase in wealth as it is maintained in the hadith of Prophet Muhammad SAW narrated by Muslim from Abu Hurairah:

ما نَقَصَتْ صَدَقَةٌ مِنْ مَالٍ

Sadaqah does not cause reduction in wealth.[13]

---

[13] El-Islamiy. *The Reward of Giving Sadaqah.*

- In addition to Quranic interpretation, zakat and *sadaqah* are not just charitable instruments to seek the pleasure of Allah and for the purpose of wealth purification. In fact, both become factors from several influences that can establish socio-economic sustainability and social changes that result in the well-being of an individual and society in this world and the next.[14]
- Moreover, both zakat and *sadaqah* are Islamic social finance instruments which are able to be institutionalized and hence might assist in enhancing financial inclusion.[15]

3.2.2 Differences between zakat and sadaqah

Before proceeding to the discussion on the differences between zakat and *sadaqah*, a general overview of Islamic social finance instruments related to this discussion should be provided. The broad term for charity and philanthropy in Islam is *sadaqah*. *Sadaqah* is in the nature of free donation without any strings attached. When compulsorily mandated on an eligible Muslim, *sadaqah* is called zakat. When *sadaqah* results in flow of benefits that are expected to be stable and permanent (such as through endowment of a physical property), it is called *sadaqah jariya* or *waqf*.[16] Hence, both zakat and *sadaqah* are charitable acts. The primary distinction between them is that zakat is compulsory as the third pillar of Islam. So long as Muslims fulfill specific requirements, performing this obligation is a requirement for all Muslims. If the wealth under ownership or surveillance of Muslims exceeds *nisab* (minimum amount of items that is subject to mandatory zakat), they should donate a portion for zakat. Meanwhile, giving saqadah is voluntary and there is no minimum amount required to be given as *sadaqah*. Prophet (PBUH) says the following:

لاَ يَتَصَدَّقُ أَحَدٌ بِتَمْرَةٍ مِنْ كَسْبٍ طَيِّبٍ إِلاَّ أَخَذَهَا اللَّهُ بِيَمِينِهِ فَيُرَبِّيهَا كَمَا يُرَبِّي أَحَدُكُمْ فَلُوَّهُ أَوْ قَلُوصَهُ حَتَّى تَكُونَ مِثْلَ الْجَبَلِ أَوْ أَعْظَمَ

No one gives Sadaqa of a date out of his honest earning, but Allah accepts it with His Right Hand, and then fosters it as one of you fosters

---
[14] Awang, S. A. et al. The concept of charity in Islam: An analysis on the verses of Quran and Hadith.
[15] Zauro, N. A., Saad, R. A., & Sawandi, N. Enhancing socio-economic justice and financial inclusion in Nigeria: The role of zakat, *Sadaqah* and Qardhul Hassan.
[16] Obaidullah, M. Enhancing food security with Islamic microfinance: Insights from some recent experiments.

the colt or a young she-camel, till it becomes like a mountain or even greater.[17]

Muslims are encouraged to donate *sadaqah* even a single date. This cannot be applicable in the case of zakat. Regarding Zakat al-Maal, it requires a minimum of 82 g pure gold for Muslim to give 2.5% of it.

Another divergence between zakat and *sadaqah* is the types of both and the minimum waiting period to disburse. There are many kinds of zakat, including zakat fitrah, *maal*, and gold, and each has a certain requirement for the portion they should pay, depending on the *nisab*. The wealth must also be held for at least a year before it can be counted under zakat. It is not necessary to pay zakat from wealth if it cannot pass the *nisab* for a year. Furthermore, there are specific times when zakat must be paid, such as the zakat fitrah that is gathered at the end of Ramadan. *Sadaqah*, in contrast, is a voluntary action. There are no strict guidelines regarding the amount you must donate, and there is no set period of time. *Sadaqah* is more flexible. *Sadaqah* can be made at any time.

Similarly, zakat recipients are eight beneficiaries and cannot be changed while *sadaqah* beneficiaries are not specific and it can be given to anyone who deserves it.

Sadaqah (charity) is one of the noble actions taught by Islam. *Sadaqah* technically refers to the act of giving someone in need in order to gain a reward and get closer to Allah. It differs from other admirable philanthropic acts prescribed in Islam, such as Zakat, primarily in how it is administered. Institutionalization is required for Zakat, but it is not required for *sadaqah*.[18]

3.3 Similarities and Differences between Zakat and *Waqf*

3.3.1 *Similarities of zakat and waqf*

Zakat and *waqf* have similarities as both belong to the same genus of social protection and social peace.[19] Both could be utilized to contribute to poverty eradication. During the time of crisis, including the recent

---

[17] Al-Naysaburi. *Sahih Muslim*.
[18] Dasar, M. & Sujimon, M. S. The classical Islamic view of *sadaqah*: A preliminary study.
[19] Bugaje, U. & Ali, D. The administration of zakat and management of *waqf* in the sharia implementing states: 1999–2015.

COVID-19 pandemic, zakat and *waqf*, as part of Islamic social finance (ISF) instruments, were proven to aid affected people in stabilizing their financial constraints.[20] Throughout history, *waqf* has played an important role in the provision of social goods, such as education and health, public goods (roads, bridges, and national security), commercial business, utilities (water and sanitation), religious services (building and maintenance of mosques and graveyards), assisting the poor, orphans, and the needy, creating employment, and supporting the agricultural and industrial sectors at no cost to the government.[21] The same social impacts exist when the practice of zakat is enhanced. Zakat should have a favorable impact on investment since it provides an incentive for people to invest their money rather than keep investable resources inert. Zakat is said to affect aggregate supply in three ways: labor supply, capital supply, and resource allocation. The impact of zakat on labor supply can be achieved by improving the poor's health, nutrition, and other living situations.[22]

From a wealth management perspective, generating income may, consciously or unknowingly, contain non-shariah-compliant elements. Hence, zakat and *waqf* are meant to purify wealth.[23] It is also observed that zakat and *waqf* can be categorized as a method of wealth distribution and redistribution necessary to ensure that the wealth will circulate in the economy for the benefit of society. Moreover, by providing appropriate financial instruments to net-deficit households, zakat and awqaf can play an important role in alleviating emergencies.

3.3.2 *Differences between zakat and* waqf

From both nature and object of conduct, zakat is mandatory alms and the third pillar of Islam that includes paying away 2.5% of an individual's net monetary income or wealth to eight vulnerable categories in society each year. It is payable as a required requirement on at least 14 wealth items and assets of individuals who have attained the minimum taxable amount known as *nisab* in Islamic jurisprudence. *Waqf*, on the other hand, refers

---

[20] Ascarya, A. The role of Islamic social finance during COVID-19 pandemic in Indonesia's economic recovery.
[21] Thaker, M. T. *et al.* Developing cash *waqf* model as an alternative source of financing for micro enterprises in Malaysia.
[22] Wahab, N. A. & Rahim Abdul Rahman, A. A framework to analyse the efficiency and governance of zakat institutions.
[23] Ariff, M. & Mohamad, S. *Islamic Wealth Management: Theory and Practice.*

to a religious endowment established by the wealthy to provide free relief services, socio-economic benefits, and solace to the vulnerable elements of society.[24]

With regard to specific nominal or threshold, there is no minimum requirement for Muslims to give *waqf* as it is not compulsory. Also, the objects of *waqf* are not limited items as compared to zakat. *Waqf* can be in the form of immovable property (lands, masjids, funerals, schools, etc.) and movable items, such as weapons, animals, shares, and cash.[25] With reference to cash, numerous studies have been conducted regarding the importance and the huge potential of cash *waqf*. Cash *waqf* can finance not only religious places but also various goods and services that are required internationally, such as education, health, social care, and commercial activities, as well as basic infrastructure, in addition to creating jobs for the majority of people.[26]

---

[24] Raimi, L., Patel, A., & Adelopo, I. Corporate social responsibility, *waqf* system and zakat system as faith-based model for poverty reduction.

[25] Sanusi, S. & Shafiai, M. H. M. The management of cash *waqf*: Toward socio-economic development of Muslims in Malaysia.

[26] Abdel, M. I. Financing through cash-*waqf*: A revitalization to finance different needs.

Self-Assessment Quiz (MCQs)

Question 1 The broad term for charity and philanthropy in Islam is called as...
(a) zakat
(b) *waqf*
(c) *sadaqat*
(d) qurban
(e) tax

Question 2
1. Mandatory action
2. Voluntary action
3. Distributed only to asnaf
4. The wealth must not reach *nisab* and haul

   From the statements above, which are the characteristics of zakat?
   (a) 1 and 2
   (b) 1 and 3
   (c) 1 and 4
   (d) 2 and 3
   (e) 2 and 4

Question 3
1. Mandatory action
2. Voluntary action
3. Distributed only to asnaf
4. The wealth must not reach *nisab* and haul

   From the statements above, which are the characteristics of *waqf*?
   (a) 1 and 2
   (b) 1 and 3
   (c) 1 and 4
   (d) 2 and 3
   (e) 2 and 4

Question 4
1. The relationship between the state and its citizen
2. It implies imposition, estimation, and charge
3. The payment rations remain constant and can't be adjusted
4. It stimulates purity, holiness, and progress

From the statements above, which are the characteristics of tax?
(a) 1 and 2
(b) 1 and 3
(c) 1 and 4
(d) 2 and 3
(e) 2 and 4

Question 5: From the following surahs, which surah does not mentione about charity (sadaqa, zakat, and *waqf*)?
(a) Al Baqarah: 43
(b) Al Maidah: 55
(c) Al Hajj: 31
(d) Al Baqarah: 263
(e) At Taubah: 60

Question 6: Zakat and tax are similar on the following:
(a) Both zakat and tax are compulsory
(b) Both zakat and tax to be managed by the government
(c) Both zakat and tax are not commercial exchanges between payers and recipients.
(d) Recipients of both zakat and tax are the same

Question 7: Zakat and tax are different on the following:
(a) Tax to be collected by the state, zakat to be given voluntarily
(b) Tax to be spent on public services, zakat to be given to specified recipients
(c) Tax rate is changeable, zakat rate is fixed
(d) Tax to be collected from both Non-Muslims and Muslims, zakat to be collected only form Muslims

Question 8: The following statement is not correct about zakat and *sadaqah*:
(a) Zakat and *sadaqah* are Islamic social finance instruments
(b) Zakat and *sadaqah* are compulsory due
(c) Both zakat and *sadaqah* would not reduce the wealth of their payer
(d) Zakat and *sadaqah* are charitable instruments

Question 9: The following statement is not correct about zakat and *waqf*:
(a) Zakat and *waqf* can be utilized to contribute to poverty eradication
(b) Zakat and *waqf* can stabilize financial constraints during pandemic
(c) Zakat and *waqf* are remarkable financial products to finance public utilities
(d) Zakat and *waqf* are alternative institutions to *riba*

Question 10: The rate of zakat on wealth once it exceeds the *nisab* is
(a) 2.5%
(b) 3.5%
(c) 4%
(d) 5%

Self-Assessment/Recall Questions

Question 1: Discuss the similarities between zakat and tax.
Question 2: Discuss the differences between zakat and tax.
Question 3: Illustrate with diagrams showing the impact of tax and zakat on prices.
Question 4: Discuss the similarities and differences between zakat and *sadaqat*.
Question 5: Discuss the similarities and differences between zakat and *waqf*.

Answers to Self-Assessment Quiz (MCQs)

1. c
2. b
3. e
4. a
5. c
6. d
7. a
8. b
9. c
10. a

Chapter 4

Types of Zakat and Zakatable Wealth

Learning Outcomes

At the end of this chapter, students must be able to

- know the types of zakat in general,
- understand the objective of zakat al-fitr,
- classify the types of zakatable wealth,
- discuss the contemporary issues on zakatable wealth.

4.1 Types of Zakat

Zakat is a unique feature in Islamic economics as it is endogenously embedded as a socio-economic mechanism that can redistribute wealth among the society, which is also one of the foundational worships in Islam. It is also directly linked to the concept of ethical economy that emphasizes norms and sentiment that inspires individuals or institutions to conduct their rights and responsibilities in an economic system with respect to others in developing an ethical society based on the concepts of brotherhood and sharing principles.[1] In this regard, zakat embodies Islamic values that essentialize the welfare of the individual alongside the public interest. Moreover, zakat as one of the ethical socio-financial instruments is an essential tool in articulating and practicing social justice

---

[1] Sayer, A. (2000). Moral economy and political economy. *Studies in Political Economy*, Vol. 61, No. 1, pp. 79–103. https://doi.org/10.1080/19187033.2000.11675254.

without curbing the motivation of people to achieve worldly success along with success in hereafter or *falah,* which aligns with the ideal concept of Islamic economics.[2]

Historically speaking and with a sincere adherence and effective implementation of zakat system, poverty was almost completely wiped out, and thus, achieved socio-economic and spiritual advancement and wider well-being[3] as discussed in Chapter 2. Zakat is an Islamic religious "tax" charged to the rich and middle class of the society for redistributing it to the poor and the needy and other recipients as specified in al-Quran.[4] Unlike conventional tax, zakat is viewed by Muslims as a means of 'purification' and not just an obligation. Ethically, zakat promotes sharing of wealth and eliminates greediness, while collectively, it helps reduce poverty within Muslim community.[5]

Islam requires the Muslims to pay zakat so that the money collected can help the poor to get their basic needs to sustain them alive.[6] There are two types of zakat, zakat al-fitr and zakat on wealth as detailed in the following.

4.2   Zakat Al-Fitr and Its Objective

Zakat al fitr is derived from the Arabic word fatara which means to become, to make, to provide, or to breakfast.[7] *Fitr* also means to open or

---

[2] Tripp, C. (2006). *Islam and the Moral Economy: The Challenge of Capitalism.* Cambridge: Cambridge University Press.
[3] Nazri, F. A. A., Rahman R. A., & Omar, N. (2012). Zakat and poverty alleviation: Roles of zakat institutions in Malaysia. *International Journal of Arts and Commerce,* Vol. 1, No. 7, pp. 61–72.
[4] Al-Mamun, A., Haque, A., & Jan, M. T. (2019). Measuring perceptions of Muslim consumers toward income tax rebate over zakat on income in Malaysia. *Journal of Islamic Marketing,* Vol. 11, No. 2, pp. 368–83. https://doi.org/10.1108/JIMA-12-2016-0104.
[5] Gambling, T. E. & Karim, R. A. A. (1986). Islam and 'social accounting'. *Journal of Business Finance & Accounting,* Vol. 13, No. 1, pp. 39–50. https://doi.org/10.1111/j.1468-5957.1986.tb01171.x.
[6] Mohammed, J. A. (2007). Corporate Social Responsibility in Islam. Auckland University of Technology Doctoral Thesis. https://doi.org/10.2139/ssrn.2593945.
[7] Munawwir, A. W. (1997). *Kamus Al-Munawwir Arab Indonesia.* Surabaya: Pustaka Progresif.

to reveal, clean, pure, and original. It represents how humans revert back to their original state when their mothers give birth to them.[8] Then, zakat al fitr can be understood as a form of zakat that is levied upon the wealth of a Muslim to purify their soul and remediate any misbehaving or misconduct done during fasting in Ramadhan.[9] The main objectives of zakat al fitr are two. First, it is a form of *ibadah* that purifies Muslims from their sins during the month of Ramadhan.[10] Second, make all people Muslims happy during this day including the poor and needy, that is why it must be paid before *'Eid al-Fitr* (Islamic holy day).[11] Ibn Umar reported: The Messenger of Allah, peace and blessings be upon him, prescribed the payment of Zakat-ul-Fitr (on breaking the fast) of Ramadan for people, every freeman, or slave, male and female among the Muslims one saa' of dried dates or one saa' of barley[12] (note that one saa' is equivalent to 3 kg approx.)

Islam requires zakat al-fitr or fitrah which is a compulsory levy that requires one *saa"* or an equivalent of 2.5 kg of rice, wheat, dates, sago, or other staple food. It is compulsory for every Muslim, whether they are men or women, young or old, as long as they live during the Ramadhan, and it is only eligible to be levied during Ramadhan until they stand up for 'Eid al-Fitr prayer.[13] A hadith by Ibnu Umar explains who is required to pay zakat al fitr:

عَنْ ابْنِ عُمَرَ رضي الله عنهما قَالَ: «فَرَضَ رَسُولُ اللَّهِ ﷺ زَكَاةَ الْفِطْرِ مِنْ رَمَضَانَ صَاعًا مِنْ تَمْرٍ، أَوْ صَاعًا مِنْ شَعِيرٍ عَلَى الْعَبْدِ وَالْحُرِّ، وَالذَّكَرِ وَالْأُنْثَى، وَالصَّغِيرِ وَالْكَبِيرِ مِنَ الْمُسْلِمِينَ». رَوَاهُ الْجَمَاعَةُ

وَعَنْ ابْنِ عُمَرَ رضي الله عنهما: أَنَّ رَسُولَ اللَّهِ ﷺ أَمَرَ بِزَكَاةِ الْفِطْرِ أَنْ تُؤَدَّى قَبْلَ خُرُوجِ النَّاسِ إِلَى الصَّلَاةِ. رَوَاهُ الْجَمَاعَةُ إِلَّا ابْنَ مَاجَهْ

---

[8] El-Bantany, R. H. (2014). *Kamus Pengetahuan Islam Lengkap*. Depok: Mutiara Allamah Utama.
[9] Azzam, A. A. M. & Hawwas, A. W. S. (2015). *Fiqh Ibadah*. Jakarta: PT Kalola Printing.
[10] Mursyidi. (2006). *Akuntansi Zakat Kontemporer*. Bandung: PT Remaja Rosdakarya.
[11] Hudaefi, F. A., Caraka, R. E., & Wahid, H. (2022). Zakat administration in times of COVID-19 pandemic in Indonesia: A knowledge discovery via text mining. *International Journal of Islamic and Middle Eastern Finance and Management*, Vol. 15, No. 2, pp. 271–86. https://doi.org/10.1108/IMEFM-05-2020-0250.
[12] Sahih Muslim. Book 5, Number 2149.
[13] Az-Zuhaili, W. (2007). *Fiqh Islam Wa Adillatuhu*. Damaskus: Dar al-Fikr.

Ibn Umar said, "The Messenger of Allah (PBUH) required zakat fitrah of 1 saa' of dates or 1 saa' grain to all Muslims, whether free or slave, male or female, young or old".

Ibn Umar said, "He ordered that this zakat be paid before people left for prayer (Eid). It is an accepted zakat. Whoever pays it after the prayer, it is an ordinary charity (see also Abu Dawud).[14]

The majority of Islamic scholars both *Salaf* and *Kalaf* state their unanimous agreement upon the compulsory nature of zakat al fitr.[15] Maliki, Shafi'i, and Hambali schools argue that the word *faradha* on the above hadith means compulsory. Abu Aliah and Imam Atha dan Ibnu Sirin also share the same judgment.[16]

Moreover, the Prophet (PBUH) specified the type and amount of zakat al fitr. According to a hadith narrated by Ibnu Umar, the Prophet (PBUH) stipulated zakat al fitr for one *saa'* of dates or wheat for every Muslim. In another hadith narrated by Abu Sa"id al-Khudri,

Abu Sa'id al-Khudri said: "At the time of the Prophet (PBUH), we paid zakat fitrah as much as 1 saa' of food or 1 saa' of dates, or 1 saa' of wheat, or 1 saa' of raisins." Then during Muawiyah's reign, when Sham's wheat flour came, he said, "In my opinion, 1 mud (wheat flour) is equal to 2 mud (dates)."[17]

Food that is eligible for paying zakat fitrah is wheat flour, dates, wheat, raisins, and *aqith* (a kind of cheese). For Muslims living in regions or countries with staple foods other than these five foods, the Maliki and Shafi'i schools allow paying zakat with other staple foods, such as rice, corn, sago, and sweet potatoes.[18] According to Shaikh Salih bin Fauzan al-Fauzan in the book Mulakhkhas Fiqhi, Shaykhul Islam Ibn Taimiyah said that zakat fitrah might be paid using staple foods in the area where the payers live, such as rice and others, even if they can pay using the type of food mentioned in the hadith.[19] Further, the amount of one *saa'* is equal

---

[14] Imam Abi Abdillah Muhammad bin Ismail Ibnu Ibrahim bin Maghirah bin Bardazibah Al-Bukhari. (1992). *Shahih Al-Bukhari*. Beirut: Darul Kitab al-„Ilmiyah.

[15] Al-Qaradawi. *Fiqh Al-Zakah: A Comprehensive Study of Zakah Regulations and Philosophy in the Light of the Qur'an and Sunna*.

[16] *Ibid*.

[17] Al-Bukhari. *Op. cit*.

[18] as-Sayyid Sabiq, S. (2005). *Panduan Zakat*. Bogor: Pustaka Ibnu Katsir.

[19] Al-Fauzan, S. S. B. F. (2011). *Mulakhkhas Fiqhi*, Jilid 1, T. Jakarta: Pustaka Ibnu Katsir.

to four *mud*, whereby one *mud* is more or less 0.6 kg. Hence, one *saa'* is equal to 2.4–2.5 kg.[20]

4.3 Zakat on Wealth

With reference to all kinds of zakat on wealth or zakatable wealth, it is very clear that only few kinds have been clarified in Quran while others are left to the Prophet (PBUH) to explain. The following are some of the zakatable wealth that has been mentioned by Allah (SW) as mentioned in the following Quranic verses:

وَفِي أَمْوَالِهِمْ حَقٌّ لِلسَّائِلِ وَالْمَحْرُومِ

In their wealths and properties is the right of the poor, he who asks, and he who is deprived. Surat al-Dhariyat (51:19)

As mentioned in the above Quranic verse, money is one of the zakatable wealth.

وَالَّذِينَ يَكْنِزُونَ الذَّهَبَ وَالْفِضَّةَ وَلاَ يُنفِقُونَهَا فِي سَبِيلِ اللَّهِ فَبَشِّرْهُم بِعَذَابٍ أَلِيمٍ

…and those who hoard gold and silver and spend it not in the way of Allāh — give them tidings of a painful punishment. Surat al Tawbah (9:34)

Hence, gold and silver are zakatable wealth as clearly mentioned in the above verse.

وَهُوَ الَّذِي أَنشَأَ جَنَّاتٍ مَعْرُوشَاتٍ وَغَيْرَ مَعْرُوشَاتٍ وَالنَّخْلَ وَالزَّرْعَ مُخْتَلِفًا أُكُلُهُ وَالزَّيْتُونَ وَالرُّمَّانَ مُتَشَابِهًا وَغَيْرَ مُتَشَابِهٍ كُلُواْ مِن ثَمَرِهِ إِذَا أَثْمَرَ وَآتُواْ حَقَّهُ يَوْمَ حَصَادِهِ وَلاَ تُسْرِفُواْ إِنَّهُ لاَ يُحِبُّ الْمُسْرِفِينَ

And He it is who causes gardens to grow, [both] trellised and untrellised, and palm trees and crops of different [kinds of] food and olives and pomegranates, similar and dissimilar. Eat of [each of] its fruit when

---

[20] Kurnia, H. & Hidayat, A. (2008). *Panduan Pintar Zakat*. Jakarta: Qultum Media.

it yields and give its due [zakah] on the day of its harvest. And be not excessive. Indeed, He does not like those who commit excess. Surat al-An'am (6:141)

Similarly, from the above Quranic verse, crops and fruits are zakatable wealth.

يَا أَيُّهَا الَّذِينَ آمَنُوا أَنفِقُوا مِن طَيِّبَاتِ مَا كَسَبْتُمْ وَمِمَّا أَخْرَجْنَا لَكُم مِّنَ الْأَرْضِ وَلَا تَيَمَّمُوا الْخَبِيثَ مِنْهُ تُنفِقُونَ وَلَسْتُم بِآخِذِيهِ إِلَّا أَن تُغْمِضُوا فِيهِ وَاعْلَمُوا أَنَّ اللَّهَ غَنِيٌّ حَمِيدٌ

O you who believe, you shall give to charity from the good things you earn, and from what we have produced for you from the earth. Surat al-Baqarah (2:267)

The above Quranic verse show that earnings of trade and other business enterprises are also among the zakatable wealth.

For the other kinds of zakatable wealth which has not been mentioned in al-Quran, it has been assigned to the Prophet (PBUH) to highlight them to the Muslims as highlighted in the following Quranic verses:

وَأَنزَلْنَا إِلَيْكَ الذِّكْرَ لِتُبَيِّنَ لِلنَّاسِ مَا نُزِّلَ إِلَيْهِمْ وَلَعَلَّهُمْ يَتَفَكَّرُونَ

And we have sent down unto thee the message that thou mayest explain clearly to people what is sent for them and that they may give thought. Surat al Nahl (16:44)

خُذْ مِنْ أَمْوَالِهِمْ صَدَقَةً تُطَهِّرُهُمْ وَتُزَكِّيهِم بِهَا وَصَلِّ عَلَيْهِمْ إِنَّ صَلَاتَكَ سَكَنٌ لَّهُمْ وَاللَّهُ سَمِيعٌ عَلِيمٌ

Of their goods (wealth), take alms, that so thou mightest purify and sanctify them; and pray on their behalf. Verily thy prayers are a source of security for them: And Allah is One Who heareth and knoweth. Surah al-Taubah (9:103)

With reference to the Hadith, as narrated by Abu Dawod in his Sanad, from Samurah bin Jundub the Prophet (PBUH) said the following:

كَانَ رَسُولُ اللَّهِ يَأْمُرُنَا أَنْ نُخْرِجَ الزَّكَاةَ مِمَّا نُعِدُّهُ لِلْبَيْعِ

The Messenger of Allah (PBUH) commanded us to give zakat on what we prepared to sell.

Hence, all these are types of zakatable wealth and the following hadith mentioned a severe punishment for those who have the wealth but do not give their zakat:

> Narrated Abu Huraira: Allah's Apostle said, "Whoever is made wealthy by Allah and does not pay the Zakat of his wealth, then on the Day of Resurrection his wealth will be made like a bald-headed poisonous male snake with two black spots over the eyes. The snake will encircle his neck and bite his cheeks and say, 'I am your wealth, I am your treasure.' " Then the Prophet recited the Holy Quranic verses:- 'Let not those who withhold . . .' (to the end of the verse). (Surat 'Imran 3:180).[21]

Following the Quranic and the Sunnah of the Prophet (PBUH), 10 types of zakatable wealth are presented in the following which are subject to zakat once the wealth reaches *nisab*/the minimum amount/threshold after one *hawl*/a lunar year passed which are listed in Figure 4.1.

4.3.1 *Zakat on gold and silver*

Gold and silver are useful precious metals which were used for centuries as money and as a measure of value. In Islam, gold and silver are considered as growing wealth by definition, and they are *zakatable* wealth whether they are used in the form of coins or gold bars, or even as ornaments and decorative materials.[22] However, they carry a different ruling when they are used as women's jewelery,[23] i.e., no zakat on women's jewelry. Regarding the *nisab* for gold and silver, it is 20 dinars of gold and 200 dirhams of silver which is equivalent to 85 grams of gold. Regarding the percentage of zakatable wealth on gold and silver, there is a consensus among Muslim scholars that the rate of zakat for gold and silver money is 2.5%.

---

[21] Al-Bukhari. *Shahih Al-Bukhari*. Vol. 2, Book 24, Number 486.
[22] al Qardawi, Y. *Fiqh al-Zakat: A Comparative Study of Zakat, Regulations and Philosophy in the Light of Qur'an and Sunnah*, Vol. I. Trans. by Monzer Kahf. Scientific Publishing Centre King Abdulaziz University Jeddah, Saudi Arabia.
[23] Al-Kahlani, M. I. I. (1960). *Subulus Salam*. Toha Putra.

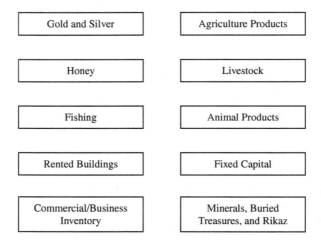

Figure 4.1. List of zakatable wealth.
Source: Yusuf al Qardawi, *Fiqh al-Zakat,* vol 1.

4.3.2 *Zakat on agriculture products*

The obligation of zakat was imposed on the second year after hijrah. Thus, zakat on agriculture is very relevant to the Muslim community in Madinah because the main earnings of people in Madinah come from the agricultural sector. Moreover, zakat on crops must be paid on the day they are harvested as mentioned in al Quran:

كُلُواْ مِن ثَمَرِهِ إِذَا أَثْمَرَ وَآتُواْ حَقَّهُ يَوْمَ حَصَادِهِ

Eat of [each of] its fruit when it yields and give its due [zakah] on the day of its harvest. Surat al-An'am (6:141)

Similar to other types of zakatable wealth, there is no zakat on the agricultural products unless they are for trading purposes. With reference to its zakatable portion, it is very clearly stated in the hadith of Ibn' Umar who narrated that the Prophet (PBUH) said, *"On that which is watered by the sky or by springs, one-tenth is obligatory, and on that which is irrigated by carried water a half-tenth is obligatory.*"[24] Hence, this hadith is clearly stating that zakat is obliged upon agricultural products and it also stipulates the ratio for zakat on agricultural products of one-tenth or half-tenth dues based on the type of irrigation system carried.[25] Hence, we can say that zakat on agriculture products is 10% zakat on agricultural products irrigated with rainwater and a 5% zakat is charged other than that.

4.3.3 *Zakat on honey*

Honey is a versatile product that brings many benefits to humanity. It is a food, medicine, as well as sweet at the same time. Regarding the mandatory zakat on honey, Al Athram says Ahmad was asked whether he believes that honey is zakatable, and he answered. *Yes indeed; 'Umar collected zakat on honey.*[26] Moreover, Amr bin Shu'aib, from his father to his grandfather, narrates that the Prophet (PBUH) *collected the one-tenth due from honey.* With reference to *nisab*, Abu Yusuf considers it equal to five wasq of the cheapest grain, such as barley. And with reference to its zakatable percentage, there is consensus if honey is produced naturally in valleys and plains, its zakatable is 10%, while for honey produced in the mountains, its zakatable is 5%.[27]

4.3.4 *Zakat on livestock*

For centuries, livestock has been used for various purposes. It is used as a source of food, means of transportation, the source for clothing, and many more. Thus, livestock ownership represents a valid amount of one's wealth.[28] Five general conditions for zakat on livestock have been specified: First, the lapse of a full Hijra year while the animals are with

---

[24] Muhammad bin Ali bin Muhammad Al-Syaukani and Muhammad Salim Hasyim. (2011). *Nail Al-Awtar.* Dar al Kutub al Ilmiyyah.
[25] Ala' al-Din Al-Kasani (1996). *Bada'i' Al-Sana'i'.* Dar al-Fikr.
[26] Qudamah. *Al-Mughni.*
[27] Al-Kasani (1996). *Bada'i' Al-Sana'i'.* Dar al-Fikr.
[28] Al-Qaradawi. *Op. cit.*

the owner. Second, it must be grazed livestock. A grazed camel is that which is fed by eating from plants of the earth and permissible grass, i.e., that which grows by Allah's command without being cultivated by anybody. However, if it feeds on cultivated crops, then it is not regarded as a grazed camel and zakat is not due on it. Third, it must be kept for some benefit, either from its milk or offspring and not used as a working camel. A working camel is that which is employed by its owner to till or irrigate the land, carry goods, or lift loads. Fourth, zakat is not payable on a working camel because they are counted as part of the basic needs of man, like clothing. *If it is rented/hired to others, Zakat is due on whatever rent is derived from it (after a Hijri year has lapsed on it).* And the last one is that the cattle must attain the *nisab* prescribed by the Prophet (PBUH).[29]

Once these conditions have been fulfilled, then zakat on livestock, such as camels, cows/buffalos, and sheep/goats, is clearly specified in the Sunnah of the Prophet (PBUH) and as seen in Tables 4.1–4.3.

Table 4.1. *Nisab* and zakat on camels.

Numbers of camels	Zakat due
1–4 camels	No zakat due
5–9 camels	One sheep
10–14 camels	Two sheep
15–19 camels	Three sheep
20–24 camels	Four sheep
25–35 camels	One she-camel (above one year of age)
36–45 camels	One she-camel (above two years of age)
46–60 camels	One she-camel (above three years of age)
61–75 camels	One she-camel (above four years of age)
76–90 camels	Two she-camels (above two years of age)
91–120 camels	Two she-camels (above three years of age)
Above 120 camels	For every forty: A she-camel (above 2 years), and for every fifty: A she-camel (above 3 years)

Source: Zakat on live Stock: https://www.ihcproject.com/zakah-on-livestock.

---

[29] Zakat on live Stock: https://www.ihcproject.com/zakah-on-livestock.

Table 4.2. *Nisab* and zakat on cows.

Numbers of cows/bulls	Zakat due
1–29 cows/buffalos	No zakat due
30–39 cows/buffalos	One cow/bull aged one year
40–59 cows/buffalos	One cow/bull aged two years
60–69 cows/buffalos	Two cows/bulls aged one year
70–79 cows/buffalos	One cow/bull aged two years and one cow/bull aged one year
80–89 cows/buffalos	Two cows/bulls aged two years
90–99 cows/buffalos	Three cows/bulls aged two years

Source: Zakat on live Stock: https://www.ihcproject.com/zakah-on-livestock.

Table 4.3. *Nisab* and zakat on sheep and goats.

Numbers of sheep/goats	Zakat due
1–39 sheep/goats	No zakat due
40–120 sheep/goats	One sheep/goat
121–200 sheep/goats	Two sheep/goats
201–300 sheep/goats	Three sheep/goats
On every additional hundred more, an extra sheep is added	

Source: Zakat on live Stock: https://www.ihcproject.com/zakah-on-livestock.

Hence, all these are types of zakatable wealth on livestock, and the following hadith mentioned a severe punishment for those who have the wealth but do not give their zakat:

Narrated Abu Huraira: The Prophet said, "(On the Day of Resurrection) camels will come to their owner in the best state of health they have ever had (in the world), and if he had not paid their Zakat (in the world) then they would tread him with their feet; and similarly, sheep will come to their owner in the best state of health they have ever had in the world, and if he had not paid their Zakat, then they would tread him with their hooves and would butt him with their horns." The Prophet added, "One of their rights is that they should be milked while water is kept in front of them." The Prophet added, "I do not want anyone of you to come to me on the Day of Resurrection, carrying over his neck a sheep that will be bleating. Such a person will (then) say, 'O Muhammad! (please intercede for me,) I will say to him. 'I can't help you, for I conveyed Allah's Message to you.' Similarly, I do not want anyone of you to come to me carrying over his neck a camel that will be grunting. Such a person (then) will say "O Muhammad! (please intercede for me)." I will say to him, "I can't help you for I conveyed Allah's message to you."[30]

4.3.5 *Zakat on animal products*

Zakat is also imposed on animal products, such as milk and silk. al-Qardawi opines that animal products should be imposed at 10% of the net output unless the animals themselves are considered trade assets.[31] However, non-pastured animals that are nurtured for their products are subjected to zakat-like trade assets for 2.5%.

4.3.6 *Zakat on fishing*

Similar to other types of goods, if used to go and fish for their daily consumption, no zakat is applicable on it, however, if they fish for selling in the market, then zakat must be applicable to all goods which are meant to be sold in the market as mentioned in the hadith stated above.

Recently, the fishing industry is one of the most important economic sectors since it is producing millions of dollars' worth of fish. Hence, for its zakat on wealth according to the view of Abu 'Ubaid who reported from Yunus bin 'Ubaid, that S. Umar bin 'Abd al 'Aziz wrote to his governor of 'Oman, 'Do not take anything from fish until it reaches two hundred *dirhams* in value similar to *nisab* of money. Once it becomes two hundred *dirhams*, take *zakat* from it.[32]

4.3.7 *Zakat on minerals, buried treasures, and rikaz*

Minerals are anything extracted from the earth which have value, such as gold, silver, lead, iron, diamond, oil, and sulfur. This definition excludes things extracted from the sea, put in the earth by human action, things that

---

[30] Sahih Bukhari, Book 24, Vol. 2, Book 24, Number 485.
[31] Al-Qaradawi. *Op. cit.*
[32] Yusuf al Qardawi. *Op. cit.*

are of the nature of the earth, such as soil, and things that carry no value.[33] Meanwhile, rikaz refers to both minerals and buried treasures. The root of the word rikaz means "to stay still" and buried treasures are valuable items buried by people in the past and excavated in present times. Both buried items and rikaz are subjected to zakat with the ratio of one-fifth, as the Prophet said, "One-fifth is obligated on rikaz."[34]

4.3.8 *Zakat on commercial/business inventory*

Allah encourages Muslims to earn halal income through business and trade, and those activities allow the community to benefit from the exchanges of goods and services and accumulate wealth. Under that logical argument, business inventory is considered wealth that may grow from time to time, so it is subjected to zakat. The Shariah evidence for zakat on business inventory comes from Quran, Sunnah, Ijma, and Qiyas.

Allah states in Quran Surah Al Baqarah: 267, *O you who have believed, spend from the good things which you have earned and from that which We have produced for you from the earth*. Further, Imam Tabari argued that Muslims should pay zakat from the wealth that they raised from business and trade activities, including business inventory, gold or silver.[35] The shariah evidence of zakat on business inventory from Sunnah refers to Abu Daud reports from Samurah bin Jundub that *The Prophet (PBUH) used to order us to pay al sadaqah out of what we have for sale*. In this regard, business inventory is considered as wealth that comes under the word "mal" used in the sayings "*give zakat on your wealth*". It is because business inventory is a general term and may refer to anything purchased for sale.[36] When it comes to the *nisab*, the value for business inventory is equivalent to 85 grams of gold at the end of zakat year.[37]

---

[33] Qudamah. *Op. cit.*

[34] Al-Syaukani & Hasyim. *Op. cit.*

[35] Abo Ja'far Muhammad B. Jarlr Al-Tabarl. *The Commentary on the Quran*, ed. Ahmad & Mahmud Shakir, 3rd edn. (Oxford University Press, 1989).

[36] Syaih Musthafa bin Said al Sayuti Al-Ruhyibani. *Mathalib Uli Al Nuha Fi Syarah Ghayah Al Muntaha*, 2nd edn. (Dar al Kutub al Ilmiyyah, 2013).

[37] Abu Zakaria Yahya Ibn Sharaf An Nawawi. *Al Majmu' Syarah Al Muhadzdzab* ('Idārat 'al-Ṭibā'ah 'al-Munīrīyah, 1925).

4.3.9 Zakat on rented buildings

There is no zakat on plots purchased to build houses for giving out on rent and earning income. But there is zakat on the savings from the rental income just as any other income if the income exceeds the *nisab* criteria.

If the building is for rent, then 2.5% of the gross annual rent must be paid as zakat. All properties in which real estate agents invest are subject to zakat, except the office they work in and the house they live in. It is obligatory for Muslims to pay zakat after one year and after deducting any debts.

4.3.10 Zakat on fixed capital

A fixed capital is one that on its own is not income generating but helps other assets generate income. All stock in trade is liable for zakat, including land and real estate that have been bought for the purpose of resale. Raw materials and goods produced for sale are also subject to zakat. However, the buildings, machinery, vehicles computers, tables, and so on that are essential for the business are exempt from zakat.

4.4 Contemporary Issues on Zakatable Assets

As presented above, it is well understood that zakatable wealth includes gold and silver, agriculture products, honey, livestock, fishing, rented buildings, fixed capital, commercial/business inventory, minerals, buried treasures, and rikaz. Additional zakatable wealth is added by contemporary Muslim scholars, such as zakat on monthly salary, zakat on earning of laborers or professionals, zakat on bonds and Shares, and zakat on cryptocurrencies.

4.4.1 Zakat on monthly salary

At the present time, income in terms of salaries, wages, profit, and professional incomes becomes the most important source of living for the majority of Muslim population.[7] As such, these categories of people cannot be excluded from the compulsory due. This raises the following questions: Is the current salary, which is the most important source of income today, subject to zakat? Can zakat be given on monthly basis? To answer these questions, let us first highlight the five conditions that must be observed while imposing zakat on income in general and zakat on salaries in particular.

Full Possession: Every Muslim who is of a certain age and has full and legal ownership of enough assets is required to pay zakat.

Fulfilling one's Basic Needs: Fulfilling the basic needs mentioned above is a very important requirement before imposing zakat on income. The person who reaches the *nisab* but still does not fulfill his basic need is not subject to pay zakat.

Fulfilling the *Nisab* (Minimum Amount Liable to Zakat): There is a consensus among Muslim scholars that zakat on income can be calculated as follows: 2.5% from the total annual net income (after the actual basic needs expenses are deducted) which exceed *nisab*. The actual basic needs expenses comprise food, clothing, accommodation, education, transportation and medical expenses, and financial obligations such as outstanding debt within the same year only.

Completion of *Haul*/Lapse of a Full Year: Although the completion of *haul* (one year) is one of the conditions for the payment of zakat,[8] some Muslim scholars agreed on the permissibility to advance zakat payment because the prophet accepted the advance payment of zakat of his uncle al 'Abbas.[9] Moreover, Dr. Yusuf al-Qardawi in his book Fiqh al-Zakat[10] provided ample evidences which supported the practice of giving zakat from salaries during the early days of Islam. Besides his views on the payment of zakat on income whether salaries, wages, professional income, or return on capital invested in other than trade, such as shipping, planes, and hotels, are *zakatable* once received, without the requirement of the lapse of one year.[11]

4.4.2 *Current practices on zakat on monthly salaries*

Recently, some Muslim countries enacted laws for the collection of zakat on income on obligatory basis such as in Sudan and on voluntary basis such as in Malaysia. In Sudan, Zakat Law of 1986 gives the right to the government to collect and to distribute zakat from all wealth including wages, salaries, professional income, and other forms. This law also gives the right to the government to deduct zakat on monthly basis, besides income tax, from all Muslims' salaries working inside Sudan as well as from all Sudanese working outside Sudan.

In Malaysia, the Malaysia Tax Law via section 44(11A) of the Income Tax Act 1967 allows companies to pay zakat through tax deduction subject to a maximum of 2.5% of the aggregate income.[14]

4.4.3 *Zakat on earning of laborers or professionals*

Income from labor and professions is subject to zakat if it reaches *nisab* and one year passes. Abu Hanifah, Abu Yusuf, and Muhammad believe that *nisab* conditions must be satisfied at least in the beginning and the end of the year. Based on this opinion, zakat can be imposed on income from labor yearly.

Zakat on earning of laborers or professionals is a contemporary issue on zakatable assets. It is because there is no strong evidence in the Quran and Sunnah regarding the obligation of zakat on earning from laborers or professionals. On the other hand, a significant number of new professions emerge alongside technological advancement and civilizations. Several jobs like Youtuber, social media influencer, streamer, and many others may have not existed ten years ago. However, those jobs now produce a significant amount of money. Exempting those professions from zakat obligation may not bring justice and welfare to the community.

Al-Qardawi refers to the lecture by 'Abd al Rahman Hasan, Muhammad' Abu Zahra, and 'Abdal Wahhab Khallaf in Damascus in 1952 who argue that earning from laborers or professionals is zakatable.[38] They based the argument on the practice of rent, in which the source of income is the expertise of the laborers being hired or rented. Further, they conclude that the implementation of zakat on laborers or professionals must fulfill the condition of *nisab* between the beginning of the year and its end. They do not support the zakat calculation based on the flow of income during the year. However, there is a disagreement among the companions, such as from Ibn Abbas Abu' Ubaid reports from Ibn' Abbas

---

[38] Al-Qaradawi. *Op. cit.*

about a man who earns income, "*He must pay its zakah the day he earns it.*" Similarly, Ibn Abi Shaibah stated the same.[39]

Moreover, zakat on earned income from laborers and professions is levied from its net amount. Thus, debts and a minimum standard of living are zakat deductible because they are essential for sustaining life. Then, Al-Qardawi states that income from labor alone, such as employment compensation and professional income, has a rate of one-fourth of one-tenth only, in the application of general texts that obligate a rate of 2.5% on money, whether it takes the form of assets or earned income. However, income that is earned as a return on capital or on capital and labor together is charged one-tenth of the net income, after the deduction of all expense, debts, and allowance for essential needs.[40]

4.4.4 *Zakat on bonds and shares*

Bond is a versatile instrument that can be utilized for liquidity management by providing an alternative solution for bank's mismatch maturity between assets and liabilities. They are also considered risk management instruments, considering the associated projects, coupons, and tenors. Bonds can be issued either by governments or corporations for project financing purposes of budgetary requirements. They can be traded in the money and bond markets by institutions like banks, insurance companies, pension funds, mutual funds, and central banks. Bonds are priced using indicative yields benchmarked on reference rates.

Like bond, sukuk is an Islamic financial instrument representing ownership of the underlying assets and their cash flow. The Accounting and Auditing Organization for the Islamic Financial Institutions (AAOIFI) Shariah Standard No 17 characterizes sukuk as "certificates of equal value representing undivided shares in ownership of tangible assets, usufruct and services, assets of particular projects or special investment activity". Concerning the assets, sharia requires halal assets as the underlying of sukuk. Moreover, the asset needs to be tangible, although some of them can be intangible assets, according to some jurists. The tangible asset reduces the excessive leverage that is prohibited in Islam.

---

[39] 'Abd al-Razzaq Al-San'ani. *Musannaf of Abd Al-Razzaq* (Majlis Ilmi Takhrij Ahadith, 2016).
[40] Al-Qaradawi. *Op. cit.*

On the contrary, bonds do not need any assets for their issuance. In addition, the purpose of financing and the involved contract in sukuk issuance have to be sharia-compliant, whereas bond is not bound to any sharia rulings. Sukuk can be structured into various contracts. AAOIFI FAS 17 states four different contracts for sukuk, such as sale-based, lease-based, partnership-based, and agency-based.[41] Those various contracts result in different accounting and reporting consequences. It differs from bonds that are quite straightforwardly recognized as debt.

Regarding bonds, Shaikh' Isa states, *Since bonds represent a loan made by companies or the government of definite amounts at definite interest rates, the holder of a bond is like the creditor of a deferred debt. At the due date, when it is paid, it must be zakatable for only one year if it remains in the holding of its owner for one year or more, according to Malik and Abu Yusuf. Until the bond is redeemed, or if it is not in possession for one year, it is not zakatable.*[42]

Then, stock or common shares are equity instruments, whereas bonds are debt instruments. Equity represents partial ownership, entitles the holder to a share in profits, and provides a residual claim on the assets of an issuing company; where maturity is concerned, it is perpetual because stocks have no maturity. The criteria for the zakatability of shares are whether the corporation is zakatable and that depends on the use of its assets. Shares are evaluated at their present value. A deduction is made for the percentage of capital used in these corporations' buildings, machinery, and tools. After deducting this percentage from the present value of the share, the residual is zakated.[43]

4.4.5 Zakat on cryptocurrencies

The emergence of cryptocurrencies cannot be separated from the advancement of blockchain. Blockchain technology provides formal guarantees to participating principals and agents that address agency

---

[41] AAOIFI. *Shari'ah Standards* (Manama, Bahrain: Accounting and Auditing Organization for Islamic Financial Institutions, 2017).

[42] Al-Qaradawi. *Op. cit.*

[43] Aissa Abderahmân. *Al Mu'amalatal Hadithah Wa Ahkamuha*, 1st edn. (Cairo: Matba'at Mukhayar, 2006).

problems in corporate governance. The presence of blockchain guarantees enables a fundamentally distinct approach to addressing agency problems in corporate governance, offering a significant departure from the current finance infrastructure that is plagued by such issues. Agency problems derive from the lack of trust between principals and agents. The agency relationship can be defined as a contract between principals and agents whereby the agent acts on principals' behalf because they delegate decision-making authority to the agent. Smart contracts enabled by blockchain technology allow for the comprehensive, near error-free, and zero transaction/agency cost coordination of agency relationships. Smart contracts and smart property are blockchain-enabled computer protocols that facilitate, verify, monitor, and enforce the negotiation and performance of a contract between principal and agent. Some studies indicate that sharing information via the blockchain's distributed and complete record of past transactions provides an efficient tool to mitigate problems caused by pre-and post-contractual information asymmetries and facilitate user coordination.[44]

The advancement of blockchain is utilized for the issuance and the exchange of cryptocurrency. It is a digital currency that uses cryptography to secure transactions. Then, based on the market supply and demand, the value of a cryptocurrency fluctuates from time to time. With the analogy to money that can store wealth and may grow over time, cryptocurrency is also subjected to zakat.[45] The State Islamic Religious Council of Perlis, Malaysia, in 2020 has issued a fatwa saying that Bitcoin (one of the popular cryptocurrencies) is subjected to zakat if it exceeds the *nisab* and haul requirement.[46] On the contrary, Majelis Ulama Indonesia (MUI) has issued a fatwa stating that cryptocurrency is haram due to the existence of

---

[44] Kallberg, J. G. & Udell, G. F. (2003). The value of private sector business credit information sharing: The US case. *Journal of Banking & Finance*, Vol. 27, No. 3 (March 2003), pp. 449–69, https://doi.org/10.1016/S0378-4266(02)00387-4.

[45] Muneeza, A. & Mohsin, M. I. A. (2022). Zakat payment from cryptocurrencies and crypto assets. *International Journal of Islamic and Middle Eastern Finance and Management*.

[46] Muhsin Nor Paizin. (2021). Community views about zakat on cryptocurrencies. *Al Qalam: Jurnal Ilmiah Keagamaan Dan Kemasyarakatan*, Vol. 15, No. 2, pp. 146, https://doi.org/10.35931/aq.v15i2.724.

speculation that may harm the community.[47] Thus, under those circumstances, zakat cannot be levied from cryptocurrency because zakat should be levied from halal sources.

4.5 Disregarding Zakatable Wealth in Muslim Countries Today

As highlighted above, zakat has to be handled by the state in terms of its collection from all eligible Muslims on their wealth and to be distributed to the eight recipients of zakat as mentioned in Quran. However, at the present time and in almost all Muslim countries, zakat becomes voluntary even if it is managed by the state or the government. Besides, its distribution was left at the hands of the Muslims where they used to give their zakat to people or relatives whom they knew thinking they are among zakat recipients. This in turn deprived the actual recipients of zakat to their right to zakat and hence this creates a situation of unjust distribution since instead of giving the zakat to the right recipients, it had been given to preferable people who are not categorized as zakat recipient from shariah perspective. Similarly, this creates a huge gap between the rich and the poor, resulting in a wide spread of poverty which forced government to borrow from international organization for anti-poverty programs rather than reviving the institution of zakat which is one of the in-house financial institutions and which is meant not only to reduce the gap between the rich and the poor but also to eradicate poverty on annual basis.[48]

As realized from Table 4.4, zakat giving has become voluntary in all 24 Muslim countries as shown with the exception of Sudan. Even though in most Muslim countries zakat has been placed under governmental ministries, its collection is voluntary. For example, even in Algeria, zakat

---

[47] Emir Yanwardhana. (2021). Wapres Blak-Blakan Soal Bitcoin Cs Haram Hingga Wisata Halal. *CNBC*, December 3, 2021. https://www.cnbcindonesia.com/news/20211203095135-4-296345/wapres-blak-blakan-soal-bitcoin-cs-haram-hingga-wisata-halal.

[48] Mohsin, M. A. (2020). A fresh view on zakah as a socio- financial tool to promote ethics, eliminate *riba* and reduce poverty. *International Journal of Management and Applied Research*, Vol. 7, No. 1, pp. 55–71.

Table 4.4. Current administration of zakat in Muslim countries.

Country	Under government	Private	Collection
Afghanistan	N/A	N/A	N/A
Algeria	Ministry of Islamic affairs and Awqaf		Voluntary
Bangladesh	Ministry of religious affairs (Islamic foundation)	Private institutions and banks	Voluntary
Bahrain	Ministry of Justice and Islamic Affairs	Private charities	Voluntary
Chad	N/A	N/A	N/A
Egypt	Al-Azhar	Private charities and banks	Voluntary
Indonesia	Government	Private	Voluntary
Iran		Shia'a Imam-related agencies	Voluntary
Iraq	Prime minister – diwan of Sunni *waqf* + diwan of Shia'i *waqf*. (before that zakat was collected by ministry of Islamic affairs for all Muslim		Voluntary
Jordan	Ministry of Islamic affairs		Voluntary
Malaysia	Majlis Agama Islam MAI		Voluntary
Morocco	There is a legislation for establishing zakat fund since 1998 but has not been activated till the date.		Voluntary
Nigeria		NGO	Voluntary
Oman	Ministry of Islamic affairs (department of zakat)	Private charities and funds	Voluntary
Pakistan	Ministry of Islamic affairs (central zakat fund)		Voluntary
Senegal	N/A	N/A	N/A
Somalia	N/A	N/A	N/A
Sudan	Government Diwan al Zakat		Compulsory
Syria		Private institutions (charities) and Islamic bank	Voluntary
Tunisia	Law of establishing Bait Al zakat is under discussion at the Parliament		Voluntary
Turkey		Some private agencies	Voluntary
Yemen	Ministry of finance		Voluntary
Saudi Arabia	Ministry of finance		Voluntary
Kuwait	Ministry of Islamic affairs (Awqaf)		Voluntary
UAE	Prime Ministry		Voluntary

Source: Mohsin, *op. cit.*

management is under the Ministry of Islamic Affairs and Awqaf, in Bangladesh, it is under the Ministry of Religious Affairs, in Bahrain, it is under the Ministry of Justice and Islamic Affairs, in Jordan, it is under the Ministry of Islamic Affairs, and in Malaysia, it is under the state religious councils of each state, yet all its collection is on voluntary basis with the exception of Sudan where zakat is placed under *Diwan al Zakat* and its collection is mandatory. We also realized that zakat collection in some Muslim countries is placed under private institutions, for example, in Bangladesh it is also placed under private institutions and banks, in Bahrain, it is also collected by private charities, and in Oman, it is also placed under private charities and funds.

4.5.1 *Lack of statistical data on zakat funds*

Since zakat given becomes voluntary at the present time and as seen above, this resulted in neglecting the amount of funds to be collected from zakat as realized in Table 4.5. Even though zakat is one of the five pillars of Islam, there is lack of data not only in terms of its collection only but also in terms of its distribution too. It is also realized that even in rich countries, like UAE and Kuwait, zakat collection is quite small when compared to the income and the wealth in these countries. Hence, for the revival of this institution, we believe this necessitates the existence of official statistical bodies for zakat data in every single Muslim country.

4.5.2 *Lack of statistical data on zakat collection*

In addition, lack of statistical data on the collection of zakat from all zakatable wealth is also unavailable in almost all Muslim countries with the exception of Nigeria and Sudan on some zakatable wealth, as seen in Table 4.6.

It is obvious from Table 4.6 that zakat collection in Muslim countries is lacking due to an inefficient zakat administration or due to the zakat distribution being left to the individuals, hence no proper documentation.

Table 4.5. Zakat collection and distribution in US dollars*.

Country	Zakat collection (million USD) 2000	Zakat collection (million USD) 2015	Zakat distribution (million USD) 2000	Zakat distribution (million USD) 2015
Afghanistan	N/A	N/A	N/A	N/A
Algeria	1	12.7	N/A	N/A
Bangladesh		1400 (2014)	N/A	N/A
Bahrain	34.5 (2005)	N/A	N/A	N/A
Chad	N/A	N/A	N/A	N/A
Egypt	2.6 (2000)	2800 (2011)	N/A	N/A
Indonesia	7.2 (2002)	231.6 (2012)	N/A	N/A
Iran	N/A	N/A	N/A	N/A
Iraq	N/A	N/A	N/A	N/A
Jordan	N/A	N/A	N/A	N/A
Malaysia	87 (2000)	628 (2013)	116 (2003)	
Morocco	N/A	4000 (2013)	N/A	N/A
Nigeria	N/A	0.22 (2013)	N/A	N/A
Oman	N/A	N/A	N/A	N/A
Pakistan	87 (2000)	48** (2014)	58 (2000)	N/A
Senegal	N/A	N/A	N/A	N/A
Somalia	N/A	N/A	N/A	N/A
Sudan	135 (2004)	479 (2012)	N/A	437 (2012)
Syria	N/A	N/A	N/A	N/A
Tunisia	N/A	N/A	N/A	N/A
Turkey	N/A	N/A	N/A	N/A
Yemen	N/A	N/A	N/A	N/A
Saudi Arabia	N/A	8000 (2015)	N/A	N/A
Kuwait	N/A	70.7 (2014)	N/A	N/A
UAE	1.9 (2004)	46 (2014)	N/A	N/A

*According to official (governmental) numbers after converting to USD.
**Zakat amount in Pakistani Rupee was increased, but it decreased in USD due to depreciation of PKR/USD exchange rate.
Source: Mohsin, *op. cit.*

90 Application of Zakat: From Classical and Contemporary Perspective

Table 4.6. Lack of statistical data on zakat collection from all types of zakatable wealth.

Country	Cash	Gold	Fishing	Honey	Mining	Agr. products	Animal products	Trade	Rented buildings	Fixed capital	Salary
Afghanistan	NA	NA	NA	NA	NA	NA	NA	NA	NA	NA	NA
Algeria	NA	NA	NA	NA	NA	NA	NA	NA	NA	NA	NA
Bangladesh	NA	NA	NA	NA	NA	NA	NA	NA	NA	NA	NA
Bahrain	NA	NA	NA	NA	NA	NA	NA	NA	NA	NA	NA
Chad	NA	NA	NA	NA	NA	NA	NA	NA	NA	NA	NA
Egypt	NA	NA	NA	NA	NA	NA	NA	NA	NA	NA	NA
Indonesia	NA	NA	NA	NA	NA	NA	NA	NA	NA	NA	NA
Iran	NA	NA	NA	NA	NA	NA	NA	NA	NA	NA	NA
Iraq	NA	NA	NA	NA	NA	NA	NA	NA	NA	NA	NA
Jordan	NA	NA	NA	NA	NA	NA	NA	NA	NA	NA	NA
Malaysia	NA	NA	NA	NA	NA	NA	NA	NA	NA	NA	NA
Morocco	NA	NA	NA	NA	NA	NA	NA	NA	NA	NA	NA
Nigeria	404,250	344,375	NA	NA	NA	1,874,500	NA	NA	NA	NA	NA
Oman	NA	NA	NA	NA	NA	NA	NA	NA	NA	NA	NA
Pakistan	NA	NA	NA	NA	NA	NA	NA	NA	NA	NA	NA

Senegal	NA	NA	NA	NA	NA	NA	NA	NA	NA
Somalia	NA	NA	NA	NA	NA	NA	NA	NA	NA
Sudan	NA	31,228	NA	NA	NA	4,171,500	136,646,750	126,431,250	9,479,000
Syria	NA	NA	NA	NA	NA	NA	NA	NA	NA
Tunisia	NA	NA	NA	NA	NA	NA	NA	NA	NA
Turkey	NA	NA	NA	NA	NA	NA	NA	NA	NA
Yemen	NA	NA	NA	NA	NA	NA	NA	NA	NA
Saudi Arabia	NA	NA	NA	NA	NA	NA	NA	NA	NA
Kuwait	NA	NA	NA	NA	NA	NA	NA	NA	NA
UAE	NA	NA	NA	NA	NA	NA	NA	NA	NA

Source: Islamic Social Finance Report 2015.

Self-Assessment Quiz (MCQs)

Question 1:
1. Zakat is not just an obligation but also a means of purification
2. Honey is one of zakat *maal*
3. One sha' is equal to 3.5 kg

From the statements above, which are true statements?
(a) 1
(b) 2
(c) 3
(d) 1 and 2
(e) 1 and 3

Question 2: According to what schools (madzhab) that rice and other staple foods can be used to pay zakat fitrah?
(a) Shafi'i and Hanafi
(b) Hanafi and Hambali
(c) Shafi'i and Maliki
(d) Maliki and Hanafi
(e) Hambali and Hanafi

Question 3: What are five foods mentioned by Prophet Muhammad for zakat fitr according to hadits narrated by Abu Saaid al-Khudri?
(a) Wheat flour, dates, sagoo, corn, and aqith
(b) Wheat flour, dates, wheat, raisins, and aqith
(c) Wheat flour, dates, sweet potatoes, wheat, and aqith
(d) Corn, dates, sweet potatoes, wheat, and aqith
(e) Sagoo, dates, corn, wheat, and aqith

Question 4: From the following choices, what is the zakatable asset from contemporary issue?
(a) Zakat on earning of professionals
(b) Zakat on honey
(c) Zakat on animal products
(d) Zakat on business inventory
(e) Zakat on trade

Question 5: Surah at Tawbah 34-34 explained about...
(a) The obligation of zakat on livestock
(b) The obligation of zakat on business inventory
(c) The obligation of zakat on agriculture
(d) The obligation of zakat on minerals, buried treasures, and rikaz
(e) The obligation of zakat on gold and silver

Question 6: The following are the objectives of zakat except:
(a) Zakat is viewed by non-Muslims as a means of 'purification' and not just an obligation
(b) Zakat promotes sharing of wealth and eliminates greediness
(c) Zakat helps reduce poverty within Muslim community
(d) Zakat is directly linked to the concept of ethical economy

Question 7: Zakat al-fitr or fitrah is a compulsory levy which requires
(a) One saa' of rice or wheat or an equivalent
(b) 1.5 kg of rice
(c) 2 kg of wheat
(d) 1.4 kg of dates

Question 8: The following are zakatable wealth except:
(a) Gold and silver
(b) Honey
(c) Oil
(d) Water

Question 9: The following are the conditions for imposing zakat on income except:
(a) Full possession of the asset
(b) Fulfilling one's comfortable needs
(c) Fulfilling the *nisab*
(d) Completion of haul

Question 10: The current collection of zakat in this country is not
(a) Sudan compulsory
(b) Malaysia voluntary
(c) Egypt compulsory
(d) Indonesia voluntary

Self-Assessment/Recall Questions

Question 1: What is zakat al-fitr and who has to give it?
Question 2: List the types of zakatable wealth that are mentioned in al-Quran.
Question 3: Explain the types of zakat on livestock and their zakatable portion. Provide examples.
Question 4: Explain the types of zakat on agriculture and their zakatable portion. Provide examples.
Question 5: Discuss the contemporary issues on zakatable wealth explaining why it doesn't have any impact in Muslim's society today.

Answers to Self-Assessment Quiz (MCQs)

1. d
2. c
3. b
4. a
5. e
6. a
7. a
8. d
9. b
10. c

Chapter 5

Conditions to Give Zakat

Learning Outcomes

At the end of this chapter, students must be able to

- know the conditions to give zakat,
- understand the procedure to give zakat,
- justify zakat as an act of worship to the giver,
- appreciate the importance of *amil* in distributing zakat.

5.1 Conditions to Give Zakat

There are nine conditions to give zakat. First, the *muzaki*/zakat giver must be Muslim. Zakat is one of the five important pillars of Islam.[1] Thus, zakat is only obligated to Muslims. Non-Muslims are not required to perform zakat. The obligation of zakat on Muslims is also narrated on the authority of 'Umar (RA) who said:

> "*While we were one day sitting with the Messenger of Allah, there appeared before us a man dressed in extremely white clothes and with very black hair. No traces of journeying were visible on him, and none of us knew him. He sat down close by the Prophet, rested his knee against his thighs, and said, "O Muhammad! Inform me about Islam*". The Messenger of Allah PBUH said, "*Islam is that you should testify*

---

[1] Al-Qaradawi, Y. *Fiqh Al-Zakah*, Vol. 2.

that there is no deity except Allah and that Muhammad is His Messenger. Then, you should perform salah. Pay the Zakat. Fast during Ramadan. And, perform Hajj to the House, if you are able to do so". (Forty Hadith: Imam An-Nawawi)

From the above hadith, it is clear that zakat giver must be a Muslim.

Second, the one who wants to pay zakat should be free or not under slavery. Most scholars unanimously agree that enslaved people are not subject to the obligation to pay zakat. The majority of scholars opine that zakat is only obligatory for the master of the enslaved person. Since zakat is only obligatory on perfect ownership, and the master is the owner of his servant's property.[2]

Third, most scholars state that *baligh*/maturity and sane are not the necessary conditions for paying zakat. Their wealth is subjected to zakat and must be paid through their agent (wali). However, the Hanafi school believes that mature and sane are the prerequisite for someone to be subjected to the obligation of zakat. Hence, children and madmen are not required to pay zakat out of their wealth.[3]

Fourth, the condition of zakat is related to the nature of the wealth, which must have the potential to grow. Zakat is essentially a tax levied imposed on the growing wealth so that it can benefit the less fortunate in the surrounding community. The previous chapter has discussed the wealth that is subjected to zakat. On the contrary, zakat is not levied upon non-growing assets such as the clothes and vehicles we use daily or the house where we live. It is because those things are basic necessities for a human to live a decent life and become productive.

Fifth, the wealth should be perfectly owned by the *muzaki*. It means that the *muzaki* has the power to control and legally own the property or asset.[4] There is an opinion dispute regarding this condition. It is whether the owner could physically manage the property by himself using their hands. However, in contemporary examples, this condition refers to whether the owner could control the asset and be able to transfer the asset

---

[2] *Ibid.*
[3] Al-Qaradawi, Y. (1999). *Fiqh Al-Zakah: A Comprehensive Study of Zakah Regulations and Philosophy in the Light of the Qur'an and Sunna*. London: Dar Al Taqwa.
[4] Mughniyah, M. J. (2007). *Fiqih Lima Mazhab Ja'fari, Hanafi, Maliki, Syafi'i, Hambali*. Jakarta: Lentera.

to another party. For instance, one could not physically touch or grab their stocks or bonds. However, they may have full control to hold, sell, or even buy new ones. In this sense, those stocks and bonds are zakatable assets.

Sixth, another important condition of zakat is *nisab* which is the minimum threshold of assets that are subjected to zakat. The previous chapter has elaborated on the different *nisab* based on the kind of wealth. For example, the *nisab* for gold is 85 g of gold and the *nisab* for the agricultural product is equal to 2.5 kg of rice.

The seventh condition is achieving a full haul. Haul is a time limit of one hijri year or 12 (qomariyah/lunar year/twelve months) of assets ownership.

رواه ابن ماجه بإسناده عن عائشة رضي الله عنها قالت: سمعت رسول الله صلى الله عليه وسلم يقول:

"لا زكاة في مال حتى يحول عليه الحول" صححه الألباني

> The Prophet said, *There is no obligation to pay zakat on wealth until one year is complete.* (Authenticated by al-Albani)[5]

The completion of one year is a condition for zakat, except zakat from plants and fruits. As for the two goods, zakat must be paid when it has been fruitful and safe from damage if it reaches the limit that can be used even though it is not yet harvested.

The eighth condition is free of debt. The Hanafi school requires freedom from debt as the condition for one who is obligated to pay zakat. However, Syafii school suggests that it is not a necessary condition. One still must pay zakat even if they have debt as long as the debt is smaller than his accumulated wealth.[6]

The last condition is the wealth exceeding the basic needs. It is important because before helping others, the *muzaki* should make sure that they can sustain their life decently.

---

[5] Authenticated by al-Albani as narrated by al-Tirmidhi from hadith of Ibn Omar.
[6] Al-Qaradawi. *Op. cit.*

5.2 The Procedure to Give Zakat

The procedure to give zakat is quite easy and straightforward. For zakat ul-Fitr, one saa' of staple food that is usually consumed. Alternatively, an equal value of money as to those staple food can be given. The donation is still valid until the very end of Ramadhan or before the khatib of zakat Fitr raises for giving the sermon. Traditionally, zakat is given to the *amil* in the surrounding mosque so that there is nobody in hunger during the Holy ul-Fitr celebration. Moreover, the door will be open for more donations to *amil* or zakat organizations for assisting them during its distribution.

For zakat *maal*/zakat on wealth, first, the wealth needs to be assessed. This includes all the cash money, savings, bonds, stocks, etc. Then is to calculate all the liabilities that the *muzaki* have, including the expenses for daily needs and debts. If the remaining wealth exceeds the *nisab* (85 g of gold) and has been possessed for one year, then it is subjected to zakat. The amount of zakat is 2.5% of the remaining wealth. Zakat can be through *amil* or zakat organization, who in turn will distribute it to its recipients.

In contemporary examples, there are many avenues that have been developed to ease the zakat estimation for each individual. Some provide zakat calculator while others provide zakat virtual assistants as illustrated in Table 5.1.

For example, in Malaysia, they provided zakat calculator to make it easy for zakat giver to calculate their zakat, as shown in Table 5.1.

Table 5.1.   Zakat calculator.

A.	Gross income (per year)	.............RM
B.	Less expenses (per year)	.............RM
	Selves	.............RM
	Number of wives (from one to four)	.............RM
	Number of children (from one to twenty)	.............RM
	Grant to parent (per year)	.............RM
	EPF911% × year)	.............RM
	Contributions to charity organization agency list	.............RM
	Total deduction (B)	.............RM

Source: Pusat Pungutan Zakat (PPZ) Majlis Agama Islam Wilayah Persekutuan (MAIWP): www.zakat.com.my.

For the payment of zakat through salary scheme, as explained in the previous chapter, 2.5% zakat is obligatory on every Muslim who owns the *nisab* for one lunar year. For this scheme, zakat giver must calculate the cost of his personal wealth and holdings, and as seen above, if the balance is more than the *nisab*, he/she is eligible to give zakat from their salary. Once the amount of zakat is calculated for a whole year, then zakat giver can divide it into 12 months for easy payment throughout the year. Not only this but in Malaysia, the zakat portion will be deducted from the income tax.

In Indonesia, zakat virtual assistant is provided via Badan Amil Zakat Nasional (BAZNAS). The virtual assistant is an artificial intelligence-based application that can interact with people and give the correct zakat estimation based on the Shariah. This development can attract more millennials to pay zakat. This app is available in Line Chat Application and it is very relevant for young generation. When users are willing to pay zakat, the apps will direct users to payment page integrated with banking services. This is shown in Figure 5.1.

Figure 5.1. Zakat virtual assistant.

Source: https://republika.co.id/tag/zakat-virtual-assistant.

Figure 5.2. Zakat metaverse.
Source: Badan Amil Zakat Nasional website: https://baznas.go.id/Press_Release/baca/BAZNAS_Mulai_Layanan_Zakat_Metaverse/1002.

After figuring out the amount of money to be paid, zakat giver can proceed with the payment through various methods. First, zakat giver can go to the zakat counter and pay it in cash. Alternatively, zakat givers can ask *amil* zakat to come to their homes or offices to pick up their zakat. Some companies also facilitate their employee to pay zakat through an automatic zakat deduction payroll system. In this regard, the employee's salary has been deducted with a certain amount of zakat, so they do not need to worry about their zakat obligation.

Nowadays, many channels have been developed to ease online zakat transactions. The zakat organizations collaborate with banks, payment gateways, point of sale, marketplace, and many other applications. This development has eased *muzaki*/zakat giver to donate and indirectly induced a positive campaign for zakat and giving behavior. In contemporary case, zakat also has embraced metaverse. In this regard, the metaverse is utilized to give education on zakat, create zakat campaign, and allow zakat donation through this sophisticated realm. BAZNAS has started this initiative since Ramadhan 2022 and has received positive feedback from public.[7]

---

[7] BAZNAS. (2022). Zakat Metaverse. www.baznas.go.id. https://baznas.go.id/Press_Release/baca/BAZNAS_Mulai_Layanan_Zakat_Metaverse/1002.

Zakat Metaverse is an educational platform for zakat campaign. On this platform, *muzaki* or public can interact with *amil* zakat regardless their distance. It is an enhanced virtual meeting with avatar for each participant. The interaction in the platform is beyond talking but also virtual handshake and other body language and interaction as you can see in Figure 5.2.

5.3 Zakat Is an Act of Worship to the Giver

Zakat is one of five inseparable practices and identities in Islam, as stated in a hadith narrated by Umar ibn Khatab.[8] It is an annual premium upon one's accumulated wealth that surpasses the minimum threshold amount (*nisab*) and is dedicated to the eight classes of recipient or *mustahiq*.[9] Etymologically, zakat originates from the word zaka, which means to grow or increase. When it relates to things, zaka means to increase, but when it relates to a person, it becomes to grow or betterment of a person — righteousness such as *tazkiyah* process. Another meaning of zakat in Arabic words is cleanliness or purity from dirt. Hence, zakat can be comprehended as the purification process along with the growth of wealth.[10]

Moreover, paying *zakat* is equally important with *salah,* which is the practice that determines the nature of being a Muslim.[11] *Zakat* is mentioned 30 times in Qur'an, of which 27 are directly placed after the injunction of *salah,* emphasizing the mutual importance between *salah* and *zakat*. Moreover, in the early history of Islam, the first caliph Abu Bakar as Siddiq embattled the apostates who had neglected the compulsory of *zakat* even if they still performed *salah*.[12] On the contrary, once a nonbeliever reverts to Islam performs *salah* and pays *zakat*, they automatically become brother/sister in Islam, as stated in Quran 9:11. This shows

---

[8] An Nawawi, A. Z. Y. (1976). *Forty Hadith*. Damascus: The Holy Koran Publication House.
[9] Farishta G. de Zayas. (1960). *The Law and Philosophy of Zakat*. Damaskus: Al-Jadidah Printing Press.
[10] Al-Qaradawi. *Op. cit.*
[11] Jabir bin Abdullah says: I heard the Messenger of Allah (peace be upon him) saying this: The difference between a man (Muslim) and *shirk* and *kufr* is the abandoning of *salah* (Muslim, 1998).
[12] Ali Muhammad As Sallaabee. (2010). *The Biography of Abu Bakr As-Siddeeq*. Dar us Salam.

that *zakat* plays a significant role as an identity for Muslims both as an individual as well as a community.

Zakat represents the idea of moral economy where economic activity is submerged into the social formation in a society and is determined by non-economic factors or as the well-known concept of embeddedness brought upon by Polanyi[13] and Thompson.[14] Under this assertion, the obligatory of *zakat* derived from Divine source (Quran and Sunnah) determines the wealth redistribution from the rich to the poor and strengthens the social cohesion among society by emphasizing kinship, neighborhood, and reciprocity as opposed to the notion of market economy that merely focused on creating economic value regardless of the consequences. Likewise, the *zakat* institution endogenously aligns with IME, which aims to create a just ambience whereby the less fortunate can be elevated, can function, and has a space to grow as *ihsani* behavioral norms suggest.[15]

Zakat inherently embodied the objectives of *shari'ah* (*maqasid shari'ah*) in its operation by achieving the ultimate human well-being, both material and spiritual.[16] At the micro level, *zakat* operation redistributes wealth among the society. It emancipates the less fortunate parallel with the intention of Islamic law, which is safeguarding and essentializing human faith, self, intellect, progeny, and wealth.[17] Under this assertion, *zakat* is a valid and reliable mechanism to present a just and equitable growth in a society. Zakat endogenously aligns with the Islamic moral economy, which aims at creating a just ambience whereby the less fortunate can be elevated, can function, and has a space to grow as *ihsani*

---

[13] Polanyi, K. (1944). *Origins of Our Time: The Great Transformation*. London: Farrar & Rinehart.

[14] Thompson, E. P. (1971). The moral economy of the English crowd in the eighteenth century. *The Past and Present Society*, Vol. 50, pp. 76–136. http://www.jstor.org/stable/650244.

[15] Zaman, N. & Asutay, M. (2009). Divergence between aspirations and realities of Islamic economics: A political economy approach to bridging the divide. *IIUM Journal of Economics and Management*, Vol. 17, No. 1, pp. 73–96.

[16] Asutay, M. (2007). Conceptualisation of the second solution in overcoming the social failure of Islamic banking and finance: Examining the overpowering of homoislamicus. *IIUM Journal of Economics and Management*, Vol. 15, No. 2, pp. 167–95. http://ssrn.com/abstract=1693608.

[17] Chapra, M. U. (2008). *The Islamic Vision of Development in the Light of Maqāṣid Al-Sharī'ah*. Jeddah: IRTI-IDB.

behavioral norms suggest.[18] Zakat is an Islamic obligation representing the third of Islam's five pillars. It obliges a 2.5% payment of yearly tax on the productive wealth of Muslim individuals and commercial firms that have reached the *nisab* (full ownership) and haul (one lunar year) of owning the wealth.[19] Zakat is a right of the poor people of society. Another point of view is that it is an obligatory financial duty of the rich people in the society.[20]

Zakat is a form of worship that involves wealth. When a Muslim person's earnings reach a prescribed amount (*nisab*) in excess of his needs, that person is required to pay a portion (on monetary wealth and on gold and silver, it is 2.5% or the 40th part of the wealth) of his earnings to the poor and needy.[21] The Quran clearly states the obligation of zakat payment as stated in At Taubah 103: *Take Sadaqah (alms) from their wealth in order to purify them and sanctify them with it, and invoke Allah for them. Verily! Your invocations are a source of security for them, and Allah is All-Hearer, All-Knower (At Taubah: 103)*. Zakat is also equally important as salat (prayer). It is represented in many verses in the Quran that states zakat and salat together in one verse. For instance, in Al Baqarah: 43, the Quran says: *And establish prayer and give zakāh and bow with those who bow [in worship and obedience]*. From both verses, it can infer that zakat is an important worship in Islam.

Further, Prophet Muhammad (PBUH) also emphasizes the obligation of zakat in his sayings, *There is no envy except in two: a person whom Allah has given wealth and he spends it in the right way, and a person whom Allah has given wisdom (i.e. religious knowledge) and he gives his decisions accordingly and teaches it to the others.*[22]

---

[18] Zaman & Asutay. *Op. cit.*
[19] Hudaefi, F. A. & Beik, I. S. (2021). Digital Zakāh campaign in time of Covid-19 pandemic in Indonesia: A netnographic study. *Journal of Islamic Marketing*, Vol. 12, No. 3, pp. 498–517. https://doi.org/10.1108/JIMA-09-2020-0299.
[20] Kafh, M. (1997). Potential effects of zakat on government budget. *IIUM Journal of Economics and Management*.
[21] Hossain, M. Z. (2012). Zakat in Islam: A powerful poverty alleviating instrument for Islamic countries. *International Journal of Economic Development Research and Investment*, Vol. 3, No. 1, pp. 1–11.
[22] Imam Abi Abdillah Muhammad bin Ismail Ibnu Ibrahim bin Maghirah bin Bardazibah Al-Bukhari. (1992). *Shahih Al-Bukhari*. Beirut: Darul Kitab al-„Ilmiyah.

The above hadith illustrates that zakat is an important avenue for Muslim to get closer to Allah (SW) and earn His blessings. In this sense, Muslims show their gratitude to Allah for what he gets by practicing zakat. In addition, zakat purifies the giver and his wealth as mentioned in the following hadith:

عن معاذ بن جبل قال: قال النبي صلى الله عليه وسلم: الصوم جنة والصدقة تطفئ الخطيئة كما يطفئ الماء النار. (رواه الترمذي)

On the authority of Muadh bin Jabal, he said: The Prophet (PBUH) said: *Fasting is a shield, and charity extinguishes sin as water extinguishes fire.* (Narrated by Al-Tirmidhi)

This hadith emphasizes the Surat At Taubah (9:03) whereby Allah (SW) states that zakat purifies the soul of the giver.

5.4 Zakat Given to *Amil* of Zakat

One may ask the following question: Should the zakat be given to an organization or directly to the eligible recipients? Essentially, zakat should be given from *muzaki* to *amil* or zakat organization for them to disburse it later to the eligible recipient. In this regard, *amil* plays as the *wakil* of the *muzaki* so that they can help disburse it to the *mustahik* on behalf of the *muzaki*. There are five reasons why zakat should be given to *amil* or zakat organization.

First, it is closer to the practice according to Shariah. In At Taubah 103, Allah (SW) commands to take zakat from the *muzaki*, represented by the word "*hudz*" or "take from". This verse shows that there is a special entity, in this case, *amil*, that is mandated to take the wealth from *muzaki*. *Amil* works under the ruling government and has effective authority and instruments to conduct the practice of zakat.

The existence of *amil* is also clearly stated in the history of Prophet Muhammad (PBUH). For instance, once Prophet Muhammad ordered Muadz, his companion, to Yemen to collect zakat. In a hadith narrated by Ibnu Abbas, the Prophet says, *And tell them if Allah (SW) requires zakat to be taken from the wealth of the rich among them and returned to the poor among them.*[23]

---

[23] *Ibid.*

In addition, the Prophet (PBUH) forbids *amil* to take any benefit from *muzaki* while collecting zakat. The Prophet (PBUH) appointed a man from the tribe of Al-Azd, called Ibn Al-Lutabiyya, for collecting the Zakat. When he returned, he said, "This (i.e. the Zakat) is for you and this has been given to me as a present." The Prophet (PBUH) said,

ثم خطبنا، فحمد الله وأثنى عليه، ثم قال: أما بعد، فإني أستعمل الرجل منكم على العمل مما ولاني الله، فيأتي فيقول: هذا مالكم وهذا هدية أهديت لي، أفلا جلس في بيت أبيه وأمه حتى تأتيه هديته، والله لا يأخذ أحد منكم شيئا بغير حقه إلا لقي الله يحمله يوم القيامة، فلأعرفن أحدا منكم لقي الله يحمل بعيرا له رغاء، أو بقرة لها خوار، أو شاة تيعر ثم رفع يده حتى رئي بياض إبطه، يقول: اللهم هل بلغت (صحيح بخاري)

Why hadn't he stayed in his father's or mother's house to see whether he would be given presents or not? By Him in Whose Hands my soul is, whoever takes something from the resources of the Zakat (unlawfully) *will be carrying it on his neck on the Day of Resurrection; if it be a camel, it will be grunting; if a cow, it will be mooing; and if a sheep, it will be bleating.* The Prophet (PBUH) then raised his hands till we saw the whiteness of his armpits, and he said thrice, "*O Allah! Haven't I conveyed Your Message* (to them)?" (Sahih Bukhari. Chapter 49, Gifts)

Second, zakat should be given to *amil* or zakat organizations because *amil* zakat can play an intermediary role between the surplus unit (*muzaki*) and the deficit unit (*mustahik*), as illustrated in Figure 5.3. In this regard, pooling the zakat to *amil* allows more money to be structured for a long-lasting program.

As an illustration, in a community, there is a *mustahik* with a monthly basic need equal to $2000 and his neighbor, a *muzaki*, is subjected to zakat for $250 per month. If the *muzaki* gives the zakat directly to the *mustahik*, the zakat may not be sufficient to sustain his life. However, suppose in that community there are at least eight *muzaki* with the same amount of zakat, and they proceed the zakat through *amil*. In that case, *amil* can generate larger funds to fulfill the *mustahik* basic needs. Further, *amil* even can create a poverty alleviation program by giving him initial funds to start a business and technical assistance or business mentoring along the program. In this regard, giving the zakat to *amil* improves the effectiveness of helping and empowers *mustahik*.

Figure 5.3. Paying zakat through *Amil*.
Source: Baznas website: https://baznas.go.id/.

As seen in Figure 5.3, the surplus unit is a person or group of people that has surpassed *nisab* and then subjected to pay zakat. The intermediary unit is *amil* zakat that collects zakat funds from *muzaki* and creates various programs for *mustahik* based on their needs. The deficit unit refers to *mustahik* which is a person who is eligible to receive zakat (8 *Asnaf*).

Third, giving zakat through *amil* will reduce moral hazards for *muzaki* and *mustahik*. From the *muzaki* side, this mechanism prevents the *muzaki* from feeling meritorious by giving the zakat directly to the *mustahik*. It will guard the pureness of his intention in practicing zakat. On the other side, proceeding zakat through *amil* will avoid the *mustahik* of feeling indebted. It is because the money does not belong to *amil*, and the *mustahik* does not directly meet the *muzaki* who gives the money. In contemporary cases, giving zakat through *amil* avoids social jealousy and prevents any harm and risk to the *muzaki*. If the *mustahik* knows who gives the zakat fund, he may repeatedly come to that *muzaki* to beg for money, which in some circumstances may not be convenient.

Fourth, paying zakat to *amil* or zakat organization will allow fairer distribution. *Amil* and zakat organizations have a standardized screening mechanism to select eligible zakat recipients.[24] They also have resources,

---

[24] Center of Strategic Studies BAZNAS. (2018). *Kajian Had Kifayah 2018*, 1st edn. Jakarta: BAZNAS. https://drive.google.com/file/d/1FyKcMiIW9btjHAkKAf8pfTpLx8Vl o7C-/view.

such as tools and staff with vast experience in screening the *mustahik*. Moreover, *amil* and zakat organizations have a wider span of work authority, which may allow them to send the zakat fund to remote areas where the zakat collection is fewer than the needs of zakat distribution. In this sense, zakat can be allocated from the zakat surplus area to the zakat deficit area. By doing so, it creates fairer zakat distribution.

Lastly, paying zakat through *amil* may increase the magnitude of the program via inter-institution collaboration. Zakat institution can create a bigger impact by collaborating with various institutions and mobilizing resources efficiently. For instance, during the early COVID-19 pandemic, for example, PPZ in Malaysia and BAZNAS in Indonesia worked together with hospitals, ambulance providers, mosques, small and medium enterprises, and other institutions to dampen the effect of the pandemic.[25] Such collaboration is extremely difficult to be done individually if *muzaki* directly gives zakat to *mustahik*.

---

[25] BAZNAS (2020). Laporan Kegiatan Penanggulangan Bencana COVID-19 Situation Report #40. Jakarta. https://baznas.go.id/pendistribusian/respon-bencana/sitrep/3509-sitrep-40-respon-covid-19.

Self-Assessment Quiz (MCQs)

Question 1
1. *Muzaki* can be Muslim or non-Muslim
2. *Muzaki* should be free (not under slavery)
3. Children are obligated to pay zakat directly
4. Zakat from plants and fruit can be paid without achieving complete haul

From the statements above, which are true?
- (a) 1 and 3
- (b) 2 and 4
- (c) 1 and 2
- (d) 3 and 4
- (e) 2 and 3

Question 2: How many times is zakat mentioned in Qur'an?
- (a) 20
- (b) 25
- (c) 30
- (d) 35
- (e) 40

Question 3: Which surah in Qur'an mentions zakat should be given to *amil* or zakat organization?
- (a) Al Baqarah: 186
- (b) Al Baqarah: 267
- (c) At Taubah: 60
- (d) At Taubah: 103
- (e) At Thalaq: 7

Question 4: What is the definition of *nisab*?
- (a) Time limit of one hijri year of assets ownership
- (b) Standard minimum of wealth to pay zakat
- (c) People who pay zakat
- (d) People who manage zakat
- (e) People who receive zakat

Question 5: Which school does not require freedom one who is obligated to pay zakat?
- (a) Shafi'i
- (b) Hanafi

(c) Maliki
(d) Shafi'i and Hanafi
(e) Hanafi and Maliki

Question 6: These are the conditions to give zakat except:
(a) The *muzaki*/zakat giver must be Muslim
(b) Enslaved Muslims must give zakat
(c) Zakat is imposed on the growing wealth
(d) The wealth should be perfectly owned by the *muzaki*

Question 7: Zakat *maal*/zakat on wealth include the following except:
(a) Cash money
(b) Saving
(c) Bonds
(d) Cows

Question 8: The payment of zakat through salary deduction scheme must follow
(a) 2.5% on every Muslim who own the *nisab*
(b) 2.5% from the grows income
(c) 2.5% after adding the contribution of EPF
(d) 2.5% after deducting last year expenditure

Question 9: Which statement is not correct about zakat?
(a) Zakat is mentioned 30 times in Qur'an
(b) Paying zakat is equally important with *sadaqah*
(c) Zakat represents the idea of moral economy
(d) Zaka means to increase

Question 10: The following are the reasons for the *amil* to manage zakat:
(a) *Amil* plays an intermediary role between the *muzaki* and the mustahik
(b) Giving zakat through *amil* will increase moral hazards for *muzaki* and mustahik
(c) *Amil* has a standardized screening mechanism to select eligible zakat recipients
(d) Giving zakat through *amil* avoids social jealousy and prevents any harm and risk to the *muzaki*

Self-Assessment/Recall Questions

Question 1: List and discuss the conditions to give zakat.
Question 2: When to be given and how much is zakat Fitr?
Question 3: "Zakat as an act of worship to the giver", do you agree with this statement? Elaborate.
Question 4: Should the zakat be given to an organization or directly to the eligible recipients? Why?
Question 5: Discuss the positive and negative aspects of giving zakat directly from its giver to its recipients.

Answers to Self-Assessment Quiz (MCQs)

1. b
2. c
3. d
4. b
5. a
6. b
7. d
8. a
9. b
10. b

Chapter 6

Zakat Socio-financial Products for Its Recipients and Their Economic Impact

Learning Outcomes

At the end of this chapter, students must be able to

- know who are the legal recipients of zakat,
- highlight zakat socio-financial products for its recipients,
- understand the economic impact of giving zakat to its recipients,
- identify the recipients who are not eligible to receive zakat.

6.1 Zakat Socio-financial Products via Zakat Recipients

Along with Allah's (SW) commandment to Muslims to pay zakat, Islam clearly regulates the management of zakat. With efficient zakat management, it can guarantee the success of circulating Muslims' wealth from the rich to the poor. Hence, in this case, it will promote the welfare of Muslim societies, specifically as a means of achieving social justice and eliminating poverty, besides preventing the accumulation of wealth among certain people.

Given the importance of zakat in society, the state is obligated and responsible for the management of zakat. Allah (SW) has determined certain groups who are entitled to receive zakat, as specifically mentioned in the following Quranic verse:

إِنَّمَا ٱلصَّدَقَٰتُ لِلْفُقَرَآءِ وَٱلْمَسَٰكِينِ وَٱلْعَٰمِلِينَ عَلَيْهَا وَٱلْمُؤَلَّفَةِ قُلُوبُهُمْ وَفِى ٱلرِّقَابِ وَٱلْغَٰرِمِينَ وَفِى سَبِيلِ ٱللَّهِ وَٱبْنِ ٱلسَّبِيلِ ۖ فَرِيضَةً مِّنَ ٱللَّهِ ۗ وَٱللَّهُ عَلِيمٌ حَكِيمٌ

Alms-tax is only for the poor and the needy, for those employed to administer it, for those whose hearts are attracted 'to the faith', for 'freeing' slaves, for those in debt, for Allah's cause, and for 'needy' travellers. 'This is' an obligation from Allah. And Allah is All-Knowing, All-Wise. (Surah al-Taubah 9:60)

As explicitly and clearly stated eight zakat recipients, and as mentioned that the management of zakat must be handled by the state, this will give the responsibility to the state to establish eight financial products, each according to its zakat recipient.

6.1.1 *Zakat socio-financial products for fuqara and its economic impact*

The *faqir* (plural *fuqara*)/poor people are the first group mentioned in the Qur'an. *Fuqara* refers to poor people who do not own property and do not have jobs or people whose basic needs are not met. A person who cannot meet his needs because he is too lazy to work, despite having the effort, is not considered poor (should not receive zakat).[1]

According to the Hanafi school, the poor are people who have little wealth, less than the *nisab* of zakat or equivalent to *nisab* but not enough to meet their needs. Meanwhile, the poor, according to the Hambali school, are people who have assets that are less than sufficient in comparison to general limits. Even if his wealth exceeds the *nisab*, he is entitled to receive zakat and is obligated to pay zakat from his wealth. However, if he is one of the people who are obliged to earn a living and the person who is obliged to provide for him is classified as a rich person, then he cannot get zakat. In contrast to the two preceding schools, the Maliki and

---

[1] Malahayatie, M. (2016). Interpretasi Asnaf Dalam Konteks Fiqih Kontemporer (Studi Analisis Fungsi Zakat Dalam Pemberdayaan Ekonomi Umat). *Al – Mabhats*, Vol. I, No. I, pp. 48–73.

Shafi'i schools believe that the *fuqara* are in worse condition than the *masaakin*. The *faqir* is a person who does not have enough money to cover even half of his needs. The amount of zakat given to the poor is until he has enough. Zakat should be enough to last a lifetime.[2]

From the above discussion, it can be deduced that the *fuqara*/poor are people who are impoverished and unable to meet their basic needs. Unlike the wealthy and well-off. Rich people have assets that exceed their basic needs for themselves and their children, whether in the form of food, drink, shelter, clothing, vehicles, business tools, or other staples. As a result, people who do not have the income to meet their minimum limit are among those who are eligible to receive zakat.[3] Hence, for this category of people, a socio-financial product via zakat has been provided to finance and assist these *fuqara*.

With reference to the economic impact of zakat on this category, *fuqara* socio-financial product is provided to assist the poor individuals who are without any means of livelihood and material possessions; besides, it must support them until they will become active members of the society and hence they become zakat giver rather than zakat receiver. Only then in this case their poverty will be eradicated.[4]

Recently, several studies have been conducted to review the impact of zakat on *fuqara*. A well-managed mosque that utilizes zakat funds could decrease poverty and improve the welfare of *mustahik*.[5] Similarly, research in five states of Malaysia reveals that zakat has a positive and significant influence on human development.[6] Likewise, empirical study

---

[2] Al-Qardawi, Y. (2009). A comparative study of zakah, regulations and philosophy in the light of Qur'an and Sunnah. *Fiqh Al Zakah*, pp. 1–351.

[3] Sabiq, S. (1973). *Fiqh As-Sunnah*. Beirut: Darul Kitab Al Arabi.

[4] Mohsin, A. & Magda, I. (2013). Potential of zakat in eliminating *riba* and eradicating poverty in Muslim countries (case study: Salary deduction scheme of Malaysia). *Islamic Management and Business*, Vol. 5, No. 1.

[5] El Ayyubi, S. & Saputri, H. E. (2018). Analysis of the impact of zakat, infak, and *sadaqah* distribution on poverty alleviation based on the CIBEST model (case study: Jogokariyan Baitul Maal Mosque, Yogyakarta). *International Journal of Zakat*, Vol. 3, No. 2, pp. 85–97.

[6] Suprayitno, E., Aslam, M., & Harun, A. (2017). Zakat and SDGs: Impact zakat on human development in the five states of Malaysia. *International Journal of Zakat*, Vol. 2, No. 1, pp. 61–69. https://ijazbaznas.com/index.php/journal/article/download/15/12/.

toward 200 recipients finds that zakat program promotes poverty alleviation in West Sumatra.[7]

6.1.2 Zakat socio-financial products for masakin and its economic impact

Miskin (plural *Masaakin*)/needy people is the second category mentioned in the Qur'an. A *miskin* is a person who lacks sufficient wealth to meet his basic needs, despite having little ability to obtain it. They have something that can provide for their basic needs, but it is in very small quantities and far from sufficient to simply survive.[8] So, it can be concluded that the condition of *fuqara* is worse than *masaakin*. The *masaakin* still have income even though it is very little and insufficient. Meanwhile, the *fuqara* do not have any ability to get the basic necessities of life.

According to the Hanafi school, the *miskin* is one who has no wealth at all and must beg in order to eat or cover his body with clothes. The *fuqara* should not beg because he has food to eat on a daily basis while the *masakin* are permitted to beg. The *masaakin* are people who have no wealth, according to the Hambali school of thought. This group is lower than the *fuqara* and requires more assistance. Meanwhile, according to the Maliki school of thought, a *maskin* is someone who has enough wealth to meet half of his needs or more. That is also true of the Shafi'i school. The *masakin* are people who have a lot of assets or halal income that can cover half of their expenses. He is entitled to zakat despite having a home and clothes. Furthermore, poor women with little jewelry or students with a large number of books are eligible for zakat.[9]

Similarly, for this group of zakat recipients, *masakin* socio-financial product is provided to finance and assist the *masakin*. This socio-financial product is meant to finance the *masakin* according to their basic necessities either in cash or in kind or both. They may have a job but their income is below the minimum requirement. So, in this case, financing this category of people can be in terms of providing them with skills and means to

---

[7] Sari, D. F., Beik, I. S., & Rindayati, W. (2019). Investigating the impact of zakat on poverty alleviation: A case from west Sumatra, Indonesia. *International Journal of Zakat*, Vol. 4, No. 2, pp. 1–12.
[8] Arifin, G. (2016). *Zakat, Infak, Sedekah: Dalil-Dalil Dan Keutamaan*. Jakarta: Gramedia.
[9] Al-Qardawi. *Op. cit.*

find better jobs not only to meet their basic necessities but also to improve their overall situation. Similar to *fuqara*, through this financial product, this category of zakat recipient will be a giver of zakat in the following years.

With reference to the economic impact of zakat on *masakin*, several zakat production-based programs were conducted which improve several aspects of their life. For instance, in Malaysia and Indonesia, after receiving zakat for one year, it increases their material and spiritual conditions threefold.[10] Similarly, disbursement of zakat in the form of productive program can be positively correlated with strengthening the potential of rural *mustahic* entrepreneurship.[11]

6.1.3 Zakat socio-financial products for amilin and its economic impact

The management of zakat is usually carried out by the *amil* zakat/zakat manager so that the practice of zakat can be carried out properly according to the guidance of Islamic law. Zakat collected from *muzakki*/zakat giver is directly distributed to *mustahik*/zakat receiver.

According to al-Qardhawi, zakat *amil* are those who manage all zakat matters, starting from zakat collection, calculation, and distribution.[12] Meanwhile, according to Wahbah Al Zuhayli, zakat *amil* are people who work to collect zakat. *Amil* zakat can also be referred to as a party appointed by the authorities or association bodies to manage zakat.[13] *Amil* zakat, according to the Hanafi school, is a person appointed by the leader as a representative who receives and collects zakat. *Amil* zakat can properly participate in zakat based on the task he performs. *Amil* zakat,

---

[10] Ayuniyyah, Q. *et al.* (2017). The comparison between consumption and production-based zakat distribution programs for poverty alleviation and income inequality reduction. *International Journal of Zakat*, Vol. 2, No. 2, pp. 11–28. https://doi.org/10.37706/ijaz.v2i2.22.

[11] Kinanti, K., Noviyanti, & Zaenal, M. H. (2018). The role of zakat to strengthen the rural Mustahiq community based on entrepreneurship. *Puskas Working Paper Series*, January, pp. 1–14.

[12] Al-Qardawi, Y. (2000). *Fiqh Al Zakah: A Comparative Study* (Vol. I). King Abdulaziz University, p. 309.

[13] Kelana, R. R. A. (2020). Efektivitas Program Penyaluran Dana Bagi Siswa Muslim Oleh Badan Amil Zakat.

according to the Maliki school of thought, is a person who collects and distributes zakat to those who are entitled to it. Even though *amil* is wealthy, he is entitled to a share of a portion of the zakat based on his earnings. *Amil*'s requirements are to be knowledgeable and well versed in all zakat laws. Furthermore, according to the Shafi'i school, the *amil* zakat is a person who is involved in the management of zakat assets. It doesn't matter who collects it, looks after it, writes it down, shares it, and so on. The *amil* zakat, on the other hand, receives no wages other than that zakat. According to the Hambali school, an *amil* zakat is a zakat administrator who is paid in zakat for his services.[14] Hence, for this category of zakat recipient, a socio-financial product is provided.

This socio-financial product is meant to pay *amil* zakat income based on the services provided in terms of collecting, keeping records, gathering information, and distributing to the mentioned zakat recipients. For efficient zakat management, the state must appoint its staff based on the dignity of each individual in terms of his ethics, honesty, and responsibilities toward himself and his society at large. Consequently, this efficient management will result not only in earning lawful earnings and gaining good reputation but also in increasing their earings through collecting more zakat from all eligible Muslims, hence zakat fund will increase which can help in satisfying the needs of all zakat recipients.

There is an urgency for *amil* zakat capacity building that will in turn enhance the successfulness of zakat practices in the future.[15] A study finds that several variables, such as internal control, information technology, and audit, have a significant and positive impact on good *amil* governance.[16]

6.1.4 Zakat socio-financial products for Muallaf and its economic impact

Muallaf/revert to Islam are people who have had their hearts softened so that they are drawn to Islam because their faith is not yet established, or

---

[14] Arifin. *Op. cit.*

[15] Adnan, M. A. (2017). The need of establishment of professional *amil* zakat to enhance the future zakat development. *International Journal of Zakat*, Vol. 2, No. 1, pp. 71–79. https://doi.org/10.37706/ijaz.v2i1.16.

[16] Yolanda, F., Zaenal, M. H., & Pramono, S. E. (2020). The effect of internal control, information technology and audit on good *amil* governance practices. *International Journal of Zakat*, Vol. 5, No. 2, pp. 67–82. https://doi.org/10.37706/ijaz.v5i2.223.

to avoid harming Muslims, or to take advantage of opportunities that may be used to their advantage. Fiqh scholars divide converts into two categories: Muslims and non-Muslims.[17] According to Yusuf Qardhawi, *muallaf* refers to people whose hearts or beliefs are expected to increase their inclination toward Islam or hinder their evil intentions against Muslims, as well as converts who are persuaded by their hearts in the hope of benefiting the Muslim from the enemy.[18] Meanwhile, people who are weak in their intentions to embrace Islam, according to Wahbah Al Zuhayli, are included in this group.[19] The margin of disagreement between these two figures is razor thin. Since *Muallaf* are linguistically interpreted as people who have recently converted to Islam.

According to the Hambali school, *muallaf* is divided into two groups. First, there are non-Muslims who are given zakat in the hope that they will convert to Islam. Second, converts are people who have recently accepted Islam. They may be given zakat to strengthen their Islamic faith. According to the Shafi'i school, there are four types of *muallaf*. First, there are those who have recently converted to Islam but whose faith is still weak. He was given zakat to strengthen his faith. Second, people who have recently converted to Islam, and he is a respected member of his community, and it is hoped that by giving him zakat, his people who are still kafirs will immediately embrace Islam. Third, a Muslim with a strong faith is hoping that by giving zakat to him, his influence will be able to stop the evil of the disbelievers. Fourth, a Muslim with strong faith, but it is hoped that by giving him zakat, the effect will be to discourage Muslims who refuse to pay zakat. Furthermore, the Hanafi school defines *Mu'allaf* as someone who is about to become Muslim or is new to Islam. Since the caliph Abu Bakr As-Shidiq, they have not received zakat. According to the Maliki school of thought, *mu'allaf* is a kafir who wishes to convert to Islam, whereas others believe he is a Muslim who has recently accepted his religion.[20]

With reference to the economic impact of zakat on this category, a *mualaf* socio-financial product is provided to strengthen the faith of the people who are inclined to enter or have already converted to Islam. Besides, it also helps in financing *da'wah*/spreading the words of Allah

---

[17] Sabiq. *Op. cit.*
[18] Al-Qardawi. *Op. cit.*
[19] Az Zuhaily, W. (2015). *Fiqh Islam Wa Adillatuhu 3, Darul Fikr*, Vol. 7. Darul Fikr.
[20] Arifin. *Op. cit.*

globally to reach all individuals living in this world. Moreover, using this share in spreading the knowledge of the prohibition of *riba* globally, e.g., through a global channel, this can help people to stop dealing with *riba*.[21]

Recently, to improve zakat program on *mualaf*, BAZNAS apostasy vulnerability index was to measure and evaluate zakat program for *mualaf*.[22] Several best practices of zakat program for *mualaf* include legal aid and aqidah support.[23] Moreover, economic empowerment program for *muallaf* is equally important to make a long-lasting impact for them.[24]

6.1.5 *Zakat socio-financial products for riqab and its economic impact*

Riqab (plural *raqabah*)/slaves/captives is a term that refers to both male and female slaves.[25] This term is explained in relation to liberation as if the Qur'an is signaling with this figurative word that slavery for humans is no different than the shackles that bind them with the hope that they, like humans in general, will be free. Meanwhile, according to Wahbah Al Zuhayli, the majority of scholars refer to slaves as Muslim slaves who have made a pact with their master to be freed and do not have the money to pay a ransom for themselves, despite having worked hard.

The four schools of thought divide *riqab* into the following categories: *Riqab* are slaves, according to the Hanafi school, especially those who try to repay a certain amount of property to their master in exchange for their release one day. Meanwhile, he is a Muslim slave, according to the Hambali school. He may be given zakat fund to free himself from slavery and Muslim guardianship. If he passes away without heirs, the

---

[21] Mohsin & Magda. *op cit.*
[22] BAZNAS. (2018). *Apostasy Vulnerability Index*, First. Jakarta: Badan *Amil* Zakat Nasional. https://drive.google.com/file/d/11IYcqSGw1LV3B5DcJCz3GWikUXjpAZYf/view.
[23] Abdillah, A. N. (2020). Pemberdayaan Mualaf Pasca Konversi Di Mualaf Center Yogyakarta. *Jurnal Tarbiyatuna*, Vol. 11, No. 1, pp. 23–30. https://doi.org/10.31603/tarbiyatuna.v11i1.3200.
[24] Satria, M. A. & Qulub, A. S. (2020). Program Pemberdayaan Ekonomi Mualaf: Studi Kasus Program Kampung Inspiratif Dan Mandiri Desa Klepu Oleh LMI. *Jurnal Ekonomi Syariah Teori Dan Terapan*, Vol. 6, No. 3, p. 555. https://doi.org/10.20473/vol6iss20193pp555-567. January 15, 2020.
[25] Al-Qardawi. *Op. cit.*

property is given to Baitul Mal. The Maliki school and the Shafi'i madhhab believe that *riqab* is a slave who pays the cost of his release in installments even though he has not paid any installments. He is entitled to zakat assets until he can pay off all of his release costs.

Recently, there is a problem with how to rediscover this group of zakat recipients, namely slaves, since several countries have abolished the slave trade. Nevertheless, several studies urge the recategorization of *riqab*. One of them argues that freeing a person from an oppressive ruler and freeing a prisoner of war are among the top in this research.[26] Another study defines *riqab* as elder neglect victims, child abuse victims, children involved with crime, and domestic violence victims.[27]

With reference to the economic impact of zakat on this category, *riqab* socio-financial product is provided to assist in liberating prisoners of war or educating criminal prisoners and providing them with the skills to find jobs once they are out of prison or financing their families while they are in prison and help provide education to their children. This share will also stop this category of recipients from borrowing with *riba*.

6.1.6 *Zakat socio-financial products for gharimin and its economic impact*

Gharim (plural *gharimin*)/Debtors are people who are in debt and are having difficulty repaying it. They are divided into several groups. People who bear the burden of debt to settle disputes, or guarantee other people's debts until the obligation to pay the debt forces them to spend all of their assets, or someone who is forced into debt because he is in a state of urgency by the necessities of life, or someone who is in debt because he wants to free himself from an immoral act is among them. As previously stated, all debtors are justified in receiving zakat until they can pay off their debts.[28]

---

[26] Ismail, Y., Awang, A. B., & bin Mhd Sarif, S. (2020). Re-categorizing recipients of zakat under riqab for. *International Journal of Zakat and Islamic Philanthropy*, Vol. 2, No. 1, pp. 125–33.

[27] Rosli, M. R. B., Salamon, H. B., & Huda, M. (2018). Distribution management of zakat fund: Recommended proposal for asnaf riqab in Malaysia. *International Journal of Civil Engineering and Technology*, Vol. 9, No. 3, pp. 56–64.

[28] Sabiq. *Op. cit.*

According to the Hanafi school, *gharim* is a person who has assets that reach the *nisab* but after the property is handed over to pay debts, his wealth no longer reaches the *nisab*. Giving zakat to *gharim* is more important than giving it to the *fuqara*. *Gharim*, according to Hambali school of though, is a person who is in debt and does not have enough assets to pay off his debt. Such a person may be given zakat in order to pay his debts. However, there are several conditions for him before receiving zakat. Namely, Muslim, independent, and the debt is not for disobedience. If he is in debt because of disobedience such as buying liquor, he is not allowed to receive zakat unless he has repented of his actions. The Maliki school of thought divides the *gharim* into two parts. First, people with debts should work together to improve their situation. Second are people who have debts for their own good in fulfilling something that is permissible or prohibited but have repented of their actions. One more type was added by the Shafi'i school. Specifically, a person who owes money for destroying someone else's property and is having difficulty repaying it. This includes *gharim* who are obligated to pay zakat.[29]

With reference to the economic impact of zakat on this category, *gharmin* socio-financial product is provided to finance those who have financial difficulties in repaying their borrowed loan to meet their crucial needs and also to assist them in finding an extra job to meet their needs in the future.[30]

Recently, zakat share on *gharmin* has been utilized in some of the Islamic banks to help some genuine debtors. In Indonesia, zakat share for *gharmin* played an important role in preventing and overcoming the *riba* from online illegal fintech financing through financial literacy, da'wah on *riba*, and giving financial assistance to close the debt.[31] Dompet Dhuafa has created a model of gharimin empowerment program that involves legal education, mediation, and monitoring.[32]

---

[29] Arifin. *Op. cit.*
[30] Mohsin & Magda. *Op cit.*
[31] Muhammad Indra Saputra *et al.* (2020). Mustahik Terjerat *Riba* Fintech: Apa Peran Zakat? *Policy Brief Pusat Kajian Strategis BAZNAS*, pp. 1–9. https://drive.google.com/file/d/1xbChqfArCZTAzBA3lhtMa_LBA1c_-Ed5/view.
[32] Nulhaqim, S. A. & Saepulrahman, A. (2013). Pelayanan Advokasi Bebas Rentenir Bagi Masyarakat Dhuafa Oleh Lembaga Sinergi Dompet Dhuafa Jabar Kota Bandung. *EMPATI: Jurnal Ilmu Kesejahteraan Sosial*, Vol. 2, No. 1, pp. 35–48. https://doi.org/10.15408/empati.v2i1.9754.

6.1.7 Zakat socio-financial products for fisabilillah and its economic impact

Muslim scholars have interpreted that the share of zakat for *fisabilillah* is meant for war in the context of jihad. According to the Hanafi school, *fisabilillah* refers to poor people who have run out of money because they are too busy fighting in Allah's name. Meanwhile, the Hanbali school defines *fisabilillah* as the *mujahid* who fights in Allah's way. Even if he is wealthy, he may be eligible for zakat to cover his supplies and *jihad* expenses until he returns home. According to Maliki, *fisabilillah* are Muslims who struggle in the path of Allah. Although he does not require financial assistance to meet his needs, he is entitled to zakat until the *jihad* is over and he returns to his home country. According to the Syafi'i school, a *mujahid* who does not receive special funds from the state has the right to receive zakat to cover all of his *jihad* expenses.[33]

According to Al-Qardawi, *fisabilillah* means not only *jihad* with weapons or war but also *jihad* with the pen (writing), verbal, thought, education, socio-economic, political, and so on.[34] The important thing, according to him, is that this meaning does not abandon its fundamental condition, namely *fisabilillah*; in other words, all jihad that is intended to uphold and uphold Allah's word is *fisabilillah*.

With reference to the economic impact of zakat on this category, *fisabilillah* socio-financial product is provided to finance any form of struggle or work for the love of Allah. Therefore, it can finance the fighters and the border guards, buy weapons and military ships, build barracks, etc. without depending on any external borrowing with *riba* to finance this category.

6.1.8 Zakat socio-financial products for Ibnu Sabil and its economic impact

Ibn Sabil/stranded are people who travel for good deeds such as education and healthcare and face financial difficulty in returning back to their home country. According to Al-Majmu', *Ibn Sabil* is a person who does not have

---

[33] Arifin. *Op. cit.*
[34] Monica, I. S. & Abidah, A. (2021). Konsep Asnaf Penerima Zakat Menurut Pemikiran Yusuf Al-Qardawi Dan Wahbah Al-Zuhayli. *Jurnal Antologi Hukum*, Vol. 1, No. 1, pp. 109–124. https://doi.org/10.21154/antologihukum.v1i1.246.

sufficient provisions when he is interrupted, as well as people who intend to travel without provisions for non-immoral reasons.[35]

According to the Hanafi and Hambali schools of thought, *Ibn Sabil* is a person who traveled long distances but ran out of money. A traveler may be given zakat but only to cover his needs because being in debt is more important to him than receiving zakat. Meanwhile, the Maliki school of thought contends that *Ibn Sabil,* who runs out of provisions, has the right to zakat even though he is a very wealthy man in his country and there are people willing to lend him money. If his journey does not lead him to disobey Allah, he is entitled to zakat. The Shafi'i school explained that Ibn *Sabil* is a traveler who traveled far from his country. So, he has the right to receive zakat, especially when he runs out of provisions whether he is still in his country or in other countries where zakat collection is there, as long as the purpose of the trip does not violate the Shariah.[36]

With reference to the economic impact of zakat on this category, *Ibn Sabil* socio-financial product is provided to help travelers who face difficulties in continuing their journey due to reasons such as loss of their money or their belongings. Hence, this will encourage more travelers to travel in order to explore, share, and gain the latest knowledge and technology that can benefit their Muslim Ummah at large.[37]

6.2 Those Who Are Not Eligible to Receive Zakat

In general, four categories of people are not eligible to receive zakat[38]; they are the Prophet (PBUH) and his family, the rich people, relatives of zakat giver, and atheist and kafir harbi.

6.2.1 *The Prophet's family*

Some fiqh scholars, including Shafi'i, believe that the *ahlul bait*/Prophet's Family is not permitted to receive zakat. The prohibition of zakat on Ahlu Bait due to their glory with Allah's Messenger. According to some Maliki

---

[35] Malahayatie. *Op. cit.*
[36] Arifin. *Op. cit.*
[37] Mohsin & Magda. *Op cit.*
[38] Sabiq. *Op. cit.*

school of thought, *ahl al-bait* are only permitted to receive zakat in an emergency, namely a condition that allows them to eat carrion.

6.2.2 *Rich people*

Rich people are not entitled to zakat because they can meet their own and their dependents' needs. Giving zakat to the rich defeats the purpose of zakat, which is to help the needy and poor. Zakat is also prohibited for people whose living expenses are met by the rich, such as children, wives, or relatives. Since they are considered sufficient with the living and the wealthy who provide sufficiency. However, according to the Shafi'i and Hanabilah scholars, zakat may be paid to *amil*, converts, fighters, and *gharim* in order to improve relations between the two parties, even if they are wealthy.

According to Hanafi scholars, the rich have the size of one *nisab* in excess of their basic needs from any property. As a result, even if they are healthy, strong, and able to work, people with less wealth than the *niab* are given zakat. Since he is poor, and poor people cover all zakat distribution objects. A rich person, according to Maliki scholars, is one who has enough wealth for the next year. Meanwhile, a poor person is defined as having less wealth than his or her needs for one year. As a result, even if a person has one or more *nisab* but not enough for a year, zakat is still paid. Furthermore, rich people, according to Shafi'i scholars, are people who are well-off in their general age, which is 62 years. Unless he has traded assets, the profit is calculated per day. If his profit is less than half of his daily needs, he is considered poor. Similarly, if he is over the age of 62, he is seen separately every day. If he has wealth or work that he cannot complete in half a day, he is a poor person.[39]

6.2.3 *Relatives of zakat giver*

It is not permissible for individuals to pay zakat to their immediate family members, such as fathers, grandfathers, mothers, grandmothers, sons, grandsons of sons, daughters, and grandchildren of daughters. This is because it is the responsibility of zakat payers to financially support and provide for their immediate family members. Zakat payers should take

---

[39] Az Zuhaily. *Op. cit.*

care of the needs of their parents, children, and grandchildren by providing them with a living and fulfilling their shopping needs. Therefore, zakat should be directed towards those who are eligible to receive it and are not immediate family members of the zakat payer. Even though they are poor, they are considered wealthy due to the wealth of those who pay zakat (from their own families). So, if he pays zakat to them, he has cheated himself by ignoring the obligation to provide a living. Furthermore, zakat should not be paid by a husband to his wife because the husband is required to provide a living for his wife.

Imam Malik excludes grandfathers, grandmothers, and grandchildren. According to him, zakat may be given to them because they are not required to provide a living. This is, if they are in poor condition. If they are rich and fight *fisabilillah* as volunteers, then the zakat payer is allowed to give zakat to them from the *fisabilillah* share, just as they can also be given zakat as part of the *gharimin*. Since people who give zakat are not required to pay their debts. Likewise, it is permissible for him to give them from the *amil* division if they serve as *amil*.

6.2.4 *Atheist and Kafir Harbi*

According to the Maliki and Hambali scholars, those who receive zakat must be Muslims and are not permitted to give zakat to non-Muslims except *muallaf*. According to Abu Yusuf, Zufar, Shafi'i, and the majority of scholars, it is not permissible to give alms other than zakat to kafir dzimmi, as is the case with zakat. It is also forbidden to give it to *kafir harbi*.

Self-Assessment Quiz (MCQs)

Question 1: Which surah in Qur'an mentioned certain groups to receive zakat?
(a) Al Baqarah: 186
(b) Al Baqarah: 267
(c) At Taubah: 60
(d) At Taubah: 103
(e) At Thalaq: 7

Question 2: The poor are people who have little wealth, less than the *nisab* of zakat, or equivalent to *nisab* but not enough to meet their needs is the definition from… school.
(a) Shafi'i
(b) Maliki
(c) Hanafi
(d) Hambali
(e) Maliki and Shafi'i

Question 3
1. People who do not have money to live
2. People who converted their religion into Islam
3. Orphan

From the statements above, who are categorized as asnaf zakat?
(a) 1, 2, and 3
(b) 1 and 2
(c) 1 and 3
(d) 2 and 3
(e) 1

Question 4
1. People who bear the burden of debt to settle disputes
2. Guarantee other people's debts until the obligation to pay the debt forces them to spend all of their assets
3. Someone who is forced into debt because he is in a state of urgency by the necessities of life
4. Someone who is in debt because he wants to free himself to do an immoral act

From the statements above, who are definition of gharim?
- (a) 1, 2, 3, and 4
- (b) 1, 2, and 3
- (c) 1, 2, and 4
- (d) 1, 3, and 4
- (e) 1 and 2

Question 5
1. The Prophets' family
2. Atheis
3. The family of *muzaki*
4. Poor widow

From the statements above, who are not eligible to receive zakat?
- (a) 1, 2, and 3
- (b) 1, 2, and 4
- (c) 2, 3, and 4
- (d) 1, 3, and 4
- (e) 1, 2, 3, and 4

Question 6: The definition of faqir (plural fuqara) includes the following except:
(a) Poor people who do not own property
(b) Poor people who do not have jobs
(c) Poor people whose basic needs are not met
(d) Poor people who do not like to work

Question 7: The definition of miskin (plural masaakin) includes the following except:
(a) The miskin is a person who lacks sufficient wealth to meet his basic needs
(b) The miskin has every small quantities but not sufficient to simply survive
(c) The miskin can still have income but is very little and insufficient
(d) The miskin do not have any ability to get basic necessities of life

Question 8: The definition of muallaf includes the following except:
(a) People who have had their hearts softened so that they are drawn to Islam
(b) People whose hearts or beliefs are expected to increase their inclination toward Islam

(c) Converts who are persuaded by their hearts in the hope of benefiting the non-Muslim from the enemy
(d) People whose hearts or beliefs are expected to hinder their evil intentions against Muslims

Question 9: The definition of riqab (plural raqabah) includes the following except:
(a) Slaves who are working to repay to their master in exchange for their freedom
(b) Elderly neglected victims
(c) Child abuse victims
(d) Prisoners of crime

Question 10: The definition of gharim (plural gharimin) includes the following except:
(a) A Muslim who borrows to buy luxury needs
(b) A Muslim who is in debt and having difficulty repaying it
(c) A Muslim who is forced into debt because he is in a state of urgency by the necessities of life
(d) A Muslim who is in debt because he wants to free himself from an immoral act are among them

Self-Assessment/Recall Questions

Question 1: Explain who are the legal recipients of zakat.
Question 2: Discuss the impact of the eight socio-financial products under zakat.
Question 3: How can zakat eradicate the poverty of the poor and needy?
Question 4: Why do you think Islam provides a share of zakat to zakat manager?
Question 5: Discuss those who are not entail to receive zakat and why?

Answers to Self-Assessment Quiz (MCQs)

1. c
2. c
3. b
4. b
5. a
6. d
7. d
8. c
9. d
10. a

Chapter 7

Calculation of Zakat

Learning Outcomes

At the end of this chapter, students should be able to understand the following:

- standards guiding zakat calculation,
- approaches in zakat calculation,
- issues in zakat calculation,
- innovative ways to assist zakat calculation.

7.1 Standards Guiding Zakat Calculation

Calculation of zakat is the procedure of computing the exact amount or quantity to be given out of particular zakatable wealth in order to discharge the obligation of paying/giving out zakat. "Zakatable wealth" comprises properties or wealth that is rightfully subject to the payment of zakat as an obligatory charity. Calculation of what is due from or to be given out of one's wealth as zakat needs to be precise and done in an exclusive manner in accordance with established rules of zakat in the Quran and sunnah. This is to ensure *certainty* and leave out any room for *arbitrary estimation* to determine what is due from a given wealth.[1] The calculation of zakat is as important as the payment of zakat.

---

[1] Dhar, P. (2013). Zakat as a measure of social justice in Islamic finance: An accountant's overview. *Journal of Emerging Economies and Islamic Research*, Vol. 1, pp. 1–11.

The calculation is an obligation of zakat that needs to be understood and carried out with all certainty. It is remarkable to note that any method of calculation of zakat that is used would ultimately give the same result in assessing the amount to give out. This understanding is important because it makes the computation and payment of zakat easier for administrators and payers of zakat, respectively.[2]

7.2 Approaches in Zakat Calculation

To calculate zakat of wealth (*zakat al-mal*), the first step is to understand the *nisab* of the *zakatable wealth* under consideration and understand its *zakat base*. A *nisab* is the threshold of minimum wealth that a person or an entity must own, from which zakat is due and determined at the end of a zakat year.[3] A zakat year is a period of one lunar year of the Hijrah calendar (*hawl* or *haul*) as a minimum time frame of a zakat payer's ownership of zakatable wealth.[4] Zakatable wealth for this purpose is categorized into five types: (1) personal wealth (money and stocks), (2) business wealth (trading goods), (3) agricultural produce, (4) livestock/animals (raised for commercial purpose), and (5) treasure troves. A zakat base refers to the net adjusted amount of assets derived from or used for business activities and represents a zakat payer's total value of wealth owned and/or possessed. Zakat base refers to the zakat payer's total funds and business/trade goods excluding fixed assets and, according to some Islamic jurists, bad debts.[5]

7.2.1 Calculating zakat of business including cash, receivables, and precious metals

It has been narrated in authentic hadith/sunnah of the holy prophet Muhammad (PBUH) that the rate of zakat of gold and silver is a quarter of one-tenth, that is, 2.5% of *nisab* or 1/40 thereof, and the *nisab* is 20 gold dinar or 200 silver dirt. This rate applies to stocks or trade goods and

---

[2]Mushfiqur Rahman (2012). *Zakat Calculation: Based on Fiqh-uz-Zakat by Yusuf al-Qaradawi*. Markfield: The Islamic Foundation, p. 128.
[3]*Ibid.*
[4]Beik, I. S. *et al.* (2016). *Core Principles for Effective Zakat Supervision — Consultative Document*. Jakarta: BI, BAZNAS & IRTI-IDB, p. 42.
[5]*Ibid.*, pp. 11–17.

currency. The *nisab* of trade goods and currency is valued as the equivalence of 85 g or 3 ounces of pure gold, out of which the 2.5% or 1/40 is given out as zakat.[6]

On the rate of 2.5% or 1/40, Hadith No. 1572 of Sunan Abi Dawud reports as follows:

> "Narrated from 'Ali (may Allah be pleased with him) that the Prophet (blessings and peace of Allah be upon him) said: "If you have two hundred dirhams (silver coins) and one full year has passed, then five dirhams are due on them. You do not have to pay anything, i.e., on gold, unless you have twenty dinars (gold); if you have twenty dinars and one full year has passed, then half a dinar is due on them, and if the number increases, then work it out on this basis"[7] (a *sahih* hadith).

Note that in reckoning a zakat year, it can be a lunar year (about 354) or solar year (about 365 days). The significance of these two lies in the fact that the number of days in these years differs, which affects the zakat due. Accordingly, a zakat payer is required to pay a rate of 2.5% of the zakat base if the zakat year is determined by a lunar year or a rate of 2.5775% where the zakat year is a solar year (to accommodate the 11 days difference). This latter rate is designed to compensate for the fewer number of days per year in the Islamic calendar.[8] The formula to calculate the zakat due in this case is as follows:

$$\text{Zakat Due} = \text{Zakat Base} \times 2.5\% \text{ (or } 2.5775\%)$$

7.2.2 Calculating zakat of agricultural produce

Agricultural produce or crops are likewise zakatable. For this purpose, Zakat is due on every farm produce that can be stored and eaten, including grains, legumes, and fruits. Their *nisab* is five *wasqs*, and their rate varies according to the farming mode of the crops, i.e., whether produced through irrigation or by rain (unirrigated), which are stated at 5% and 10%, respectively. The *nisab* is fixed by the prophet (blessings and peace of Allah be

---

[6] See footnote 2.
[7] Qadhi, Y. (2008). *English Translation of Sunan Abu Dawud*. Beirut: Darussalam Publishers and Distributors.
[8] Beik, I. S. *et al.* (2016). *Core Principles for Effective Zakat Supervision — Consultative Document*. Jakarta: BI, BAZNAS & IRTI-IDB, p. 42.

upon him) in several hadiths. One instance is the narration in Hadith number 2139 (Book 5) of Sahih Muslim where the holy Prophet (blessings and peace of Allah be upon him) said the following: "There is no Zakat on grains or dates until such items weigh five *wasqs*" (Sahih Muslim).[9]

A *wasq* is a unit of weight measure equivalent to 130.56 kg. Therefore, five wasqs equal 653 kg (5 × 130.56 = 653), equivalent to 1439 lbs, which is the *nisab* to be paid at harvest time as enshrined in the holy Quran "…but pay the due thereof on the day of their harvest" (Quran, Surah Al-an-am, verse 141).

Moreover, the rate of zakat and *nisab* of zakat vary in accordance with zakatable asset and the reckoning period (zakat year) as stated. For this purpose, agricultural produce is categorized into two: those produced via irrigation and those produced using rain, i.e., without irrigation.

- **Irrigated land output/produce**: The zakat rate for these farm products is 5% of the net value of *nisab* as harvested, to be calculated after deducting costs, including expenses for irrigation, fertilizer, and general operations.
- **Unirrigated land output/produce**: The zakat rate for these farm products is 10% of the gross value of *nisab* as harvested. These produce often incur less expenses as the land is being irrigated by natural springs or rain.[10]

Note that, for the purpose of time computation with respect to agricultural produce, a zakat year is not to be considered because what matters is the harvesting of the produce rather than an actual year's time frame.

Summing up, zakat due for business/trade goods, currency, and precious metals is calculated as 2.5% of the value of zakatable assets (zakat base) after one lunar year or 2.5775% thereof after a solar year, using any of the methods to determine zakat base, i.e., net assets method, net invested funds, adjusted working capital, and adjusted growth method. Then, the zakat due is calculated by multiplying *zakat rate* with *zakat base*.[11]

---

[9] Al-khattab, N. (2007). *English Translation of Sahih Muslim*. Houston: Darussalam Publications.

[10] Beik, I. S. et al. (2016). *Core Principles for Effective Zakat Supervision — Consultative Document*. Jakarta: BI, BAZNAS & IRTI-IDB, p. 42.

[11] MASB (2006). Technical Release *i* − 1 Accounting for Zakat on Business. https://www.masb.org.my/pdf.php?pdf=Accounting%20for%20Zakat%20TRi-1.pdf&file_path=uploadfile.

7.2.2.1 Standards and guiding principles governing zakat calculation

There are standards and guiding principles that govern zakat calculation. As a matter of regulation, the standards and guiding principles are synthesized from the Quran or sunnah and provided in regulatory instruments.[12] Under these standards and principles, some approaches or methods of zakat calculation are formulated and designed, as will be explained subsequently. The following are the standards that guide zakat calculation:

1. Financial Accounting Standard (FAS) 9 of the Accounting and Auditing Organization for Islamic Financial Institutions (AAOIFI),
2. Technical Release *i* – 1 Accounting for Zakat on Business of Malaysian Accounting Standards Board (MASB),
3. Guidelines on Financial Reporting for Islamic Banking Institutions of the Bank Negara Malaysia (BNM),
4. Zakat Management Manual of the Jabatan Wakaf, Zakat dan Haji (JAWHAR), Malaysia,
5. Zakat Calculation Standards of the National Zakat Foundation Worldwide.

Islamic financial institutions, business entities, and individuals alike are guided by the methods and directions comprised in these standards/guidelines. These standards/guidelines are issued by regulators and standard-setting bodies across jurisdictions for the calculation and/or assessment of zakat.

The most popular standard currently in use for zakat accounting is AAOIFI's FAS 9 (for zakat). AAOIFI is a private, not-for-profit standard-setting body on accounting and auditing based in Bahrain.[13] AAOIFI issued FAS 9 (as it is generally known) for zakat, effective 1st January 1999,

---

[12] Zakat Foundation of America (2007). *The Zakat Handbook: A Practical Guide for Muslims in the West*. Bloomington: AuthorHouse Publishing Co., p. 119.

[13] Accounting and Auditing Organization for Islamic Financial Institutions (AAOIFI) is a not-for-profit standard-setting organization established in 1990 and based in Bahrain. It is established to maintain and promote Shariah standards for the overall Islamic financial services industry and all its participants. See AAOIFI. Available at https://aaoifi.com/?lang=en. Accessed September 20, 2022.

Table 7.1. Zakatable wealth, *nisab*, and rate for zakat calculation.

Class of wealth (Zakatables)	*Nisab*/Threshold (value)	Rate
1. Personal wealth (cash and receivables)	85 g/3 ounce of pure gold	2.5% (1/40) of value
Gold	85 g/3 ounce of pure gold	2.5% (1/40) of value
Silver	595 g	2.5% (1/40) of value
2. Business Wealth (trade assets)	85 g/3 ounce of pure gold	2.5% (1/40) of value
3. Agricultural produce		
Irrigated crops	653 kg/1439 lbs	5% (2/40) of harvest
Non-irrigated crops	653 kg/1439 lbs	10% (4/40) of harvest
4. Animal/Livestock		
Goat/Sheep & all ovine	40–120	1
	121–200	2
	Every 100 more	+1 per 100
Buffalo/Cattle & all bovine	30–39	1 (1-year-old)
	40–59	1 (2-year-old)
	60–69	2 (1-year-old)
	70–79	2 (a 2-year-old & a 1-year-old)
5. Treasure troves (hidden precious metals & mined natural resources)	85 g/3 ounce of pure gold	20% of Value

Source: Compiled and adapted from AAOIFI's FAS 9 (1999), The Islamic Foundation (2003), National Zakat Foundation Worldwide (2020).

for Islamic banks. The AAOIFI's standards are predominantly used in many countries (Table 7.1).[14]

Similarly, the Malaysian Accounting Standards Board (MASB) developed its own standards in 2006 for Malaysia, based largely on the AAOIFI's standards, and is currently in use. The MASB, in some terms,

---

[14] AAOIFI. Financial Accounting Standard Number (9) Zakah. Available at https://aaoifi.com/financial-accounting-standard-no-9-zakah/?lang=en. Accessed September 20, 2022.

has deemed certain provisions of the AAOIFI's standards as inappropriate for the Malaysian context, such as the ones that require Islamic financial institutions to act as zakat collectors and distributors. This goes contrary to Malaysian legislation (state and federal) on the matter.[15] So, MASB developed its own standards, issued via Technical Release $i-1$, known as Accounting for Zakat on Business, to make zakat calculation and payment more viable to Malaysian businesses. The MASB standards on zakat calculation were based on recommendations of the Malaysian Islamic Development Department (JAKIM).[16]

For Islamic banks and financial institutions in this regard, in addition, the MASB standards are to be used alongside the Bank Negara Malaysia (BNM)'s Guidelines on Financial Reporting for Islamic Banking Institutions.[17] The BNM's guidelines in this regard seek to attain the same objective for Islamic banks as the MASB's standards.

Additionally, the Jabatan Wakaf, Zakat dan Haji (JAWHAR) Malaysia has prepared and issued a Zakat Management Manual, a standard to cater for zakat accounting and calculation by zakat paying businesses and entities.[18]

The National Zakat Foundation Worldwide (NZFW) is a multilateral organization and its membership comprises Muslim minority countries of Europe. The NZFW was established in 2011 in the UK. As a zakat

---

[15] Malaysian Accounting Standards Board (2009). Presenting Financial Statements of Islamic Financial Institutions, Technical Release I-3. http://www.masb.org.my/index.php?option=com_content&view=article&id=155&Itemid=25. Accessed September 20, 2022.

[16] Tajuddin, T. S. & Muhammad, I. (2021). Business zakat reporting: Evidence from the Islamic financial institutions. In Qadri, H. M., & Bhatti, M. I. (Eds.) *Contemporary Issues in Islamic Social Finance*. London: Routledge, pp. 234–245; Nurul'Iffah, M. A., & Hassan, R. (2020). Calculation, distribution and disclosure of zakat in Malaysian Islamic banks. *Journal of Islam in Asia*, Vol. 17, No. 2, pp. 162–181.

[17] Bank Negara Malaysia (BNM). (2016). Financial Reporting for Islamic Banking Institutions. Available at BNM. http://www.bnm.gov.my/guidelines/01_banking/02_financial_reporting/Financial_Reporting_for_Islamic_Banking_Institutions.pdf. Accessed September 20, 2022.

[18] JAWHAR (2009). Zakat Calculation Management Manual. Available at https://e-penerbitan.jawhar.gov.my/manual-pengurusan-pengiraan-zakat/. Accessed September 22, 2022. See also Ali, H. M., Basir, S. A., & Ahmadun, M. (2015). The issues of implementing Islamic quality management system MS1900: 2005 certification at the department of Awqaf, Zakat and Hajj. *Journal of Research in Islamic Studies*, Vol. 2, No. 1, pp. 14–28.

organization, it issued its Zakat Calculation Standards largely for the use of individuals and also for institutions and entities that find them relevant in their respective jurisdictions and contexts.[19]

As a matter of accounting and audit, it is noteworthy that all the standards require disclosure of the method used by reporting entities (businesses and Islamic banks) in assessing zakat base for calculating their zakat.[20]

7.2.2.2 Approaches in calculation of zakat

Under the standards and guidelines on the calculation of zakat highlighted above, certain approaches and/or methods are established to determine and/or calculate zakat as follows:

1. net asset method,
2. net invested funds method,
3. adjusted working capital method,
4. adjusted growth method.

These approaches and/or methods are mainly for the determination and/or calculation of zakat base as would be seen in the following explanations:

(1) **Net Asset Method**: To determine zakat base under AAOIFI's FAS 9 from which the net asset method gains prominence, combine all zakatable assets and then subtract all liabilities due together with investment accounts' unrestricted equity, minority interests, assets value under ownership of government, equity of endowment reserves, equity of non-profit organizations, and charities excluding the equity of individuals. In this method, all assets are valued as cash equivalent while liabilities are valued as per their book value.[21] However, under MASB (2006) standards,

---

[19] National Zakat Foundation Worldwide (2020). Calculating your Zakat. Available at https://nzf.org.uk/zakat-calculator/. Accessed September 22, 2022.

[20] Nurul'Iffah, M. A. Z. & Hassan, R. (2020). Calculation, distribution and disclosure of Zakat in Malaysian Islamic banks. *Journal of Islam in Asia*, Vol. 17, No. 2, pp. 162–181; see also Mannan, M. A. (2000). Effects of Zakah assessment and collection on the redistribution of income in contemporary Muslim countries. In Imtiaz, *et al.* (Eds.) *Management of Zakah in Modern Muslim Society*. Jeddah: IRTI-IDB, pp. 78–89.

[21] AAOIFI. Financial Accounting Standard Number (9) Zakah. Available at https://aaoifi.com/financial-accounting-standard-no-9-zakah/?lang=en. Accessed September 20, 2022;

zakat-paying entities are required to measure assets as well as liabilities based on the measurement used in their financial statements.[22] The net assets method is formulated and expressed as follows:

> Zakat Base = Assets Subject to Zakat
>   – All Liabilities Including Intangible Assets

(2) **Net Invested Funds Method**: According to the net invested funds method, also under AAOIFI's FAS 9, zakat base can be determined through the sum of paid-up capital, things and funds acquired which are not separated from the assets, any and all balance earnings, total income value, and liabilities not due for payment by the year ended on financial statement date. From this sum, the following are subtracted: net fixed assets together with non-trading investments (e.g., real assets meant for renting) as well as losses accrued from the sum above.[23] For the net invested funds method, the formula is expressed as follows:

> Zakat Base = (Paid up capital + reserves + provisions not
>   separated from assets + retained earnings + net income
>   + liabilities not due by the year ended) – (net fixed assets
>   + non-trading investments + accumulated losses)

(3) **Adjusted Working Capital Method**: The MASB standards determine zakat base using the adjusted working capital method whose formula is expressed as follows:

> Zakat Base = Net Current Assets

---

see also Adnan, M. A., & Bakar, N. B. A. (2009). Accounting treatment for corporate zakat: A critical review. *International Journal of Islamic and Middle Eastern Finance and Management*, Vol. 2, No. 1, pp. 32–45.

[22] Ismail, A. G., Tohirin, A., & Ahmad, M. A. J. (2013). Debate on policy issues in the field of zakat on Islamic bank business. IRTI Policy Paper, No. 3, pp. 13–15.

[23] AAOIFI. Financial Accounting Standard Number (9) Zakah. Available at https://aaoifi.com/financial-accounting-standard-no-9-zakah/?lang=en. Accessed September 20, 2022; see also Obaidullah, M. (2016). Revisiting estimation methods of business zakat and related tax incentives. *Journal of Islamic Accounting and Business Research*, Vol. 7, No. 4, pp. 349–364.

(Adjusted for items that do not meet the conditions for zakat assets and liabilities.)[24]

(4) Adjusted Growth Method (MASB, 2006): MASB standards state the formula for adjusted growth method of determining zakat base in the following expression:

Zakat Base = (Owners' Equity + Long-term Liabilities)
— (Non-Current Assets including equipment and plant)

(Adjusted for items that do not meet the conditions for zakat assets and liabilities.)[25]

The adjusted growth and adjusted working capital methods are also endorsed and adopted by JAWHAR. It is notable as earlier mentioned that all these calculation methods provide the same figure of zakat base and would eventually provide the same result.

7.3 Issues in Zakat Calculation

(1) Fluctuation in value of zakatable assets/wealth

Zakat can be calculated only after a year when zakatable wealth reaches *nisab*. It is necessary to keep record of the increase and fluctuation from *nisab* level to determine zakat due. For this purpose, a record needs to be kept of one's own or business entity's wealth from the *nisab* level and then note the date of any increase above the *nisab*, on a regular basis, from where the reckoning begins. Where fluctuation of value is recorded at one point so that the wealth in question is below *nisab*, then the ongoing reckoning of a year is negated until when another increase above *nisab* is

---

[24] Malaysian Accounting Standards Board (2009). Presenting Financial Statements of Islamic Financial Institutions, Technical Release I-3. http://www.masb.org.my/index.php?option=com_content&view=article&id=155&Itemid=25. Accessed September 20, 2022.; see also Obaidullah, M. *op cit.*, pp. 360–361.

[25] Malaysian Accounting Standards Board (2009). Presenting Financial Statements of Islamic Financial Institutions, Technical Release I-3. http://www.masb.org.my/index.php?option=com_content&view=article&id=155&Itemid=25. Accessed September 20, 2022; see also JAWHAR (2009). *Zakat Calculation Management Manual*. Available at https://e-penerbitan.jawhar.gov.my/manual-pengurusan-pengiraan-zakat/. Accessed September 22, 2022.

recorded at other points. Then, the reckoning of a year begins from there again.[26]

(2) Business/company income tax and shareholders' religion

Many countries including Malaysia do not have an integrated system of taxation that combines tax and zakat for businesses/companies. Accordingly, separate calculations and deductions are made out of a business/company's earnings, trade goods, and assets to determine tax and zakat. The two are distinct and separate responsibilities here. While the former is a legal obligation required by laws of the land, the latter is an Islamic religious obligation upon high-net-worth Muslims/Islamic business entities recognized by the law equally. On this note therefore, zakat can only be calculated out of Muslims' shareholding in the business/company's earnings, trade goods, and assets to determine zakat. These amount to double payment/deductions out of the same earning for Muslim. There is zakat rebate for this purpose (section 6A(3) Income Tax Act 1967 [Malaysia]). Nonetheless, there is issue with this as well. The rebate is subtracted from payable tax only to a certain limit. By this, it means for every ringgit given for zakat, it is deducted from tax in the same assessment year. When zakat is less than tax, balance is paid to tax authority, but when zakat is more than tax, the difference cannot be claimed from the authority.[27]

(3) Debt and liabilities for zakat accounting

The status of business/company's debt and liabilities needs to be ascertained in assessing zakat base and calculating zakat due from zakatable wealth. Zakat can be assessed and paid inclusive of strong or good debt, i.e., receivable including loan or money owed to the business/company where the debtor is solvent and capable of repaying. However, some Islamic scholars allow such debt to be considered as part of zakat base only when it is collected. Moreover, where a loan is ascertained as a bad debt, such a loan cannot be assessed as part of zakat base. Another issue arises from the fact that in practice zakat accounting method and business

---

[26] Beik, I. S. *et al.* (2016). *Core Principles for Effective Zakat Supervision – Consultative Document.* Jakarta: BI, BAZNAS & IRTI-IDB, pp. 45–46; Yusoff, M. B. (2006). Fiscal policy in an Islamic economy and the role of Zakat. *International Journal of Economics, Management and Accounting*, Vol. 14, No. 2, pp. 12–14.

[27] Nasir, M. N. & Hassan, S. (2005). Zakat on business in Malaysia: Issues and current treatment. In Shanmugam, B. *et al.* (Eds.) *Issues in Islamic Accounting.* Serdang: UPM Press, pp. 165–178.

tax deduction for business/company are based on different data/information. While business tax deduction is based on income statement, zakat accounting is based on information from balance sheet. Since the duo demonstrates no relationship, it affects the benefit of tax deduction accorded to business/company due to zakat payment. Zakat is payable by the business/company regardless of profit so long as the business/company has its working capital within zakat *nisab*. Here, the business/company only suffers loss, same as where its tax is less than the zakat it pays. Since zakat is paid on accumulated earnings (excluding productive fixed assets) and income tax is paid on current earnings, the case of granting tax benefit on tax liability due to paying zakat is not strong enough.[28]

7.4 Innovative Ways to Assist Zakat Calculation

(1) Standard zakat assessment and calculation form

In order to provide guidance and facilitate zakat calculations, zakat assessment and calculation forms and worksheets are designed to be used by prospective individual and business enterprise zakat payers. Several models of such forms are designed taking into consideration juristic differences to calculate zakat accurately and easily. The forms and worksheets are tailored to meet the zakat calculation needs of zakat payers who are salaried employees, small and medium entrepreneurs, investors in stock market, etc. Zakat calculation forms cover common zakat issues in the contemporary world. These forms can be found in governmental and not-for-profit zakat administration agencies around the world; examples include Zakat Foundation of America and National Zakat Foundation Worldwide, UK.

For bigger corporate business entities including Islamic financial institutions, there are regulations for compiling information on zakat among other things on which reports have to be filed to regulators on regular basis. The compilation of zakat information is statutorily designed forms as a matter of regulatory reporting and compliance.

---

[28] Obaidullah, M. (2014). Business zakat accounting and taxation in Malaysia. Available at https://www.iiibf.com/business-zakat-accounting-taxation-in-malaysia/. Accessed September 28, 2022; Beik, I. S. *et al.* (2016). *Core Principles for Effective Zakat Supervision — Consultative Document*. Jakarta: BI, BAZNAS & IRTI-IDB, pp. 46–47.

(2) Technology — Leveraging Internet, PC, and mobile applications

Through the Internet and digitalization, personal computer (PC), mobile, and web-based applications have been developed to provide different kinds of stand-alone tools for the zakat assessment and calculation. Several Islamic banking institutions provide such tools on their websites. They are tools that operate as zakat calculators. These tools provide knowledge on zakat calculation using texts and videos for demonstration among other facilities that use an algorithm to run a wizard that calculates zakat and various zakatable wealth. The tools enable users to analyze assets and find ones qualified for zakat and to be calculated accordingly by asking simple questions according to a particular Islamic school of jurisprudence. Users enter minimum inputs like the total amount of currency (cash), gold or silver, and/or the kind and total number of livestock owned, value business goods owned, and debts. The tools then analyze the inputs/answers supplied by the users, work out an answer (calculate) automatically according to rules of Islamic jurisprudence, and post total assets and/or amount to be paid as Zakat. Examples in this regard include the mobile application of United Nations High Commission for Refugees (UNHCR) called GiveZakat and web-based applications like Zakat Foundation of America's zakat calculator,[29] Kuwait Finance House's zakat calculator,[30] and Pusat Pungutan Zakat (PPZ)'s zakat calculator.[31]

---

[29] Zakat Foundation of America. (n.d.). Available at https://www.zakat.org/resource-center/zakat-calculator. Accessed September 28, 2022.
[30] KFH. (n.d.). Available at https://www.kfh.com.my/malaysia/personal/tools-and-services/calculators/zakat-calculator.html. Accessed September 28, 2022.
[31] PPZ. (n.d.). Available at https://www.zakat2u.com.my/kiraan/zakat/pendapatan. Accessed September 28, 2022.

Self-Assessment Quiz (MCQs)

Question 1: Zakat needs to be precisely calculated in order to avoid ………. and ensure ………. .
(a) Arbitrary estimation ……. certainty
(b) Certainty …… Arbitrary estimation
(c) Assessment …… calculation
(d) Calculation …… estimation

Question 2: Which of the following is the rate of zakat for currency and receivables?
(a) 2.2%
(b) 2.5%
(c) 2.6%
(d) All of the above

Question 3: Which of the following is not an instrument for standards that guide zakat calculation?
(a) MASB Technical Release $i - 1$ Accounting for Zakat on Business
(b) AAOIFI's FAS 9
(c) JAWHAR's Zakat Management Manual
(d) General Zakat Brief & Manual

Question 4: Which of the following is the zakat rate where zakat year is a solar year?
(a) 2.5775%
(b) 2.775%
(c) 2.557%
(d) None of the above

Question 5: Which zakat calculation method is expressed by the formula, "Zakat Base = Assets Subject to Zakat – All Liabilities Including Intangible Assets"?
(a) Net Invested Funds Method
(b) Net Asset Method
(c) Adjusted Growth Method
(d) All of the above

Question 6: A threshold of minimum wealth that a person or an entity must own from which zakat is due and assessed at the end of a zakat year is called …………..
(a) Hawl
(b) *Nisab*
(c) Wasq
(d) All of the above

Question 7: In order to provide guide and facilitate zakat calculations, the following are used by prospective individual and enterprises zakat payers except?
(a) Zakat calculation form
(b) Computer applications
(c) Zakat manipulation form
(d) Mobile device application

Question 8: Tax and zakat are two separate responsibilities. While the former is an obligation imposed by laws of the land, the latter is ……… on net-worth persons/entities.
(a) Socio-religious option
(b) Socio-economic choice
(c) Moral obligation
(d) Islamic religious obligation

Question 9: Malaysian Accounting Standards Board (MASB) developed its own standards for businesses via Technical Release $i - 1$ to make zakat calculation and payment …………. .
(a) Affordable to Malaysian businesses
(b) More viable to Malaysian businesses
(c) Attractive to Malaysian businesses
(d) Simple for Malaysian businesses

Question 10: Zakat can be assessed and paid inclusive of strong or good debt, i.e., receivables including money owed to an entity where the debtor is ……………..
(a) Solvent and capable of repaying
(b) Insolvent and likely to wind up
(c) Bankrupt to liquidation
(d) All of the above

Self-Assessment/Recall Questions

Question 1: Why is accurate calculation of zakat required of business entities?

Question 2: Identify any three Standards Guiding Zakat Calculation and highlight the objective of their issuance.

Question 3: Critically discuss why MASB issued Technical Release $i-1$ Accounting for Zakat on Business for Malaysian enterprises instead of wholly adopting AAOIFI's FAS 9.

Question 4: Identify any two approaches in calculation of zakat and explain them with an illustration of their methods and formula.

Question 5: Define zakat base and zakat *nisab* and explain how the two can be determined for the purpose of calculating zakat for money/currency in Islamic banks.

Answers to Self-Assessment Quiz (MCQs)

1. a
2. b
3. d
4. a
5. b
6. b
7. c
8. d
9. b
10. a

Chapter 8

Administration of Zakat

Learning Outcomes

At the end of this chapter, students should be able to know

- approaches in zakat administration,
- history of zakat administration,
- governance and account requirements for zakat organizations,
- issues in zakat administration,
- a case study on zakat administration.

8.1 Zakat Administration

Zakat administration refers to the management, control, and supervision of all activities pertaining to identification and selection of zakat recipients/beneficiaries and collection and distribution of zakat.[1] These activities are very crucial for ensuring a functional zakat system in the society. The Quranic verse on eligible beneficiaries of zakat mentions *amilin alayha* (the workers administering zakat) which signifies that collection and/or administration of zakat generally is the function of an organized body of people who can be given compensation to their work irrespective of whether they are poor or not.[2] This typically supposes a government (Islamic state) or

---

[1] Beik, I. S. *et al.* (2016). *Core Principles for Effective Zakat Supervision – Consultative Document*. Jakarta: BI, BAZNAS & IRTI-IDB, p. 42.

[2] Yudha, A. T. R. C., Wijayanti, I., Ryandono, M. N. H., & Petra, D. H. S. P. H. (2021). Financial inclusion through zakat institution: Case study in Indonesia and Brunei

government agency or any trustworthy organized people to be in charge of zakat administration. Historically, the Islamic state and/or government had always spearheaded zakat administration and the prophet of Islam had championed the tradition and established its practice.[3]

Legally speaking (Shariah wise), zakat is compulsory and, given its economic role, its payment is not to be left to individual desires, hence the relevance of a government role in its administration. Zakat is not an individual function according to the Shariah but a collective function only akin to the responsibility of the Islamic government/state. As such, zakat administration requires efficient manpower for efficiency in the administration. Therefore, where practicable, an Islamic government is responsible for establishing an agency that manages collection and distribution of zakat on the government's behalf.[4]

8.1.1 Approaches in zakat administration

Collection and distribution of zakat are generally understood to be the function of (1) an Islamic state where one exists and (2) a Muslim community, where such a community lives without an Islamic state. The latter is largely the case today with Muslims who are outside Islamic lands.[5] Thus, they independently determine whom to give or where to send their zakat.[6] Therefore, in reality, three forms of zakat administration systems have been identified for zakat in the world today. These are as follows:

Darussalam. *International Journal of Islamic Business and Economics*, Vol. 5, No. 2, pp. 129–141.

[3] Saad, R. A. J. & Farouk, A. U. (2019). A comprehensive review of barriers to a functional zakat system in Nigeria: What needs to be done? *International Journal of Ethics and Systems*, Vol. 35, No. 1, pp. 24–42.

[4] Masyita, D. (2018). Lessons learned of zakat management from different era and countries. *Al-Iqtishad Journal of Islamic Economics*, Vol. 10, No. 2, pp. 441–456.

[5] Rahmat, R. S. & Nurzaman, M. S. (2019). Assessment of zakat distribution: A case study on zakat community development in Bringinsari village, Sukorejo district, Kendal. *International Journal of Islamic and Middle Eastern Finance and Management*, Vol. 12, No. 5, pp. 743–766.

[6] Mahmud, M. W. & Haneef, S. S. S. (2008). Debatable issues in Fiqh Al-Zakat: A jurisprudential appraisal. *Jurnal Fiqh*, Vol. 5, pp. 117–141.

1. Zakat administration system operated by state or government.
2. Zakat administration system operated by government-sponsored agencies.
3. Zakat administration system operated by NGOs and volunteer communities.

Each of these three systems above can have an administration approach which can generally be centralized, decentralized, distributed, delegated, and isolated (unsupervised) among others. Actually, there are no hard and fast rules governing the classification of these approaches. Therefore, taking into consideration certain specific contexts, other approaches might be obtainable as well.

8.1.1.1 *Centralized approach to zakat administration*

A centralized approach to zakat administration tends to have the highest central authority or council that is charged with responsibility of overseeing zakat administration over a whole country in accordance with a designated hierarchy of statutorily conferred authority. Often time, there is reservation of the authority to direct, manage, and control activities, often concentrated in the central leader. This approach highly depends on the central leader or authority for direction and decision-making.[7] Countries that adopt centralized zakat administration include Pakistan, Saudi Arabia, Brunei, and Morocco, among others.[8]

8.1.1.2 *Decentralized approach to zakat administration*

A decentralized zakat administration approach uses a devolved system of authority shared by many zakat institutions established by governments or communities and controlled by the government. Typically, decentralization entails the establishment of subsidiaries to administer certain aspects of zakat corporate management. Often time, institutions of different capacities partake in the collection and distribution of zakat at various administrative units of the society, each given some statutory power over

---

[7] Hudayati, A. & Tohirin, A. (2010, January 16). Management of zakah: Centralised vs decentralised approach. In *Seventh International Conference – The Tawhidi Epistemology: Zakat and Waqf Economy*, Bangi, Malaysia, pp. 351–374.
[8] *Ibid.*

the unit it administers zakat. There is systematic dispersal of authority and responsibility, and direction and decision-making are shared in equal terms among authorities of respective and dispersed zakat institutions.[9] Countries that adopt decentralized zakat administration include Indonesia, Malaysia, UAE, and Yemen, among others.

8.1.1.3 Distributed approach to zakat administration

A distributed approach of zakat administration involves transferability and assignment of tasks to various intermediaries including institutional agents who are required to work based on specified guidance and strategy. The distributed approach is sometimes a centralized approach that decentralizes without actually conferring statutory power but rather assigning the same to intermediaries and agents. As such, they are subject to government control. The intermediaries and/or institutional agents often provide an acceptable level of reliability in performance at reduced cost.[10] Countries that adopt distributed approach to zakat administration include Bahrain, Kuwait, and Qatar, among others.

8.1.1.4 Delegated approach to zakat administration

A delegated approach involves assignment of accountability to an intermediary institution for carrying out specified zakat administration activities and tasks as agreed upon while retaining ultimate responsibility thereof. This approach shares certain semblance of distributed approach with respect to assignment/transfer of responsibility. Designated zakat institutions in several countries do adopt the delegated approach as a matter of administrative procedure to procure professional zakat administrative services on behalf of government.[11]

---

[9] Schaeublin, E. (2014). Zakat practice in the Islamic tradition and its recent history in the context of Palestine. *Histories of Humanitarian Action in the Middle East and North Africa*, pp. 19–26.

[10] Wahab, N. A. & Rahim Abdul Rahman, A. (2011). A framework to analyse the efficiency and governance of zakat institutions. *Journal of Islamic Accounting and Business Research*, Vol. 2, No. 1, pp. 43–62.

[11] Lubis, M., Lubis, A. R., & Almaarif, A. (2019). Comparison of the approach in zakat management system. *Journal of Physics*, Vol. 1235, No. 1, pp. 12048–12049.

8.1.1.5 *Isolated (unsupervised) approach to zakat administration*

An isolated (unsupervised) approach to Zakat administration obtains where self-independent institutions establish mechanisms to manage and control zakat collection and distribution, including accountability thereon, for a period of time in a localized community, usually on an *ad hoc* basis. In this approach, a team is often raised in a mosque-to-mosque network of people which administers zakat, particularly among congregants of the network. It is characterized with financial crisis that occurs mostly because it depends on voluntary participation of unprofessional people in the community. Moreover, the team is not subject to monitoring or any supervision and works on the sole trust of the congregants.[12] This approach is rather informal and practiced in countries where governments do not partake in religious activities and no professional zakat NGOs or agencies are readily available. The approach is obtained in Nigeria, Azerbaijan, and Mozambique, among others.

8.1.2 *History of zakat administration*

The holy prophet of Islam, Muhammad (PBUH), was himself the first zakat administrator of the Islamic world. He appointed zakat collectors and distributors for every region as more people accepted Islam and the Islamic world expanded, a tradition that continues till date. Zakat was historically collected from among the wealthy individuals from a particular locality and given to the needy and poor residents in the same locality. Where there was excess, which was usually determined after a thorough local disbursement, it was to be deposited at *bait al-mal* (treasury). It was on record that during the time of Calip Abu Bakr, the first caliph of the Islamic world; he appointed Umar ibn Khattab as a state zakat administrator, who in turn directed residents of big cities to select among themselves the most trustworthy individuals as zakat collectors.[13]

---

[12] *Ibid.*, pp. 12049–12050. See also Farouk, A. U., Idris, K., & Saad, R. A. J. (2017). The challenges of zakat management: A case of Kano state, Nigeria. *Asian Journal of Multidisciplinary Studies*, Vol. 5, No. 7, pp. 142–143.

[13] Tahir, I. N. & Oziev, G. (2018). Zakat administration: An analysis of the past approach. *International Journal of Economics, Management and Accounting*, Vol. 26, No. 1,

Zakat administration of the first caliph Abu Bakar marked the beginning of institutionalized zakat. The importance of zakat management via an institutionalized system was realized after the demise of the Prophet when certain tribes of Arab declined to give zakat, expelled some *amils* (zakat workers) appointed by the prophet, and were only willing to remain Muslim if no zakat was to be collected from them. The caliph led a fight against these tribes successfully and zakat was collected from them. These strides of caliph Abu Bakr left a lesson from which later caliph, Umar ibn Khattab, continued the dynamic institutionalization of zakat and its administration which culminated in the formal reorganization of the *bait al-mal* (public treasury) by 638 AD or 15 A.H. in the Islamic empire. The last episode of this system was epitomized by the Muslim Ottoman Empire in 1925. Zakat administration has always been an important government function throughout Islamic history. Along the way however, European colonial interference in Muslim countries and governments spelled radical changes. Due to this interference, state administration of zakat is greatly diminished, and zakat is left as a personal and individual obligation.[14]

Consequently, zakat administration obtains differently among contemporary Muslim countries. Thus, in Malaysia, Sudan, Libya, Yemen, Iran, and Pakistan, where Islam is the state religion, a compulsory zakat system has been in place and administered by either state authorities or central government ministry of religion and ministry of finance. Likewise, in some Middle Eastern countries including Kuwait and Saudi Arabia, ministries on zakat and *waqf* have been established and charged with the administration of zakat.[15] However, in countries where secularism holds sway religious activity is regarded as a private matter, zakat has been left as purely an individual affair[16] so that in some counties such as South

---

pp. 57–90; National Zakat Foundation (2021). The History of Zakat. Available at https://nzf.org.uk/knowledge/history-of-zakat/. Accessed October 2, 2022.

[14] Meirison, M. (2020). Administration and finance system of the Ottoman empire. *Jurnal Ilmiah Al-Syir'ah*, Vol. 18, No. 2, pp. 91–111.

[15] Adachi, M. (2018). Discourses of institutionalization of zakat management system in contemporary Indonesia: Effect of the revitalization of Islamic economics. *International Journal of Zakat*, Vol. 3, No. 1, pp. 25–35.

[16] Gamon, A. D. & Tagoranao, M. S. (2018). Zakat and poverty alleviation in a secular state: The Case of Muslim minorities in the Philippines. *Studia Islamika*, Vol. 25, No. 1, pp. 97–134.

Africa and India, for instance, trust organizations are set up to administer zakat.[17] Nonetheless, in many non-Muslim countries, zakat is voluntary, left as a choice of an individual. Yet, in some countries such as Mali, Nigeria, and Bangladesh, zakat is administered by non-governmental voluntary organizations with the help of voluntary contributions from zakat payers. In other countries yet, zakat administration is taken local community mosque committees because no zakat agencies exist.[18]

8.1.3 Governance and accounting requirements for zakat organizations

Governance of zakat entails all actions and processes of overseeing the operations and administration of zakat organizations. Governance is very crucial for zakat to achieve its objective and purpose. Zakat administrators are required to be just and accountable about their handling of zakat and administering it.[19] As the first zakat administrator in Islam, the holy prophet (PBUH) had characterized and epitomized the standards of manners in terms of accountability while carrying out zakat function as a matter of trust.[20] Therefore, accountability is integral to zakat governance and the holy prophet had set the precedent.[21] For the purpose of just and competent governance of zakat, Shariah stipulates certain qualities that are desired of a zakat collector and, by necessary implication, zakat administrator.

As individuals, the minimum qualities for zakat collectors are the following: being Muslims, sane, past puberty age, trustworthy, righteous/

---

[17] Alam, S. & Ahmed, M. U. (2020). A critique of zakat practices in India. *International Journal of Zakat and Islamic Philanthropy*, Vol. 2, No. 2, pp. 212–113.

[18] Weiss, H. (2020). Muslim NGOs, zakat and the provision of social welfare in sub-Saharan Africa: An introduction. In Weiss, H. (Ed.) *Muslim Faith-Based Organizations and Social Welfare in Africa*. Cham: Palgrave Macmillan, pp. 1–38. Saad & Farouk. *Op. cit.*

[19] Hardiyanto, N., Choirul Afif, N., Bayu Aji Sumantri, M., & Haizam Mohd Saudi, M. (2018). Systemic approach to solve problem of managing zakat in contemporary Muslim society in Indonesia. *International Journal of Engineering & Technology*, Vol. 7, No. 4.34, p. 261.

[20] Muhammad, S. A. & Saad, R. A. J. (2016). Determinants of trust on zakat institutions and its dimensions on intention to pay zakat: A pilot study. *Journal of Advanced Research in Business and Management Studies*, Vol. 3, No. 1, pp. 40–46.

[21] Ganiyev, A. & Umaraliyev, S. (2020). The role of zakat in the early stages of the Islamic civilisation. *EPRA International Journal of Multidisciplinary Research*, Vol. 25, pp. 441–444.

honest, and efficiently capable of their duties. Also, in their manner and character, they are not allowed to accept gifts offered by zakat payers; declare everything collected as zakat and record the same appropriately; and exhibit courtesy, kindness, and moderation in their dealings with zakat payers.[22]

It should be noted however since fact zakat today is administered by institution administrators rather than an individual, these qualities are applicable to the institution (with necessary changes) and individual persons employed to run the institutions. Additionally, as zakat collection is an obligation of the state, zakat institutions are required to be established by a Muslim government in an Islamic state. If, however, there is no such government in place to discharge the obligation, then as a communal responsibility, Muslims from each region or locality have to establish an entity (formal or informal) to administer zakat obligation.[23]

For accountability of zakat organizations, they are not to be left to do as they deem fit. For this purpose, adequate supervision of the organizations must be ensured through a check and balance system that monitors the organization's activities, especially finances. Thus, periodic reporting to relevant authorities needs to be made on their activities and finance. In this regard, routine audit of their financial accounts and databases needs to be carried out for transparency and prevention of misappropriation of zakat funds. This kind of supervision has been confirmed as a matter of rule by sunnah of the holy prophet Muhammad (PBUH).[24]

In a hadith reported in Sahih al-Bukhari, Abu Humaid Al-Sa'idi narrated that the prophet (PBUH) appointed one Ibn Al-Lubiyah to collect zakat from Bani Sulaim (a tribe). When Al-Lubiyah returned with the zakat, the prophet checked the account with him. Then, Al-Lubiyah reported to the prophet thus: "This is yours, and this is what is given to me as a gift." On hearing this, the prophet queried: "Why didn't you stay in your father's and mother's home to see whether you will be given gifts or not if you are truthful?" Thereafter, the prophet addressed the people present on the issue and warned: "… by Allah, not anyone of you takes a thing unlawfully but he will meet Allah on the Day of Resurrection, carrying that thing. I do not want to see any of you carrying a grunting camel

---

[22] Muhammad & Saad. *Op. cit.*, pp. 42–43.
[23] Mubtadi, N. A. (2019). Analysis of Islamic accountability and Islamic governance in zakat institution. *Hasanuddin Economics and Business Review*, Vol. 3, No. 1, pp. 1–12.
[24] Wahab & Rahim Abdul Rahman. *Op. cit.*

or a mooing cow or a bleating sheep on meeting Allah" [Sahih Al-Bukhari, Vol. 9 Book 89, Hadith No. 286].

By this hadith, in contemporary practice, zakat organizations are statutorily required, as a regulatory matter, to keep and maintain books of account for zakat operations, separate from books of account for their own expenditures. Likewise, all the books and accounts are subject to regulatory audit and reporting to authorities periodically. The accountability and transparency of zakat organizations are indispensable and have to be upheld always to bolster trust and confidence of zakat payers and recipients alike in zakat organizations and to zakat administration.

In Malaysia therefore, the Department of Awqaf, Zakat, and Hajj (*Jabatan Wakaf, Zakat dan Haji* [JAWHAR]) is established and charged with the responsibility of managing/administering endowments (*waqf*), properties, zakat, and pilgrimage (hajj). For effective zakat administration, the department issued guidelines for State Islamic Religious Councils (SIRCs) called Zakat Distribution Management Manual (*Manual Pengurusan Agihan Zakat* [MPAZ]) 2007 on the management of zakat.[25] It is a reference manual for zakat administration in all states, including federal territories.

The MPAZ encapsulates 15 working principles on zakat administration as sanctioned by Shariah to ensure fairness and effectiveness in all processes involved. The principles govern zakat collection and distribution, as well as the zakat institutions' operation. They are stated as follows: trust (amanah), transparency, comprehensiveness, fairness, being responsible, prudence in managing expenses, intensive supervision, separation of zakat funds from others, full information and disclosure (on funds collected, distributed, and expended), targeting essential needs of zakat recipients (had al-kifayah), immediate distribution, right and exclusiveness of zakat funds (to the eight recipients groups), priority to three groups of recipients (faqir [poor], miskin [needy], and *amil* [zakat collector]), and allowing zakat payers to nominate recipients (where they want to).[26]

These principles sum up the general shariah requirements for good governance and accountability of zakat administration practices.

---

[25] Sawandi, N., Aziz, N. M. A., & Saad, R. A. J. (2019). Discharging accountability: A case study of a zakat institution in Malaysia. *International Journal of Supply Chain Management*, Vol. 8, No. 1, pp. 676–682.

[26] JAWHAR. (2007). *Manual Pengurusan Agihan Zakat*. Putrajaya: Jabatan Wakaf, Zakat dan Haji.

Comparatively, these principles cover contemporary good governance practices as provided by regulators and standard-setting institutions.[27]

8.1.4 Issues in zakat administration

Generally, issues surrounding zakat administration are imprecise identification of zakat recipients, ineffective zakat distribution, bureaucracy, and administrative inefficiency. Other issues are rather specific to certain context and circumstances of zakat administration such as experience of administrators which varies among countries.

On the above note, Malaysia can be said to be a bit advanced/experienced in zakat management and administration. Its system and approach have received international quality recognition and accolades, earned due to diversified and enhanced zakat collection system which serves as model to many other countries.[28] Zakat administration is the responsibility of SIRCs (13 states) and Majlis Agama Islam Wilayah Persekutuan (MAIWP) for the federal territories (Kuala Lumpur, Putrajaya, and Labuan) in Malaysia. Yet, state-level centralization poses an issue. Federal Constitution confers on each state sultan's authority in zakat is the reason for the centralized administration at the state level. Though the approach is viewed positive toward zakat collection, it makes effective distribution of the same difficult.[29] Moreover, existence of just single institution of zakat in each state negates competition which helps drive innovation. This often results in laxity and inefficiency in managing zakat funds.[30]

Inefficiency of zakat administration is an issue that often results from inadequate information dissemination and lack of awareness (as to when to pay and how much to pay).[31] There is also lack of requisite awareness on part of eligible recipients about how to go about claiming zakat. This

---

[27] For instance, UNESCAP (2008). *What is Good Governance?* Available at https://www.unescap.org/sites/default/files/good-governance.pdf. Accessed September 20, 2022.

[28] Migdad, A. (2019). Managing zakat through institutions: Case of Malaysia. *International Journal of Islamic Economics and Finance Studies*, Vol. 5, No. 3, pp. 28–44.

[29] Htay, S. N. N. & Salman, S. A. (2014). Proposed best practices of financial information disclosure for zakat institutions: A case study of Malaysia. *World Applied Sciences Journal*, Vol. 30, No. 30, pp. 288–294.

[30] Ahmad Razimi, M. S., Romle, A. R., & Muhamad Erdris, M. F. (2016). Zakat management in Malaysia: A review. *American-Eurasian Journal of Scientific Research*, Vol. 11, No. 6, pp. 453–457.

[31] *Ibid.*

is coupled with inability to exhaustively identify the eligible recipients.[32] This may not be far from the reason that while categories of asnaf are known from Quran, it is challenging to find them in real world, verify their respective categories, and ensure they deserve Zakat. This results in imprecise and inexhaustive identification of recipients (*asnaf*).[33] This, coupled with apparent unnecessary bureaucracy around routine reassessment of (even of already identified recipients) before each payment, often disillusions the recipients and leads to ineffective process of distribution of zakat. These affect the performance of the zakat institutions and the impact of zakat, particularly on the poor and needy, in the name of avoiding risk of awarding wrong asnaf.[34]

Lack of creative and effective distribution system is a governance issue that portrays the zakat institutions as incompetent in the public eyes, hence the perception that the institutions are incapable of channeling zakat to the rightful recipient. This impression discourages prospective zakat payers to pay to zakat institutions. It also discourages eligible recipients from applying for zakat. Another issue in relation to identification and distribution is that zakat institutions and their collection centers appear to focus less on prospective zakat payers than recipients.[35] Hence, available records show, for instance, in Malaysia, that a smaller number of zakat payers are officially identified than there are actually, i.e., identified zakat payers are less than actual number of eligible zakat payers.[36] Thus, payments of zakat by the officially unidentified payers, where they do, are unrecorded which means inaccurate data/statistics in that regard.

---

[32] Samargandi, N., Tajularifin, S. M., Ghani, E. K., Aziz, A. A., & Gunardi, A. (2018). Can disclosure practices and stakeholder management influence zakat payers' trust? A Malaysian evidence. *Business and Economic Horizons*, Vol. 14, pp. 882–893.

[33] Sapingi, R., Nelson, S. P., & Obid, S. N. S. (2016, May 3). Current disclosure practices by zakat institutions in Malaysia: An exploratory study. In *2nd UUM Qualitative Research Conference*, pp. 408–416.

[34] Mahmood, T. M. A. T., Din, N. M., Al Mamun, A., & Ibrahim, M. D. (2021). Issues and challenges of zakat institutions achieving Maqasid Syariah in Malaysia. *AZKA International Journal of Zakat & Social Finance*, pp. 119–137.

[35] Ahmad, K. & Yahaya, M. H. (2022). Islamic social financing and efficient zakat distribution: Impact of fintech adoption among the asnaf in Malaysia. *Journal of Islamic Marketing* (ahead-of-print). DOI: 10.1108/JIMA-04-2021-0102.

[36] Wahid, H., Kader, R. A., & Ahmad, S. (2011, July 17). Localization of zakat distribution and the role of Mosque: Perceptions of *amil* and zakat recipients in Malaysia. In *Proceedings of International Zakat Forum*, Kuala Lumpur, Malaysia, pp. 1–25.

8.1.5 Case Study: Federal Territory Islamic Religious Council (Majlis Agama Islam Wilayah Persekutuan [MAIWP]) Malaysia

Federal Territory Islamic Religious Council or *Majlis Agama Islam Wilayah Persekutuan* (*MAIWP*) is the Islamic Religious Council for the Malaysian Federal Territory established in 1974. MAIWP is a statutory body that advises the Yang di-Pertuan Agong, the Paramount Ruler of Malaysia, on the religion of Islam. Therefore, all matters of zakat administration are the responsibility of the MAIWP. For this purpose, the MAIWP established a Zakat Collection Centre (*Pusat Pungutan Zakat* [PPZ]) in 1991 as an agency charged with the responsibility for zakat collection in the Malaysian Federal Territories of Kuala Lumpur, Putrajaya, and Labuan [sections 4, 5, 8, 8A Administration of Islamic Law (Federal Territories) Act 1993]. While the PPZ collects and gathers zakat funds, management and distribution of the same to eligible recipients (asnaf) are undertaken by the *Baitul-mal* or treasury department of the MAIWP. The PPZ and Baitul-mal are two subsidiaries and administrative divisions of the MAIWP.[37]

It should be noted that all operations regarding collection of zakat are conducted for and on behalf of the PPZ by a private firm called Hartasuci Private Limited which has already become synonymous with the PPZ. The PPZ is responsible for all activities of zakat collection as well as *sadaqat* (charity) in the federal territories. Over the years, PPZ has introduced a range of services aimed to encourage Muslims to settle their zakat obligation. In partnership with another firm, Pertama Digital Berhad, PPZ has introduced a mobile application called MyPay, which facilitates its zakat collection function.[38] MyPay is one among several channels for making zakat payment. Others include MyZakat application, Ride 2U, MyTemujanji, PPZ-MAIWP Portal, Digital Zakat Counter services, and Door-to-Door service. PPZ collects income zakat, business zakat, and zakat on shares/stocks, precious metals, and other kinds of zakat. As of 2021 end, MAIWP through PPZ has collected over RM816 million zakat and expended and/or channeled over RM725 million to eligible recipients and other projects

---

[37] Ibrahim, M. F. (2020). Comparison of zakat distribution as Islamic social finance tool to help Al-Gharimin group by LZS and Baitul-mal MAIWP. *International Journal of Islamic Economics and Finance Research*, Vol. 3, No. 2, pp. 1–11.

[38] See Aman, A. S. (2021). MyPay partners with PPZ-MAIWP to accelerate cashless zakat payments. *The New Straits Time*, 2 December. Available at https://www.nst.com.my/business/2021/12/750675/mypay-partners-ppz-maiwp-accelerate-cashless-zakat-payments.

through the Baitul-mal.[39] For the purpose of the channeling or distribution, PPZ has established distribution units called Zakat Distribution Centers (*Pusat Agihan Zakat* [*PAZA*]) across the federal territories.[40]

Another innovation introduced by MAIWP that helps in zakat distribution is the *Zakat Wakalah Scheme*. This is a policy that produces an arrangement whereby zakat money collected by MAIWP through PPZ is refunded to the entities who paid the money for them to distribute the same to eligible recipients of their choice. Acting as representative to MAIWP, these entities are individuals, companies/business organizations, higher education institutions, and employers who are considered to have identified eligible zakat recipients in their respective domains.[41] The scheme adds to the pool of channels for the distribution of zakat. Zakat payers incorporated into the scheme give accounts of their distribution activities by submitting a report on "Zakat Money Distribution" through MyWakalah, an online collation system for the scheme.[42]

In terms of governance, PPZ has administrative and procedural structure that ensures accountability among other good governance parameters. PPZ has an Integrity Unit which reports directly to Hartasuci's Board of Directors via Audit and Governance Committee of PPZ-MAIWP. There are six functions assigned to the Integrity Unit thus to preserve best governance, build up integrity, detect and verify misconduct, manage complaints, handle disciplinary function, and ensure compliance with applicable regulations. Additionally, there are policies against conflict of interest, gifts and hospitality for employees and stakeholders, anti-corruption, as well as general code of conduct and business ethics. Likewise, reports detailing all activities are annually published in line with the PPZ-MAIWP's policies on disclosure.[43]

---

[39] PPZ-MAIWP (2021). Annual Report 2021. Available at https://www.zakat.com.my/info-ppz/laporan/buku-laporan/#1656468999108-f6fe3b4b-9ee5. See also Azuar, A. (2022). Federal Territory's zakat collection exceeds RM800m in 2021. *The Malay Reserve*, 11 January. Available at https://themalaysianreserve.com/2022/01/11/federal-territorys-zakat-collection-exceeds-rm800m-in-2021/.

[40] Ibrahim. *Op. cit.*

[41] PPZ-MAIWP. (n.d.). Zakat Wakalah. Available at https://www.zakat.com.my/info-zakat/wakalah/. Accessed September 30, 2022.

[42] *Ibid.*

[43] PPZ-MAIWP. *Op. cit.* See also Alif, S. (2022). PPZ-MAIWP Allocates RM1.1b to Help Needy. *The Malay Reserve*, 11 April. Available at https://themalaysianreserve.com/2022/04/11/ppz-maiwp-allocates-rm1-1b-to-help-needy/.

Self-Assessment Quiz (MCQs)

Question 1: The term *"amilin alayha"* in relation to those who are eligible to receive zakat refers to one of the following categories of people. Which One?
(a) Poor and needy
(b) Zakat administrators
(c) Weary travelers
(d) Proselytizers

Question 2: Traditionally, zakat administration including collection and distribution of zakat and the control of people charged with these duties is the responsibility of ……….
(a) Islamic state/government
(b) Voluntary organization
(c) Individual volunteers
(d) All of the above

Question 3: The following are forms of zakat administration systems that are obtainable today except …………….
(a) Zakat administration system operated by state or government
(b) Zakat administration system operated by NGOs or volunteer communities
(c) Zakat administration system operated by private businesses
(d) None of the above.

Question 4: An approach of zakat administration where authority on zakat matters is devolved and shared among zakat institutions established by respective governments of states, regions, or communities is described as ……….
(a) Centralized approach to zakat administration
(b) Decentralized approach to zakat administration
(c) Delegated approach to zakat administration
(d) Distributed approach to zakat administration

Question 5: Who was the first zakat administrator of the Islamic world/empire?
(a) Prophet Muhammad
(b) Caliph Abu Bakr
(c) Caliph Umar ibn Khattab
(d) Ottoman Caliph

Question 6: Which of the following Islamic institutions assumed the responsibilities of zakat administration in zakat administration history to date?
(a) Shariah court
(b) Baitul mal
(c) Madrasah
(d) All of the above

Question 7: In which of the following zakat administration approaches would Malaysian system of zakat administration be placed?
(a) Delegated approach
(b) Decentralized approach
(c) Distributed approach
(d) None of the above

Question 8: The following are working principles of zakat administration encapsulated in the Jabatan Wakaf, Zakat dan Haji (JAWHAR)'s Manual Pengurusan Agihan Zakat (MPAZ) 2007 except ....
(a) Trust
(b) Fairness
(c) Inequity
(d) None of the above

Question 9: Good governance and accountability in zakat administration institutions require zakat institution institutions to maintain books of account for zakat operations separate from .... :
(a) Liabilities from assets
(b) External service record
(c) Contract and expenditures
(d) Books of account for own expenditures

Question 10: Inexhaustive or imprecise identification of zakat recipients and .... are general issues that militate against realizing the goals of zakat.
(a) Ineffective zakat distribution
(b) Inability to find zakat center
(c) Incapability to pay zakat
(d) All of the above

Self-Assessment/Recall Questions

Question 1: Discuss how zakat institutions can contribute to good governance and accountability in zakat administration.

Question 2: Examine the role of zakat institutions in promoting standards for zakat administration.

Question 3: Explain the rationale behind requiring accountability and good governance of zakat institutions.

Question 4: Succinctly discuss how ineffective zakat distribution and inexhaustive or imprecise identification of zakat recipients affects efficiency of zakat administration.

Question 5: Discuss any three approaches of zakat administration with examples of countries where the approaches are practiced.

Answers to Self-Assessment Quiz (MCQs)

1. b
2. a
3. c
4. b
5. a
6. b
7. b
8. c
9. d
10. a

Chapter 9

Role of Zakat in Achieving Sustainable Development Goals

Learning Outcomes

At the end of this chapter, students should be able to know

- untapped potential of zakat,
- use of zakat in achieving sustainable development goals,
- challenges in using zakat in achieving sustainable development goals,
- selected case studies.

9.1 The Sustainable Development Goals [SDGs]

The Sustainable Development Goals (SDGs) are a set of 17 universally concerted goals aimed at combatting contemporary environmental, economic, and political challenges that the world faces. Also known as the global goals, the SDGs are collectively considered a blueprint to achieve a better and sustainable future that seeks to provide an approach to addressing the challenges on a long-term basis. This is being done through joint actions and collaborations among countries, multilateral organizations, public entities, and corporate private enterprises. The SDGs were formulated in 2012 in Rio de Janeiro, Brazil, during a United Nations (UN) Conference on Sustainable Development. They were adopted by the UN in 2015 as a universal call to action to end poverty, hunger, and inequality, protect the planet, and ensure that people over the world enjoy peace and prosperity by the year 2030. The 17 goals are therefore collectively referred to as the 2030 Agenda for Sustainable Development.[1]

9.1.1 Untapped potential of zakat

According to the World Bank and World Economic Forum, there is an estimated 2.5 trillion dollars of funding for the SDGs annually. Meanwhile, according to the World Bank and IRTI-IsDB, zakat is considered a potential source of funding that could mobilize an estimated 200 billion to 1 trillion dollars per year in this regard, hence the potential of zakat is too huge to be ignored or left untapped in the global development agenda.[2]

Zakat is a powerful economic tool for redistribution of wealth and prevention of poverty if it can focus more on creating impact than as an act of charity alone. Here, zakat can empower its recipients to engage more in productive activities than individual consumption. Thus, zakat can play a significant role to complement governments' efforts to assist the people in terms of material needs as part of national development. Also, zakat charitable funds can be channeled and invested in social and economic development projects that advance economic prosperity as a means to individual and societal welfare. It is notable however that these potentials of zakat have been largely untapped, particularly as a source of funds to finance international development. It is in light of this potential that zakat can be similarly used toward achieving the SDGs.[3]

Zakat is one of the primary Islamic tools that stands for and seeks to actualize the foundational objectives of Shariah (maqasid al-shariah),[4] i.e., protection of faith, life, progeny, intellect, and wealth. This is through fair circulation/distribution of wealth to address the menace of poverty,

---

[1] UNDP. (2015). What Are the Sustainable Development Goals? Available at https://www.undp.org/sustainable-development-goals. Accessed August 20, 2022.
[2] UNDP. (2020). Zakat for the SDGS. Available at https://www.undp.org/blog/zakat-sdgs; UNDP. (2017). The role of zakat in supporting the Sustainable Development Goals. Available at https://www.undp.org/indonesia/publications/role-zakat-supporting-sustainable-development-goals.
[3] Hasan, Z. (2020). Distribution of zakat funds to achieve SDGs through poverty alleviation in BAZNAS Republic of Indonesia. *AZKA International Journal of Zakat & Social Finance*, pp. 25–43.
[4] The maqasid al-Shariah signify the objectives and purposes behind the divine order and instructions enshrined by Shariah.

hunger, inequality, and their associated vices in society. While zakat idealizes religious philanthropy, its scope is essentially capable of achieving the SDGs. Zakat can address the rising need for social and economic investments to address related challenges that the world faces.[5] Basically, zakat is Shariah's economic mechanisms for alleviating poverty, ending hunger and inequality, and addressing waste and unfair distribution of wealth among other societal ills in the contemporary time. This is a purpose coincidentally shared with some of the SDGs. Zakat can help achieve the SDGs because they are mostly enjoined by and encompassed among objectives of the Shariah according to contemporary Islamic scholars.[6]

9.1.2 *Use of zakat in achieving sustainable development goals*

Zakat can be used to achieve most of the SDGs in an order of priority because they are aligned with the foundational objectives of Shariah. For this purpose, the SDGs are hereby categorized/prioritized in hierarchies in accordance with the classes of zakat recipients as enshrined in the holy Quran and/or their needs. The first and topmost priority includes the goals of ending poverty (goal 1), ending hunger (goal 2), reducing inequality among people (goal 10), and ensuring healthy life and well-being of humanity (goal 3). The second priority includes the goals of ensuring availability of clean water/sanitation (goal 6), providing inclusive and quality education (goal 4), promoting decent work and economic growth (8), and promoting peace and justice in societies (goal 16). The third priority includes the goals of ensuring responsible consumption and production (goal 12), building resilient industry and infrastructures (goal 9), and ensuring affordable and clean energy (goal 7). The fourth priority includes the goals for ensuring sustainable cities/human communities (goal 11),

---

[5] Khan, T. & Badjie, F. (2022). Islamic blended finance for circular economy impactful SMEs to achieve SDGs. *The Singapore Economic Review*, Vol. 67, No. 1, pp. 219–244; OECD. (2018). *Making Blended Finance Work for the Sustainable Development Goals*. Paris: OECD Publishing, pp. 41–42. DOI: https://doi.org/10.1787/9789264288768-en.

[6] Laldin, M. A. & Djafri, F. (2021). The role of Islamic finance in achieving sustainable development goals (SDGs). In Hassan, M. K., Saraç, M., & Khan, A. (Eds.) *Islamic Finance and Sustainable Development*. Cham: Palgrave Macmillan, pp. 107–126. World Bank. (2018). *Sustainable Development Goals and the Role of Islamic Finance*. Available at https://blogs.worldbank.org/eastasiapacific/sustainable-development-goals-and-role-islamic-finance. Accessed August 25, 2022.

combatting climate change (goal 13), conserving marine life/ecosystem (goal 14), protecting terrestrial life/ecosystem (goal 15), and global partnerships for implementing the SDGs.[7]

It should be noted that zakat funds are used to achieve SDGs to the extent that development targets and goals can be equated to what has been enjoined in Islam to promote maqasid al-Shariah. So, in the order of these priorities, zakat contributions are basically made toward five of the goals, i.e., the goals on poverty eradication, ending hunger, improving health/well-being, quality education, and ensuring clean water and sanitation. But it is notable that the fundamental of zakat is consistent with almost all of the SDGs.[8]

Therefore, zakat institutions can direct zakat funds mostly toward issues of poverty, hunger, health, education, water, and sanitation in facilitating the attainment of the SDGs. These are in line with the first and second priorities through contributions by individual zakat payers to recipients of their choice as a private matter and often within given national boundaries. Meanwhile, another realistic means of zakat contributing to the achievement of the SDGs is by leveraging its potential as a targeted and socially impactful resource.[9] This integration, as means to an end, enables the channeling of the zakat funds into SDG-oriented activities where they are needed most around the world and thus strengthens zakat impact to play a role as an enabler to the attainment of the SDGs.

---

[7] Rehman, H. A., Hasan, H., & Muhammad, M. (2021). Compatibility of sustainable development goals (SDGs) with Maqasid al-Shariah: Are there any missing goals. *Islamic Banking and Finance Review*, Vol. 8, No. 2, pp. 109–132; see also Abdullah, M. (2021). Shari'ah, ethical wealth and SDGs: A maqasid perspective. In Billah, M. (Ed.) *Islamic Wealth and the SDGs*. Cham: Palgrave Macmillan, pp. 69–85. NB: There is one goal (SDG 5) on 'gender equality' whose parameters, as provided by the UN, differ with Shariah ruling thereon.

[8] Alfiani, T. & Akbar, N. (2020, November). Exploring strategies to enhance zakat role to support sustainable development goals (SDGs). In *International Conference of Zakat*, pp. 295–310.

[9] Djafri, F. & Soualhi, Y. (2021). Islamic Finance: Shariah and the SDGS — Thought Leadership Series Part 4 — October 2021. Available at https://www.inceif.org/news-portal/wp-content/uploads/2021/09/ISRA-UKIFC-Report-part-4-Oct-2021_compressed.pdf. Accessed August 30, 2022.

9.1.3 Challenges in using zakat in achieving sustainable development goals

Certain issues have been identified as challenges to the use of zakat to achieve the SDGs. These challenges include the following:

Lack of a framework for the integration of the SDGs with the overarching objective of Shariah (maqasid al-shariah) that zakat seeks to represent and accomplish.[10] Each of the SDGs' targets and indicators is designated to gauge attainment of that particular goal. For instance, goal 8 has an attainment target and indicator of at least of 7% annual growth rate in real GDP per capita among the least developed nations. This presents challenges that are no less theoretical than technical to achieve SDGs via zakat output as there is no mechanism in place to monitor zakat processes locally and globally for this purpose.[11] Thus, determining the share of zakat in the targeted annual growth rate is not readily ascertainable.

Similarly, there is no reliable official data on zakat collection and distribution worldwide, coupled with inaccurate assessment of its potential toward achieving the SDGs, brought about by the imprudent use of zakat funds to satisfy contemporary development and sustainability issues.[12] Besides, no SDG performance benchmarks have been specifically developed for zakat to ascertain its achievement and impact.

In addition, there is lack of adequate human capital on the part of zakat administrators for the understanding and practical application of the SDGs' value proposition in the governance, operations, and prudential requirements in zakat management. Adequate human capital is needed for proper alignment of zakat with targets and indicators of SDGs.

These challenges constrain the role of zakat toward the SDGs to some extent because they are understood to affect deployment of zakat and ascertain its actual impact on target indicators of achieving the SDGs.[13]

---

[10] Tok, E., Yesuf, A. J., & Mohamed, A. (2022). Sustainable development goals and Islamic social finance: From policy divide to policy coherence and convergence. *Sustainability*, Vol. 14, No. 11, p. 6875; Alfiani & Akbar. *Op. cit.*

[11] Riyaldi, M. H., Suriani, S., & Nurdin, R. (2020, November). Optimization of zakat for sustainable development goals. In *International Conference of Zakat*, pp. 339–354.

[12] Joint SDG Fund. (2020). Institutionalizing and Leveraging Zakat to Finance SDGs in Mauritania. Available at https://www.jointsdgfund.org/programme/institutionalizing-and-leveraging-zakat-finance-sdgs-mauritania. Accessed October 20, 2022.

[13] Islamic Finance Council UK. (2022). Islamic Finance and the SDGs: Framing the Opportunity. Available at https://www.ukifc.com/2020/05/05/ukifc-and-isra-launch-report-on-islamic-finance-and-the-sdgs/. Accessed October 20, 2022.

9.1.4 Selected case studies

9.1.4.1 UNHCR zakat for refugees

The United Nations High Commission for Refugees (UNHCR) is an agency of the UN that is responsible for more than 20 million refugees globally as of the end of 2021.[14] Muslims constitute a sizable portion of this number of refugees today. For this purpose, the agency sought and obtained Shariah legal clarification (fatwa) to ensure it gets involved as intermediary for zakat collection and distribution in a manner harmonious with the Shariah.[15] A fatwa was issued by Tabah Foundation (UAE) in accordance with Hanafi jurisprudence which appears more suitable to the context of the agency. In relation to this also several other fatwas on different issues of zakat administration were issued by fatwa bodies including Fatwa Council of Tareem (Yemen) and Shariah scholars like Sheikh Dr Ali Gomaa. The fatwas address Shariah issues on conveying zakat outside its locality, giving zakat to non-Muslims, and use of an intermediary to distribute zakat among others on which the Islamic schools of jurisprudence share different opinions. The fatwas sanctioned and lead to the establishment of a UNHCR Refugee Zakat Fund in 2019 as a source of funds for refugee management.[16]

In accordance with its fatwa, UNHCR ensures zakat funds are for the classes of zakat recipients that the Holy Quran mentions. Similarly, UNHCR distributes zakat in-kind rather than cash, ensures due process in the purchase/procurement of goods, and covers related expenses with all standards of accountability. Accordingly, UNHCR periodically publishes reports detailing the amount collected and distributed and the impact of the disbursed funds.[17]

Good governance measures were ensured for the fund that guarantees transparency of every step in its processes of collection (donation) and distribution to eligible recipients. An application called GiveZakat was

---

[14] UN. (2022). Office of the United Nations High Commissioner for Refugees. Available at https://www.un.org/youthenvoy/2013/09/office-of-the-united-nations-high-commissioner-for-refugees/. Accessed October 20, 2022.

[15] Furber, M. (2017). *UNHCR Zakat Collection and Distribution Tabah Report*, No. 1 (May). Available at https://zakat.unhcr.org/wp-content/uploads/2020/05/UNHCR-Zakat-Distribution-English.pdf. Accessed October 29, 2022.

[16] *Ibid.*

[17] *Ibid.*

launched through which interested donors/payers of zakat around the world dedicate their zakat for refugees using mobile phones in a simple and easy way. The application enables tracking of funds until it reaches eligible recipients.[18]

Several SDGs are being achieved with the involvement of international organizations serving as intermediaries for zakat and by aligning the same with certain SDGs. This not only internationalizes zakat but also promotes its impact on international development.[19]

9.1.4.2 BAZNAS and UNDP zakat for COVID-19 support/recovery

National Zakat Agency or Badan Amil Zakat Nasional (BAZNAS) Indonesia and the United Nations Development Programme (UNDP), together with PT Ammana Fintek Syariah and PT Principal Asset Management, entered into collaboration to provide support, recovery, and aid economic advancement of vulnerable communities in Indonesia post COVID-19 pandemic.[20] The collaboration is to harness zakat funds through Islamic fintech for SDG-related projects and recovery activities following the COVID-19 pandemic.

The collaboration works in this manner. As per its organizational mandate, BAZNAS zakat funds and makes grants to UNDP for the implementation of designated SDG projects. The funds and projects are executed in accordance with the global policies of the UNDP. With Principal as asset developer and Ammana as Shariah p2p fintech, the collaboration leverages on a conceptualized Innovative Financing Lab which unlocked new Islamic financing to close SDG funding gap. The lab designed and launched new financing instruments and brought about enhanced investments of zakat funds and higher returns for SDG projects and measured their progress and impact via a dedicated platform. Additionally, UNDP

---

[18] UNHCR (2021). What you may not know about Refugee Zakat Fund App. Available at https://zakat.unhcr.org/blog/en/refugee-zakat-fund/about-refugee-zakat-fund-app.
[19] Ismail, Z. (2018). Using Zakat for International Development — K4D Helpdesk Report. Birmingham: University of Birmingham. Available at https://opendocs.ids.ac.uk/opendocs/handle/20.500.12413/13647. Accessed October 29, 2022.
[20] UNDP Indonesia (2020). Leveraging Social Finance and Philanthropy to Help Indonesia Build Back Better. Available at: https://www.undp.org/indonesia/press-releases/leveraging-social-finance-and-philanthropy-help-indonesia-build-back-better.

assisted in identifying main vulnerabilities and corresponding inclusive intervention that helped in addressing them locally.[21]

This collaboration saw the provision of disaster management support to over 10,000 residents of villages in the districts of Lombok and Central Sulawesi in Indonesia. Another project of the UNDP-BAZNAS collaboration was the installation of small-capacity hydropower plants which bring electricity to remote communities for over 4,500 people. These projects and activities enabled the residents of the targeted communities to be trained and acquired new skills that improve the maintenance of their plantations with enhanced crop production. Also, access to steady and sustainable energy bolsters resilient and sustainable business practices among the local farmers that focus on local commodities (cashew, coffee, and rubber) processing into finished goods.[22]

These projects collectively contributed to achieving the SDGs on poverty, hunger, inequality, sustainable energy, and economic development. In connection with this, the UNDP provides technical assistance to BAZNAS that enhances zakat collection and administration and links it with SDG strategies.[23]

---

[21] UNDP-BAZNAS (2018). Unlocking the potential of zakat and other forms of Islamic finance to achieve the SDGs in Indonesia. Available at https://www.undp.org/indonesia/publications/unlocking-potential-zakat-and-other-forms-islamic-finance-achieve-sdgs-indonesia. Accessed October 30, 2022.

[22] UNDP. *Op. cit.*; Principal (2020). Principal and UNDP Signed Collaboration on the Utilization of Sharia Social Finance and Philanthropy. Available https://www.principal.co.id/en/principal-and-undp-signed-collaboration-utilization-sharia-social-finance-and-philanthropy-6-august. Accessed October 30, 2022.

[23] Noor, Z. & Pickup, F. (2017). The role of zakat in supporting the sustainable development goals. UNDP Brief, United Nations Development Programme, New York.

Self-Assessment Quiz (MCQs)

Question 1: As universally acknowledged goals, another popular name for sustainable development goals is ……….
(a) Global goals
(b) General goals
(c) Goals for all
(d) All of the above

Question 2: The potential of zakat toward achieving the SDGs has been described as …….
(a) Negligible to notice
(b) Too huge to ignore
(c) Important but inconsequential
(d) Noticeably fleeting

Question 3: Zakat is an Islamic economic tool for …………. of wealth and prevention ………
(a) Redistribution ……. poverty
(b) Redistribution ……. prosperity
(c) Allotting ………. rationing
(d) All of the above

Question 4: Zakat idealizes religious philanthropy, but its scope is capable of addressing the rising needs for ……………… called for by the SDGs.
(a) Intellectual and economic investments
(b) Social and religious investments
(c) Social and economic investments
(d) Entrepreneurial and knowledge investments

Question 5: In terms of target and indicator, zakat shares commonality with all the SDGs except ………
(a) SDG on gender equality
(b) SDG on inequality
(c) SDG on energy
(d) All of the above

Question 6: In order of priority, zakat funds can be used for alleviating poverty and inequality before combating climate change.
(a) False
(b) True
(c) False if in developing country
(d) None of the above

Question 7: Zakat is used to achieve an SDG to the extent its target and indicator can be equated to what has been enjoined by ....
(a) Consensus of Muslim jurists
(b) Reputable Islamic scholar
(c) Islamic Fiqh Academy
(d) Maqasid al-Shariah

Question 8: Collaboration among zakat institutions, multilateral organizations, and humanitarian agencies for global interventions has resulted in ....
(a) Localization of zakat
(b) Internationalization of zakat
(c) Islamization of zakat
(d) All of the above

Question 9: Lack of one of the following is considered a challenge to the use of zakat to achieve sustainable development goals:
(a) Framework to evaluate SDG achievement
(b) Framework to integrate SDGs with maqasid al-Shariah
(c) Evidence that supports SDGs in maqasid al-Shariah
(d) Evidence for SDGs in Shariah

Question 10: One of the following Islamic advisory bodies gave fatwa that provided legal backing for UNHCR to partake in zakat administration.
(a) Nigerian Council of Islamic Affairs
(b) BNM Shariah Advisory Council
(c) Tabah Foundation
(d) All of the above

Self-Assessment/Recall Questions

Question 1: Explain the untapped potential of zakat in relation to achieving the SDGs.

Question 2: What is the rationale for equating SDGs' targets and indicators with maqasid al-Shariah before using zakat funds to execute an SDG-related project?

Question 3: Critically evaluate how zakat can be used in achieving sustainable development goals.

Question 4: What are the challenges faced in using zakat to achieve sustainable development goals? Discuss.

Question 5: Evaluate the collaboration of BAZNAS and UNDP Zakat for COVID-19 Support/Recovery as a case study of using zakat to achieve SDGs.

Answers to Self-Assessment Quiz (MCQs)

1. a
2. b
3. a
4. c
5. a
6. b
7. d
8. b
9. b
10. c

Chapter 10

Use of Technology to Enhance Zakat Administration

Learning Outcomes

At the end of this chapter, students should be able to know

- types of technologies used to enhance zakat administration,
- how technology has been used to enhance zakat administration,
- challenges in employing technology to enhance zakat administration,
- selected case studies.

10.1 Technology and Zakat Administration

Technology has become part and parcel of the contemporary world and contributes in making life easy.[1] Technology-driven innovations have transformed the way and manner all forms of transactions are conducted and delivered to consumers. Thus, transactions, especially financial ones, are made easier by technology, hence technology becomes very crucial to financial services.[2] It is in this regard that technology becomes relevant

---

[1] Marques, G. (2019). Ambient assisted living and internet of things. Harnessing the internet of everything (IoE) for accelerated innovation opportunities. *Future Internet*, Vol. 11, No. 12, p. 259.

[2] Xuan, S., Zhang, Y., Tang, H., Chung, I., Wang, W., & Yang, W. (2019). Hierarchically authorized transactions for massive internet-of-things data sharing based on multilayer blockchain. *Applied Sciences*, Vol. 9, No. 23, p. 5159.

for zakat administration, and so it should be used to make zakat administration efficient and effective. Different innovations are introduced by financial technology (fintech) and used to facilitate transactions in the contemporary world. The technology needs to record, secure, process, recall, and store data of persons and entities sought to be served to conduct transactions or events. This makes technology-powered financial and related transactions or events to be data-centric. This means that, when any technology is used in zakat administration, there is need for it to secure the data pertaining to zakat collection, zakat distribution, as well as zakat payers and recipients' registration details.[3]

It is noteworthy that there are various forms/types of technologies that are used for the purpose of transactions like zakat collection/distribution and identification/registration of zakat recipients. These technologies include mobile telephony (GSM), Internet-of-Things (IoT), artificial intelligence, distributed ledger technology (DLT), or blockchain, among others. Technologies used for the purpose of financial dealings are termed as fintech (financial technology) and serve as mechanisms for storage, security, retrieval, and dispatch of customers' data. Since zakat involves financial dealings, fintech is a mechanism that will enhance its dealings.[4]

10.1.1 *Types of technologies used to enhance zakat administration*

The following are types of technologies that are and can be used to enhance zakat administration:

10.1.1.1 *Blockchain (digital/distributed ledger)*

What is a blockchain? A blockchain is a digital ledger of cryptographically signed transactions that operate in a distributed or decentralized fashion (i.e., without a central repository) and often without a central authority (e.g., a banking entity, company, or regulator/government).

---

[3] Salleh, M. C. M. & Chowdhury, M. A. M. (2020). Technological transformation in Malaysian zakat institutions. *International Journal of Zakat*, Vol. 5, No. 3, pp. 44–56.

[4] Elsayed, E. A. & Zainuddin, Y. (2020). Zakat information technology system design, zakat culture, and zakat performance–conceptual model. *International Journal of Advance Science and Technology*, Vol. 29, No. 9, pp. 22–24; Nailah, N., & Rusydiana, A. S. (2020, November 13). The zakat & technology. In *Proceedings of International Conference of Zakat*, Bali, Indonesia, pp. 311–330.

Information in blockchain is grouped into blocks, each one representing a distinct transaction.[5] Operations of the nodes are based on smart contract algorithms that automate all transactions. At its basic level, blockchain enables users through nodes (individual computers) to record and communicate transactions in a shared ledger within a community of users, such that no transaction can be changed once completed, validated, and published in normal operation of the blockchain network. The nodes are connected to each other and continuously exchange information. Each block embodies timestamp and transaction information and it is cryptographically linked to the previous one after validation and consensus decision. This makes the block or record tamper-evident. As transactions are performed, new blocks are added, and older blocks become more tamper resistance and difficult to modify, thus aiding auditability and transparency. New blocks are replicated across copies of the ledger within the network based on consensus, and any conflict is resolved automatically using established algorithmic rules.[6]

For all practical purposes, blockchain-based innovations have distinguishing features and qualities. These are decentralization and immutability of record, faster settlement of transactions, trusted cryptography for security, and near impossible-to-hack system.[7] Immutability renders record insusceptible to alteration while decentralization allows the same record to be distributed in an unalterable state, which enables building and maintaining consumers' trust in the system. Decentralization also means eliminating certain intermediaries and transforming the role of others in financial market which speeds up settlement process and allows for greater trade accuracy and less personnel/transaction costs in financial business.[8]

---

[5] Tapscott, A. & Tapscott, D. (2017). How blockchain is changing finance. *Harvard Business Review*, 1 March 2017, p. 17. Available at https://hbr.org/2017/03/how-Blockchain-is-changing-finance. Accessed March 5, 2022.
[6] *Ibid.*
[7] Techracers. (2018). How is blockchain disrupting the fintech industry? Medium. Retrieved from https://medium.com/@Techracer/how-is-blockchain-disruptingthe-fintech-industry-3640eaae9e89.
[8] Praveen, J. (2017). Blockchain explained: The difference between public and private blockchain. *IBM*, 31 May. Available at https://www.ibm.com/blogs/blockchain/2017/05/the-difference-between-public-and-private-blockchain/. Accessed October 7, 2022.

10.1.1.2 Web-based applications

These include websites that use the Internet to provide online zakat calculators and avenues to channel zakat contributions after ascertaining the payable amount. In addition, there are web-based zakat payment gateways that link zakat payers and banks. For instance, e-Zakat Pay system was introduced by Lembaga Zakat Selangor (Selangor Zakat Board) Malaysia.[9] More robust applications and programs are being developed in this regard, for example, an application developed by a Dublin-based fintech firm, AidTech, and the International Federation of Red Cross and Red Crescent Societies that leverages on blockchain technology.[10] On operating the application, it can prompt prospective zakat payers and provide options to select a particular Islamic school of jurisprudence the zakat payers adhere to, i.e., Maliki, Shafi', Hanafi, or Hambali. This is followed by questions, e.g., as to where the payer intends the zakat to be sent to/expended in (among specific listed projects). It is according to the selected school that calculation is made, and payable zakat is ascertained and paid to a particular project on education, poverty eradication, etc. that the payer chooses. Payers receive acceptance confirmation, keep track of payments made, and are notified when the money is utilized in the chosen projects. The underlying blockchain element of this innovation ensures the establishment of more transparent zakat management and administration.[11]

10.1.1.3 Mobile USSD/WAP/apps/digital wallets

Zakat is also paid through mobile telecommunication companies using unstructured supplementary service data (USSD) or wireless application protocol (WAP) function in any mobile cellphones operating on global system for mobile communication (GSM) cellular network. For this

---

[9] Tahir, M. N. (2015). Evaluation of Online Payment Service Quality: A Case Study of e-Zakat Online, Lembaga Zakat Selangor Online Payment Portal. Doctoral dissertation, Universiti Teknologi MARA (unpublished), pp. 14–24.

[10] LuxTag. (2019). 4 Examples of Blockchain-Based Platforms Made in Malaysia. Available at https://www.luxtag.io/blog/4-examples-of-blockchain-based-platforms-made-in-malaysia/. Accessed October 30, 2022.

[11] Mohamed, H. & Ali, H. (2022). *Blockchain, Fintech, and Islamic Finance: Building the Future in the New Islamic Digital Economy*. Boston: Walter de Gruyter GmbH & Co KG, pp. 70–87.

purpose, an SMS with a particular message is sent to a particular number or a USSD code is dialed from a cellphone to run a particular command. This is followed by prompts that affect transfer or payment of certain amount to a designated depository under the mobile telecommunication company which acts as zakat collector for a particular zakat administrator.[12] For example, Celcom Axiata's M-Fitrah service in Malaysian States of Selangor, Melaka, and Kedah, among others.[13] Similarly, leveraging on the dispersive mobile telephony services and the Internet, the use of digital wallet system for the payment of zakat has been introduced in several countries.

10.1.1.4 *Internet-of-Things (IoT)*

IoT is another versatile innovation that involves a network of devices and/or physical objects equipped with sensors or some sentient technologies and programmed to communicate with similar devices/objects and exchange information over the Internet. IoT is used to automate operations in hospitals, manufacturing, traffic, utility organization, home automation, etc.[14] With that capability, IoT can potentially determine stress level and by extension financial status of a household. From initial registration, the recipients are issued some sensor-bearing device, e.g., a smartwatch. Therefore, using IoT system, zakat administrators can potentially determine from a one-time acquired registered household's data the eligibility of the household to receive zakat any time. Stress level of the recipients will be monitored and if it shows they are eligible to receive zakat again as initially, then they will be given without another registration. Having identified its location in real time through some sensor-embedded or GPS-enabled smart gadget, distribution to such a household can be made with a QR code which is to be presented at a designated vendor or shop to withdraw money or make purchases or other related means in a hassle-free manner.[15]

---

[12] Beik, I. S., Swandaru, R., & Rizkiningsih, P. (2021). Utilization of digital technology for zakat development. In *Islamic FinTech*. Cham: Palgrave Macmillan, pp. 231–234.
[13] Muneeza, A. & Nadwi, S. (2019). The potential of application of technology-based innovations for zakat administration in India. *International Journal of Zakat*, Vol. 4, No. 2, pp. 87–100.
[14] Beik, S. & Rizkiningsih. *Op. cit.*, pp. 235–240.
[15] Muneeza, A. (2021). Enhancing zakat distribution with IoT: Eliminating multiple registration by poor to receive zakat. *Indian Centre for Islamic Finance Newsletter*, Vol. 7, No. 2, pp. 16–17.

10.1.1.5 Robo officer/Chatbot

There is need to address the stress that zakat recipients undergo such as long waiting in queues and unnecessary questions (sometimes even humiliating) during interviews and registrations. The zakat recipients are often exposed to these undeserving hassles in the manual processes of verification which leave most of them ashamed and dissatisfied. Chatbot is a type of computer programme that is designed to perform a designated function through natural conversation with texts and voice commands.[16] Robo officer is a Chatbot that provides certain services with little or no human intervention. Robo officer and Chatbot are designed and used to facilitate the verification, validation, and confirmation processes of the poverty status of zakat recipients.[17] Robo officer and Chatbot aid zakat administrators' function of identifying and validating zakat recipients in an easy manner without the usual psychological stress the poor and needy are subjected to using the manual process.

10.1.2 How technology has been used to enhance zakat administration

There are two major concerns of zakat administrators. First is identification and validation of zakat recipients. A lot of hurdles and resources go into this function of the administrators, often time with a lot of inconveniences to both the administrators and recipients. Second is distribution of zakat. For administrative convenience and ease of the processes involved, distribution of zakat would be preferred if it can be made without zakat recipients being actually present, in persons, at zakat administrators' offices or distribution centers. Appropriate innovative technologies are deployed to address these concerns, including the following.

Rice ATM: This a model ATM that dispenses rice with the use of a designated card. On registration, requisite data about zakat recipients are recorded and matched to an 'account.' Recipients are then issued a

---

[16] Khan, S. & Rabbani, M. R. (2021). Artificial intelligence and NLP-based chatbot for Islamic banking and finance. *International Journal of Information Retrieval Research*, Vol. 11, No. 3, pp. 65–77.

[17] Khan, A. & Hashim, F. (2021). Rise of Islamic robo advisory in the 21st century. In Khan, A. & Hashim, F. (Eds.) *Artificial Intelligence and Islamic Finance*. London: Routledge, pp. 193–209.

special withdrawal card. The system is designed to dispense certain quantity of rice (in kg) for users upon inserting their access card into the machine followed by a login password. For ease of access, the machine is installed in places that are close to where the poor and needy reside. This innovation has been successfully implemented in Malaysia and Indonesia. Moving forward, the rice ATM model can be used for the distribution of other grains, depending on local availability, for the purpose of zakat.[18]

Iris ATM: This is a model ATM introduced by the United Nations High Commissioner for Refugees (UNHCR) as a biometric system that leverages on the unique patterns in human irises for the registration and identification of refugees as well as delivering aid to them. Users' irises are captured at registration and linked to a bank account created for this purpose. Passcode, often a recipient's year of birth or other selected number, is assigned. Based on the users' data already in the system, the system uses a scanning system and passcode on the ATM; this validates recipients' irises and dispenses cash without a card. The system has been identified as a fraud-proof verification and authentication system of recipients' identity. The UNHCR acting in its capacity as zakat intermediary uses this system for disbursement of zakat to recipients.[19] Through this technology, zakat recipients who are refugees as well are saved from the stigma of waiting for a long time in queues only to collect food items. The system ensures and promotes recipients' freedom to spend their cash on other things than food items. Thus, it reinforces and enhances their sense of dignity.[20]

Chatbot: Indonesia's BAZNAS develops and uses 'Zaki', a chatbot that helps in administrative processes of zakat payment. It is an initiative that uses technological parameters including artificial intelligence (AI) and machine learning (ML) to control, standardize, and unify methods of asking questions to elicit and compile requisite zakat recipients' data and seeks to address all anomalies associated therewith in manual method.

---

[18] Muneeza, A. (2019). Rice ATMs: Technology based innovations for enhancement of zakat. *IF Hub*, June. Available at https://ikr.inceif.org/bitstream/INCEIF/3122/1/rice_atms_technology_based_innovations_aishath.pdf. Accessed September 20, 2022.

[19] UNHCR (2019). 100% Zakat Distribution Policy. Available at https://zakat.unhcr.org/blog/en/refugee-zakat-fund/100-zakat-policy. Accessed September 20, 2022.

[20] UNHCR (2016). Using biometrics to bring assistance to refugees in Jordan. Available at https://www.unhcr.org/innovation/using-biometrics-bring-assistance-refugees-jordan/. Accessed September 20, 2022.

It entails applying Natural Language Processing (NLP) using sentient analysis of speeches and texts via tonal recognition in an interactive voice response system to eliminate biased/objectionable human factors. Through interactive voice assistance, the chatbot calculates zakat automatically and transfers the same to a recipient. Zaki is accessed using a free instant messaging application called LINE under the name *@zakibaznas* via smartphones, tablet computers, and personal computers. This application can be developed to encompass identification and registration of the poor and needy as well as enabling them to receive zakat. Similar to zaki is the Malaysian State of Pahang Zakat Collection Center's 'ZakatChat' which functions in the same way and serves the same purpose. The ZakatChat is operated as a virtual assistant that interacts with and provides answers to customers' questions in helping them pay zakat.[21]

The foregoing technological initiatives have not only rendered administrators' functions of distributing zakat and identifying its recipients easy but also relieves the psychological stress the poor and needy are often subjected to through the manual, non-automated process. They are an aid in both ways.

10.1.3 Challenges in employing technology to enhance zakat administration

The use of technology in zakat administration requires attention to detail due to certain challenges that are generally associated with the use of technology to conduct transactions, especially those that are financial in nature. It is notable that some actual capabilities and potentialities of emerging technology-based innovations like blockchain and IoT could be hyped without regard to related practical and long-term challenges. Technological transformation is an ongoing process, and so no technology can provide an instant, one-fit-all solution to real-world problems.[22]

---

[21] Inforial. (2018). BAZNAS launches zakat virtual payment assistant for alms donors. *The Jakarta Post*, May 28. Available at https://www.thejakartapost.com/adv/2018/05/28/baznas-launches-zakat-virtual-payment-assistant-for-alms-donors.html. 20 September 2022.

[22] Soleh, M. (2020). Zakat fundraising strategy: Opportunities and challenges in digital era. *Journal of Nahdlatul Ulama Studies*, Vol. 1, No. 1, pp. 1–16.

Therefore, in employing technology to enhance zakat administration, challenges that need to be addressed include lack of awareness and proper understanding by zakat administrators of innovations sought to be introduced in relation to their underlying technologies. Zakat administrators need to understand and have requisite awareness about any technology they want to employ in order to facilitate its adoption in zakat administration.[23]

Similarly, there are legal, regulatory, and jurisdictional constraints with respect to some ideals of the technology, i.e., digitization and digitalization of money and financial assets into tokens and other sorts of encryptions. These are innovations that are not recognized under the laws of several countries.[24] As such, there are issues, i.e., legal recognition, that are not yet settled in their ownership and right in these assets/tokens as obtainable through blockchain. Moreover, existing laws/regulations on privacy do not address technology-related security and privacy concerns of personal data in cyberspace which zakat payers and recipients can be exposed to.[25] Unfortunately, on this issue too, many countries do not have requisite legal and regulatory rules to address real and potential issues therein. Also, political commitments necessary for the development and implementation of suitable legal and regulatory rules are lacking, particularly in countries where centralized zakat administration system is adopted.[26]

There is also a challenge pertaining to compliance with the rules of Shariah. Technology should not impede Shariah governance and compliance. Technology is required to foster Shariah compliance by reflecting the rules of Shariah in the automation of all transactions relating to

---

[23] Utami, P., Suryanto, T., Nasor, M., & Ghofur, R. A. (2020). The effect digitalization zakat payment against potential of zakat acceptance in national *Amil* zakat agency. *Iqtishadia*, Vol. 13, No. 2, p. 216.

[24] Kunhibava, S., Mustapha, Z., Muneeza, A., Sa'ad, A. A., & Karim, M. E. (2021). Ṣukūk on blockchain: A legal, regulatory and Shariah review. *ISRA International Journal of Islamic Finance*, Vol. 13, No. 1, pp. 118–135.

[25] Yeoh, P. (2017). Regulatory issues in blockchain technology. *Journal of Financial Regulation and Compliance*, Vol. 25, No. 2, pp. 196–208.

[26] Klapper, L. & Singer, D. (2017). The opportunities and challenges of digitizing government-to-person payments. *The World Bank Research Observer*, Vol. 32, No. 2, pp. 211–226.

identification and registration of zakat recipients and collection and disbursement of zakat.[27]

Moreover, there is security risk in the Internet-based and cyber-powered digitization initiatives used in zakat administration. This is due to the uncertainty in cyber safety and frequency of cyber-attacks.[28] Limitation of Internet coverage and its inevitability is another constraint. Most importantly, there is need to ensure protection of all parties and stakeholders in zakat matters cyber risk. This emanates from the fact that proper governance of technology is not yet available under the laws/regulations of several countries.

Cost of acquisition and maintenance of technology is another challenge to its adoption in zakat administration.[29]

The foregoing challenges, to an extent, affect deployment of technology for zakat administration. Therefore, without stifling anticipated and actual innovations sought to be brought by technology, relevant authorities and stakeholder need to appropriately identify and address these challenges with respect to zakat in this regard.

10.1.4 Selected case studies

10.1.4.1 Blockchain use case: Crypto zakat

Blockchain is referred to as an enabler technology in that it has been used as an underlying technology to introduce many innovations that facilitate various transactions including cryptocurrencies, crypto assets, and crypto exchange.[30] It is in this regard that the idea of crypto zakat is being

---

[27] Kunhibava, Mustapha, Muneeza, Sa'ad & Karim. *Op. cit.*, p. 130. See also Ulya, N. U. (2018). Legal protection of donation-based crowdfunding Zakat on financial technology: Digitalization of zakat under perspective of positive law and Islamic law. In *Proceeding of the 2nd International Conference of Zakat (ICONZ)*, pp. 132–149. DOI: 10.37706/iconz.2018.132

[28] Kumar, N. M. & Mallick, P. K. (2018). Blockchain technology for security issues and challenges in IoT. *Procedia Computer Science*, Vol. 132, pp. 1815–1823.

[29] Reier Forradellas, R. F. & Garay Gallastegui, L. M. (2021). Digital transformation and artificial intelligence applied to business: Legal regulations, economic impact and perspective. *Laws*, Vol. 10, No. 3, p. 70.

[30] Rejeb, D. (2020). Blockchain and smart contract application for zakat institution. *International Journal of Zakat*, Vol. 5, No. 3, pp. 20–29.

actualized for transparency to enhance zakat administration. Crypto zakat is described as a blockchain-based Ethereum platform that provides a decentralized alternative solution to zakat collection and distribution using crypto tokens. In other words, crypto zakat is an innovation to pay zakat out of cryptocurrencies and/or crypto assets holding as well as payment of zakat (for non-crypto assets) using crypto. Crypto zakat operates on blockchain technology which in this regard facilitates zakat collection, zakat distribution, and verification/registration of zakat payers and recipients. The technology shortens the process involved in these functions of zakat, ensures zakat money reaches recipients almost instantaneously, and makes the whole process/procedure transparent and immutable.[31]

Note that the practice of crypto zakat innovation can obtain only where zakat payment using cryptocurrency such as Bitcoin, Ether, and Tether is accepted as legal tender, for instance, in Indonesia. In Malaysia also, following the fatwa of the State of Perlis Fatwa Committee, zakat can be paid in cryptocurrencies. But it is noteworthy that, notwithstanding this fatwa, cryptocurrencies are by law not generally recognized as legal tender in Malaysia and only fiat money is used for this purpose. This position is akin to the conditional qualification required of crypto or digital assets before they are regarded as zakatable according to ruling by Shariah Advisory Council (SAC) of Securities Commission Malaysia. The ruling is to the effect that crypto or digital assets are zakatable only to the extent they can qualify as *mal* (asset) in Shariah.[32]

Let us examine an example of deploying the crypto zakat innovation in practice from the use cases of Blossom Finance Indonesia (Ethereum blockchain) and Global *Sadaqah* (crowd-funding platform), Malaysia.

Blossom Finance Indonesia: Blossom Finance was established in 2014 in USA and came to Indonesia in 2015, dealing in halal financial products. Based on a fatwa issued to Blossom Finance by its Shariah advisory organ, cryptocurrencies such as Bitcoin are zakatable wealth/money in Islam but cautions against speculation. So, Blossom acts as an intermediary and accepts direct payments in cryptocurrency via its Ethereum blockchain network from zakat payers. The payments are made

---

[31] Muneeza, A., Bin-Nashwan, S. A., Abdel Moshin, M. I., Mohamed, I., & Al-Saadi, A. (2022). Zakat payment from cryptocurrencies and crypto assets. *International Journal of Islamic and Middle Eastern Finance and Management* (ahead-of-print). DOI: 10.1108/IMEFM-12-2021-0487.
[32] *Ibid*.

into Blossom-controlled wallets held at a designated cryptocurrency exchange in Indonesia. Thereafter, the cryptocurrency is converted by Blossom into Indonesian rupiah, which then is remitted and deposited into bank accounts of non-profit partner zakat organizations and rural cooperatives in Indonesia.[33] In addition to remittance receipts, Blossom shares report on the use and impact of the contribution with contributors.[34]

GlobalSadaqah Malaysia: GlobalSadaqah is a Malaysian crowdfunding institution based on charity. As an intermediary, GlobalSadaqah collects zakat paid out of cryptocurrencies as part of a worldwide fundraising campaign. Likewise, it uses cryptocurrencies to pay zakat.[35] GlobalSadaqah has charity partners in over 60 countries. To initiate zakat campaign, prospective participating partners submit proper documents that detail information about their projects. GlobalSadaqah's in-house Shariah team then examines and analyses the information and determines if the project satisfies the criteria of zakat recipients. If approved, then a campaign is launched on the platform of GlobalSadaqah. Several campaigns for which cryptocurrencies and fiat alike were accepted have been carried out successfully by GlobalSadaqah.[36] Donations are accepted in accepting donations of Bitcoin, Ethereum, and other altcoins on its platform. GlobalSadaqah charges a negotiable 7.5% of total funds collected to cover related expenses. GlobalSadaqah also provides guidance on request about zakat calculation.[37]

---

[33] Blossom Finance. (2018). Muslims Can Now Pay Zakat in Cryptocurrency. Available at https://blossomfinance.com/posts/muslims-can-now-pay-zakat-in-cryptocurrency. Accessed October 22, 2022.

[34] Busari, S. A. & Aminu, S. O. (2022). Application of blockchain information technology in Ṣukuk trade. *Journal of Islamic Accounting and Business Research*, Vol. 13, No. 1, pp. 1–15; Delle Foglie, A., Panetta, I. C., Boukrami, E., & Vento, G. (2021). The impact of the blockchain technology on the global Sukuk industry: Smart contracts and asset tokenisation. *Technology Analysis & Strategic Management*, pp. 1–15.

[35] Global*Sadaqah*. (2022). Donate Your Crypto for a Good Cause. Available at https://www.global*sadaqah*.com/blog/donate-crypto-good-cause/. Accessed October 22, 2022.

[36] Global*Sadaqah* (2021). Bit by Bit Journey of Bitcoin. Available at https://www.global-*sadaqah*.com/blog/bitcoin-journey/. Accessed October 22, 2022.

[37] *Ibid.*

Self-Assessment Quiz (MCQs)

Question 1: All technologies used for the purpose of zakat collection and distribution can be categorized as ....
(a) InsurTech
(b) InterTech
(c) FinTech
(d) RegTech

Question 2: Blockchain technology and related transactions are distinguished by certain features and qualities which include but one .... :
(a) Immutability
(b) Decentralization
(c) Erratic Cryptography
(d) Faster Settlement

Question 3: With the exception of one, all the following are types of technologies used to enhance zakat administration.
(a) Digital ledger
(b) GSM-based USSD/WAP
(c) Internet-of-Things
(d) E-Trading

Question 4: One of the main issues of zakat administration that is sought to be addressed via technology is .... :
(a) Identification and validation of zakat recipients
(b) Identification of zakat recipients' family
(c) Identification and solicitation of zakat recipients
(d) None of the above

Question 5: Distribution of zakat would be preferred using technology that dispensed with zakat recipients' .... at zakat administrators' offices or distribution centers.
(a) Satisfactorily present
(b) Spiritual availability
(c) Physical presence
(d) Abdication

Question 6: In which type of technology is zakat recipient enabled to make cash withdrawals through biometric identification?
(a) Rice ATM
(b) Iris ATM
(c) Crypto ATM
(d) All of the above

Question 7: Two chatbots developed and used in Indonesia and Malaysia respectively to enhance zakat administration are ……….. and ………..
(a) Zaki and ZakatChat
(b) ZakatChat and EasyChat
(c) ZakiChat and ZakatChat
(d) EasyZakat and EasyChat

Question 8: Legal status and ownership of ……….. and digitized financial assets have not been settled with finality under the law in many countries where zakat administration is obtainable.
(a) Financial brief
(b) Financial dossier
(c) Digital deed
(d) Digital currencies

Question 9: All technologies for use to enhance zakat administration must guard against …………… and foster …………….
(a) Shariah compliance and cyber security issues
(b) Cyber security issues and Shariah compliance
(c) Shariah compliance and Fatwa
(d) All of the above

Question 10: Crypto zakat is not permissible in all of the following countries except …………..
(a) Indonesia
(b) Nigeria
(c) Saudi Arabia
(d) None of the above

Self-Assessment/Recall Questions

Question 1: Explain how Robo officer/Chatbot can facilitate identification and registration of zakat recipients as part of zakat administration.

Question 2: Enumerate and highlight the general role that blockchain technology can play in operation of crypto zakat.

Question 3: Critically discuss any three challenges that need to be considered about the use of technology to enhance zakat administration.

Question 4: Explain how rice ATM and iris ATM operate to facilitate zakat distribution.

Question 5: Discuss the use of mobile telephone services and Internet web-based applications in zakat collection and distribution.

Answers to Self-Assessment Quiz (MCQs)

1. c
2. c
3. d
4. a
5. c
6. b
7. a
8. d
9. b
10. a

Chapter 11

Zakat Management Programs

Learning Outcomes

At the end of this chapter, students should be able to know

- practice of zakat management programs across the world,
- impact of zakat management programs on asnaf,
- factors to consider in formulating zakat management programs,
- selected case studies.

11.1 Zakat Management Programs: What and Why

Zakat administration is a complex task whose execution requires planned action through series of activities, often by an agency of the government. Zakat management programs are a plan of action for achieving effective zakat management and attainment of zakat goals. Zakat management programs encompass a system of procedures and/or activities designated for the purpose of ensuring zakat has been efficiently managed and ultimately utilized for the benefit of intended zakat recipients (asnaf). Zakat management programs involve activities about and for zakat recipients which include identification of asnaf, compilation of their data, proper mobilization, and disbursement of zakat to them as and when due. In addition, zakat management programs can, in instances where resources permit, provide for engaging asnaf to train/impart them with skills and knowledge they need for efficient utilization of zakat being disbursed to them. Zakat management programs therefore are geared up to ensure building up and developing ethics for compliant zakat administration as a form of guidance for zakat managers/administrators as well as building conscientious and scrupulous zakat recipients/users. Zakat management programs can facilitate proper understanding of the purpose, objectives, and wisdom behind zakat as an Islamic mechanism for socio-economic empowerment of zakat recipients/users in the society.[1] In other words, zakat management programs are established for zakat optimization to ensure accountability, good governance, and impact delivery in zakat administration.[2]

Zakat management programs are important in order to maintain the role of zakat for the development of Muslim communities in particular and the Islamic economy in general.[3] The potential of zakat has been recognized globally in national and international development in regard to human and economic empowerment.[4] For its relevance and from that standpoint, zakat is managed through purposeful programs to unlock its potential and fully tap its benefits. Series of programs have been floated among national and state governments as well as non-governmental organizations in order to manage, develop, and deploy zakat for its contemporary practice. It is notable that due to the prominent role zakat plays in development, progressive awareness is being created for using zakat for the right purpose via zakat programs that establish and champion user managerial competencies. This is because such programs often equip zakat users/recipients with the needed prudence to manage, improve, and sustain their lives with zakat as starting point. Thus, zakat management programs enhance the development of zakat and help promote the impact of zakat as a development tool in the contemporary world.[5]

---

[1] Ayaaz, A. A. N. (2021). Essential Questions and Answers Regarding Contemporary Zakat. Available at https://www.madeenah.com/essential-questions-and-answers-regarding-contemporary-zakat/. Accessed October 12, 2022.
[2] Saad, R. A., Aziz, N. M. A., & Sawandi, N. (2014). Islamic accountability framework in the zakat funds management. *Procedia — Social and Behavioral Sciences*, Vol. 164, pp. 508–515.
[3] Saad, R., Farouk, A., & Abdul Kadir, D. (2020). Business zakat compliance behavioral intention in a developing country. *Journal of Islamic Accounting and Business Research*, Vol. 11, No. 2, pp. 511–530.
[4] Ismail, Z. (2018). Using Zakat for International Development. K4D Helpdesk Report. Birmingham, UK: University of Birmingham, pp. 8–9.
[5] Hassan, N. M. & Noor, A. H. M. (2015). Do capital assistance programs by zakat institutions help the poor? *Procedia Economics and Finance*, Vol. 31, pp. 551–562.

11.2 Practice of Zakat Management Programs Across the World

There are various zakat management programs around the world in both Muslim majority and non-Muslim majority countries. While zakat management programs share the common goal and objective — to improve the socio-economic conditions of asnaf — the modalities of the practices often differ due to the socio-economic exigency and other prevailing circumstances of the asnaf in any given country at a particular time. Therefore, in addition to what is commonly known about zakat in providing relief against poverty and hunger among individual asnaf, some programs address public health and educational issues that pertain to asnaf and general public. Likewise, other programs provide economic empowerment to make entrepreneurs of the asnaf. As such, the practice of zakat management programs varies in scope and scale depending on the zakat administrator involved, i.e., national or state governments, volunteers at community level, and local or international non-governmental organizations, as well as international or multilateral agencies.

Accordingly, some zakat programs are very limited in scope and cater to only an immediate community while others are state affairs whose coverage is within a particular state boundary. Yet, others are international and involve cross-border zakat funding and recipients. In this case, the zakat programs are mostly run by international non-governmental organizations as well as multilateral development agencies. In view of this, zakat management programs can be established as public or private affairs or a collaboration of both. Further, the size of zakat fund being administered is another factor to consider in zakat management practices. This is in regard to national and international regulations with respect to expending, possessing, and moving funds and the body involved, whether a private charity organization or related governmental and inter-governmental initiative.[6] Compliance expectations relate to anti-money laundering/combatting the financing of terrorism (AML/CFT) controls, economic and trade

---

[6] Nurzaman, M. S. (2017). The impact of zakat programs from human development perspectives: An empirical evaluation. In Zulkhibri, M., & Ismail, G. A. (Eds.) *Financial Inclusion and Poverty Alleviation: Perspectives from Islamic Institutions and Instruments.* Cham: Palgrave Macmillan, pp. 245–270.

sanctions, transparency, as well as exchange of tax information.[7] It is a common knowledge that after the 9/11 attacks, Muslim charities came under intense scrutiny. Since then, zakat has received considerable attention from national and multilateral intergovernmental bodies for security reasons as much as from global donors for development purposes.[8] Zakat programs risk thwarting actions and measures against their activities in response to non-compliance and enforcement actions or penalties including freezing of funds, withdrawing, or terminating correspondent banking relationships.[9] Therefore, depending on the type of body or agency running the zakat programs, national and international financial regulations that accord qualified freedom for cross-border programs need to be considered in order to advance the charitable and philanthropic goals of zakat.

In practice, zakat management programs are often established to target general or particular goals/objectives of zakat by applying the same to address particular societal problems or category of people affected by such problems. Notwithstanding the fact that zakat programs primarily target the poor and needy, in some cases, people are made poor, needy, and diseased following emergency situations. Such emergencies could be due to the outbreak of disease, devastation and displacement by natural disaster, civil unrest, and military/armed conflicts, among other calamities that results in a refugee situation. Thus, some zakat programs provide relief against such emergencies often in cross-border cases. In all these cases, zakat programs can make general cash allocation to the recipients for personal financing in relation to foodstuffs, medication, and clothing to be relieved of hunger and squalor. Other zakat programs provide cash grants following entrepreneurial training of the zakat recipients for their empowerment to self-sufficiency.[10]

In every case however, it is a global practice that zakat management programs facilitate collection, disbursement, and allotment of zakat to recipients. This is to ease access and make zakat readily available for asnaf

---

[7] Taraboulsi-McCarthy, S. & Cimatti, C. R. (2018). Counter-terrorism, de-risking and the humanitarian response in Yemen: A call for action. Working Paper. Humanitarian Policy Group and ODI, p. 3. Available at https://www.odi.org/sites/odi.org.uk/files/resource-documents/12047.pdf. Accessed September 30, 2022.
[8] Barzegar, A. & El Karhili, N. (2017). The Muslim Humanitarian Sector. British Council. Available at https://www.britishcouncil.us/sites/default/files/final_report__the_muslim_humanitarian_sector.pdf. Accessed September 30, 2022.
[9] Ismail. *Op. cit.*
[10] Hassan & Noor. *Op. cit.*

and render all its processes manageable and less formal. For this purpose, zakat management programs have to ensure better outreach to zakat recipients and aid practical application of zakat as solution to socio-economic problems (including poverty/hunger) through series of coordinated activities. While providing relief/succor against such problems through cash, food items, empowerment, and other basic needs, the zakat recipients are also engaged and prepared toward self-sufficiency. This is done through skill acquisition training sessions and expert advisory on proper management and utilization of zakat grants. Therefore, certain zakat programs are designed to make entrepreneurs out of the zakat recipients through zakat grants for businesses. In furtherance of this, such programs involve continued monitoring as part of regular efforts to develop entrepreneurial skills for running the business by the zakat recipients for a given duration.[11]

11.3 Impact of Zakat Management Programs on Asnaf

Given the socio-economic role of zakat in Islam and its obligation upon Muslims, zakat management programs are targeted to generate certain impact on all asnaf (designated zakat recipients). Different zakat management programs produce different impacts on asnaf. Generally, however, experiences from the practices of zakat management programs around the world have indicated that such zakat programs deliver the following impacts for asnaf:

1. Awareness and prudence about zakat and its use: Zakat programs create awareness among actual and potential asnaf. Through zakat programs, zakat recipients are enabled to become aware of their rights for zakat, in addition to realizing and taking cognizance of activities and initiatives provided by zakat administrators for their benefits. This enables them to follow and stay tuned for information and updates from zakat administrators and other stakeholders relevant to zakat management. Similarly, the programs not only create requisite awareness about accessing zakat on the recipients' part but also impart in them a sense

---

[11] Azani, M. & Basri, H. (2018, July 24). Implementation of norms and rules of zakat and utilization in national agency for *amil* zakat (BAZNAS) Pekanbaru based on Islamic law. *IOP Conference Series: Earth and Environmental Science*, Vol. 175, No. 012049. Available at https://doi.org/10.1088/1755-1315/175/1/012049.

of prudence so that they are judicious in their use of zakat and ensure to make the most of it for their benefit. This in effect improves the lives of the asnaf households by helping them to forge ahead out of poverty, hunger, and squalor and progressively move up to prosperity.[12]

2. Knowledge and skills' acquisition via life-transforming value proposition for self-sufficiency: Zakat management programs facilitate addition of value to the lives of asnaf and promote their welfare by guiding them on the proper use of zakat for relief against poverty and hunger or succor from disease. Most important however is the greater value where asnaf are trained in a particular business and/or transformed into entrepreneurs to practice the business with zakat take-off grant provided to run it. Here, zakat programs are the hallmark of effective zakat management administration and facilitate imparting a life-transforming impact on the asnaf.[13]

3. Motivation and inspiration to develop into zakat payers: Zakat programs can basically make asnaf to understand the purpose, goals, and philosophy of zakat as it applies to them in relation to their socio-economic development and self-reliance to potentially render them into zakat payers ultimately. Zakat program can impart conviction in asnaf for contentment over basic needs while breaking free of poverty. This motivates and inspires zakat recipients to acquire the will to support others of lesser socio-economic standing around them while they develop into prudent zakat users in accordance with Shariah and economic realities. This promotes proper utilization of zakat and ensures zakat is used for what it is meant for by advancing a collective effort toward the needs and well-being of people generally. This, in addition, prevents waste and ensures responsible consumption and/or spending by the zakat recipients.[14]

4. Understanding and reassuring disposition to zakat administration: Zakat management programs make potential asnaf become accustomed to zakat administration and develop reassuring disposition toward its processes. This influences the emergence and development of well-informed, enlightened, and unassuming asnaf who are not only familiar but also cordial to zakat administration procedures that are applicable to them. The asnaf are made to know and understand the fact that these

---

[12] Nurzaman. *Op. cit.*

[13] Afif Muhamat, Jaafar, Emrie Rosly & Abdul Manan. *Op. cit.*; See also Hassan & Noor. *Op. cit.*

[14] Afif Muhamat, Jaafar, Emrie Rosly & Abdul Manan. *Op. cit.*

procedures are necessary to manage zakat for their benefits. These include the processes of their identification, registration, and data compilation as well as disbursement or grant of zakat to them, including all actions/conduct that are necessary for that purpose. The understanding and reassuring disposition of asnaf to zakat administration help expedite the discharge of several related administrative tasks and this helps immensely toward the success of zakat program.[15]

11.4 Factors to Consider in Formulating Zakat Management Programs

The task of zakat administration mostly rests on the shoulders of the governments in a contemporary Islamic state. The complex nature of the task of zakat collection, identifying zakat recipients, and zakat distribution has warranted the governments to establish a special agency/body to whom the task of managing zakat funds is often assigned, including the task of organizing events or activities to channel these funds to the intended recipients who need them. In order to channel zakat funds appropriately, and ensure their effective utilization, the special agency would formulate and organize various programs targeted at the various asnaf. To create zakat program, there is need to consider certain factors to ensure the programs so created are actually beneficial to the target recipient and the agency. Usually, zakat programs organized for this purpose are planned top-down and cognizant of possible benefits to derive therefrom based on the needs of the targeted asnaf. For this purpose, zakat programs can be elaborately planned by considering the following factors:

1. Resources and personnel to run program by given scheme/plan: Formulating zakat management programs is a task that requires a scheme or plan of action for which requisite financial resources have to be allocated including proficient personnel. Such allocated resources and personnel need to be sufficient and proficient to run the program always or on an as-needed basis. By proficient personnel, it means experts and professionals with requisite managerial and administrative competence acquired through training and on-the-job experience.

---

[15] Harun, N. H., Hassan, H., Jasni, N. S., & Rahman, R. A. (2010). Zakat for asnaf's business by Lembaga Zakat Selangor. *Management & Accounting Review* (Special Issue) Vol. 9, No. 2, pp. 123–138.

Therefore, resources and personnel are to be made available from the onset to commence a zakat program and to be provided whenever needed in order to facilitate formulation of impeccable programs.[16]

2. Modalities of engaging with target asnaf: Modalities of engaging with target asnaf primarily involve all processes of identifying target asnaf for whom zakat would be granted. The modalities entail procedure is very important in preparing to formulate zakat management programs. The identification process would involve thorough scrutiny and careful sensitization among potential people in a given society. In this regard, the scope of potential people would include people of underprivileged financial, economic, and social standing who, given their circumstances, can be categorized into one class of asnaf or another in the society. Appropriate announcement and campaign techniques would need to be employed in order to sensitize, motivate, and attract the target asnaf to be properly identified/recorded.[17]

3. Scope/Mechanism of access and delivery: Zakat management programs need to be asnaf-oriented in their scope so that they are easily accessible and deliverable to them. Accordingly, the means or facilities via which access would be granted to beneficiaries under a particular program should be determined. Scope can vary among several areas including social sector, community development, health economic, and humanitarian support.[18] The accessibility to benefits arising from the programs should be tied to their delivery as well. For this purpose, zakat programs need to consider society's exposure to modern financial intermediation systems and related technological innovations to ensure zakat programs are accessed by and delivered to asnaf. Contemporary zakat programs leverage on the Internet and fintech to identify and document asnaf, reach out to cover them under zakat programs, and deliver zakat grants/benefits to them.[19]

4. Need for and relevance of zakat program: The need for an initiative under zakat programs should be determined by its relevance, i.e., being essential for people's lives based on the need of their circumstances

---

[16] Afif Muhamat, Jaafar, Emrie Rosly & Abdul Manan. *Op. cit.*

[17] Abd Rahman, R. & Ahmad, S. (2011). Entrepreneurship development strategy for poor and needy recipients on capital assistance through zakat distribution. *Jurnal Pengurusan*, Vol. 33, pp. 37–44.

[18] Ahmed Shaikh, S. & Ghafar Ismail, A. (2017, November 25). Role of zakat in sustainable development goals. *International Journal of Zakat*, Vol. 2, No. 2, pp. 1–9.

[19] Abd Rahman & Ahmad. *Op. cit.*

and time. Therefore, zakat management programs should be viable and appropriate enough to address contemporary and/or emerging issues in the socio-economic contexts of people's lives. It is thus observable that practical significance of zakat programs lies in their alignment with societal need as much as of individual zakat recipients in the society. It is in consideration of this factor that zakat programs are being tailored to provide funds to address issues relevant to objectives of zakat under the Sustainable Development Goals (SDGs).[20]

5. Impact and value proposition to deliver through the program: Zakat programs need to consider the impact to be delivered to zakat recipients and ensure that such impact can be lifelong and commensurate to the value proposition of zakat. Thus, in connection to relevance, zakat programs should be determined a lasting value that beneficiaries (asnaf) in the programs stand to get. In essence, the program should not only define the nature of improvement and value to impart in zakat recipients' lives but also be capable of ascertaining and measuring it at regular intervals, i.e., whether by assuaging the fangs of poverty through a lasting relief against hunger or imparting lifetime economic self-sufficiency skills whose practical deployment helps zakat recipients to attain food security, be well rid of poverty and squalor, as well as related socio-economic problems.[21]

11.5 Selected Case Studies

11.5.1 *Selangor State' Asnaf Entrepreneurial Program (Malaysia)*

Selangor is a state in Malaysia and one of the pioneers to formulate zakat programs in the country. Selangor Zakat Board or, in the Malay language,

---

[20] Harahap, L. R. (2018). Zakat fund as the starting point of entrepreneurship in order to alleviate poverty (SDGs issue). *Global Review of Islamic Economics and Business*, Vol. 6, No. 1, pp. 63–74; Noor, Z. & Pickup, F. (2017). *The Role of Zakat in Supporting the Sustainable Development Goals: A UNDP Brief.* New York: United Nations Development Programme. Available at https://www.undp.org/indonesia/publications/role-zakat-supporting-sustainable-development-goals.

[21] Mawardi, I., Widiastuti, T., Al Mustofa, M. U., & Hakimi, F. (2022). Analyzing the impact of productive zakat on the welfare of zakat recipients. *Journal of Islamic Accounting and Business Research* (ahead-of-print). DOI: https://doi.org/10.1108/JIABR-05-2021-0145.

Lembaga Zakat Selangor [LZS] is an agency responsible for zakat administration in the state. The board or LZS is a leading zakat administration agency in Malaysia that began operation as far back as 1994 under the Selangor State Islamic Council or *Majlis Agama Islam Selangor or Majlis Agama Islam Selangor (MAIS)*. The board runs a special zakat program known as Asnaf Entrepreneurial Program (AEP) or Usahawan Asnaf Program. The AEP was introduced to provide entrepreneurship assistance with zakat money as an economic development program. Through this program, zakat funds are distributed to the selected asnaf in the form of funding after training to assist them establish and run a business. The concept of entrepreneurial asnaf is said to be pioneered by the LZS in Malaysia.[22] The goal is to help asnaf through the zakat funding to grow economically via the business the asnaf are trained to practice. With progressive productivity, the Asnaf Entrepreneurial Program (AEP) aims to ultimately provide and increase opportunities for alleviating poverty and attaining economic independence by participating asnaf. The AEP is an example of a public initiative for zakat program by a state government within the state boundary in a given country (Malaysia).

For the purpose of the AEP (the zakat program), the LZS, through a pool of its dedicated staff and using a stringent procedure, conducts identification and selection exercises of eligible asnaf to benefit from the program. The selection is based on asnaf's background, interest/passion for business, and proven physical fitness to do the business. To determine the interest, LZS considers three factors in asnaf for this purpose: interest in a particular business, willingness to partake in or participate in the special training, and physical capability. The asnaf are assessed through careful screening and interviewing session conducted by the LZS.[23] The training covers subjects of marketing, personal development, and entrepreneurship in order to ensure asnaf are also prepared mentally to engage in entrepreneurship. The LZS closely monitors the participants from

---

[22] Afif Muhamat, A., Jaafar, N., Emrie Rosly, H., & Abdul Manan, H. (2013). An appraisal on the business success of entrepreneurial asnaf: An empirical study on the state zakat organization (the Selangor zakat board) in Malaysia. *Journal of Financial Reporting and Accounting*, Vol. 11, No. 1, p. 54.

[23] Shiyuti, H. A. & Al-Habshi, S. M. (2018). An overview of asnaf entrepreneurship program by Lembaga Zakat Selangor, Malaysia. In *6th ASEAN Universities International Conference on Islamic Finance (AICIF)*, Manila, Philippines, 14th & 15th November.

training to running their respective businesses. An Asnaf Zakat Entrepreneur Development Centre has been established for this purpose.

Generally, funding depends on the type of business and falls into two categories: a maximum of five thousand Malaysian ringgit as capital for starting a business and a maximum of thirty thousand Malaysian ringgit to grow the business.[24] There are six categories/types of business assistance for which training, funding (including cash/equipment/tools/rental of premises), and monitoring are provided. These are (1) agricultural and vegetable garden/orchid, (2) animal husbandry for goat and cattle farming, (3) fishery for both marine and freshwater, (4) services including vehicle workshop, spa and salon, sewing, clothing store, laundry, taxi, and school van, (5) eateries/restaurants, food trucks/mobile dining lorries, all-purpose flour, milled chilies, and chips, and (6) retail grocery stores and asnaf folk market.[25] From 2013 to July 2022, the Asnaf Entrepreneurial Program has produced a total of 1,228 asnaf entrepreneurs who, through the program, received business training in various enterprises, own their businesses, and are now zakat givers.[26]

11.5.2 *International Federation of Red Cross and Red Crescent Societies [IFRC] and Perlis Islamic Religious Council and Malay Customs (Majlis Agama Islam dan Adat Istiadat Melayu Perlis [MAIPS]) Zakat Program (Kenya)*

The Perlis Islamic Religious Council and Malay Customs (*MAIPS*) is the state agency responsible for the administration of zakat (collection and distribution) among other Islamic religious matter in the Malaysian State of Perlis. IFRC is a worldwide international humanitarian agency whose mandate includes providing emergency relief to persons in poverty, hunger, and diseases due to devastation, affliction, and/or displacement by natural disaster, civil unrest, and warfare resulting in refugee situations

---

[24] Lembaga Zakat Selangor (n.d.). LZS Experience Developing Asnaf Zakat Entrepreneurs. Available at https://www.zakatselangor.com.my/artikel/pengalaman-lzs-membangunkan-usahawan-asnaf-zakat/. Accessed November 20, 2022.
[25] *Ibid.*
[26] Lembaga Zakat Selangor (2022). 1,228 Asnaf are Now Entrepreneurs. Available at https://www.zakatselangor.com.my/terkini/1228-asnaf-kini-bergelar-usahawan/.

among other calamities across the world.[27] The IFRC and MAIS zakat program for Kenya involve the use of zakat collected by MAIPS in Perlis, Malaysia, and channeled via IFRC for emergency relief purposes to drought-stricken and crises-ridden Kenyan Kitui communities.[28] Three reasons were put forward as to why the Kitui community was chosen by MAIPS for the zakat assistance: 1. The people were in need of humanitarian assistance and Red Crescent Climate Centre had so identified them, which qualified them as asnaf, 2. the initiative provided an opportunity to demonstrate the contribution zakat can give to international humanitarian projects, and 3. the program potentially established the fact that Islamic social finance can create and sustain impact for shared prosperity in charitable relief.[29] The MAIPS-IFRC zakat program in Kenya is an example of a public initiative for zakat program in collaboration with an international agency targeted at recipients afflicted by natural disasters with humanitarian crises.[30] The scope of this program is internationalized due to the cross-border delivery of zakat.[31]

The program followed a crisis point worst drought that was experienced in Kenya in 2017 whereby an estimated 2.7 million people were affected and needed relief assistance. The people faced serious water scarcity in addition to a very poor harvest of both cash and food crops. In order to provide relief to the victims of the drought, IFRC sought to intervene and brought on board MAIPS to assist the communities in need using zakat. MAIPS issued a fatwa for Shariah approval related to

---

[27] IFRC. (2022). About the IFRC: Local Action, Global Reach. Available at https://www.ifrc.org/who-we-are/about-ifrc. Accessed November 20, 2022.

[28] IFRC (2018a). Beyond Charity – The Transformative Power of Zakat in Humanitarian Crises. Available at https://www.alnap.org/system/files/content/resource/files/main/Kenya_case_study_2018_003.pdf. Accessed November 22, 2022.

[29] IFRC (2019). Annual Report 2018. Available at https://media.ifrc.org/ifrc/wp-content/uploads/2019/08/IFRC-2018-Annual-Report.pdf, p. 153. Accessed November 22, 2022.

[30] Mahmood, J., Hassan, M. K., & Muneeza, A. (2022). The transformative power of zakat (alms) in a humanitarian crisis: A case study from Kenya. In Hassan, M. K., Muneeza, A., & Sonko, K. (Eds.) *Islamic Finance in Africa*. Edward Elgar Publishing, pp. 307–318.

[31] Mahmood, J., Hassan, M. K., & Muneeza, A. (2022). Internationalization of zakat to serve humanity in the midst of COVID-19: Using international organizations as intermediaries of zakat. In Hassan, M. K., Muneeza, A. & Sarea, A. M. (Eds.) *Towards a Post-Covid Global Financial System*. Bingley: Emerald Publishing Limited, pp. 105–127.

cross-border zakat transportation and distribution.[32] MAIPS provided zakat funds to the tune of USD$ 1.2 million to the IFRC to use in a Drought Assistance Program in Kitui, a small-scale farming population in southern central Kenya. MAIPS in partnership with IFRC executed this humanitarian project with zakat.[33]

Millions of people identified as asnaf benefited from the MAIPS-IFRC zakat program and their lives were transformed under the Drought Assistance Program. The program was two-pronged in its approach and simultaneously tackled the problems of water access and cash crop. To produce clean and accessible water, new boreholes and pumps were installed, and existing ones were repaired. This provided clean water to the community and job opportunities for those who engage in selling and distributing water through water kiosks. To assist in cash crops' production, certified green gram seeds were distributed to 175,000 families engaged in subsistence farming, where each family received 2 kgs of the seeds. A forecast-based financing approach was adopted and with the help of technological applications, it was determined that green gram seeds could be successfully grown in the community. It was estimated that at harvest each of the families produced over 180 kgs which were to be sold at a rate of USD1 per kg.[34]

The impact of the program was tremendous. The provision of clean and accessible water saved many lives that were hitherto exposed to several dangers fetching water from remote crocodile-infested rivers/streams. Similarly, with funding for water kiosks operations, water distribution businesses, and water pumps/boreholes maintenance, employment opportunities were created. Moreover, food security through the green gram crops and good revenues from the sale of the crops increased the quality of lives of the people in terms of food, clothing, education, and healthcare. This was in addition to providing the farmers with the guarantee of next round of production. Also, the farmers who participated in the project repaid for the initial two kgs of seed given to them as per initial agreement. Funds from this repayment were to be used in a similar project to assist a neighboring community that endured similar destitution. In

---

[32] Mahmood, J., Hassan, M. K., & Muneeza, A. (2022). The transformative power of zakat (alms) in a humanitarian crisis: A case study from Kenya. In Hassan, M. K., Muneeza, A., & Sonko, K. (Eds.) *Islamic Finance in Africa*. Edward Elgar Publishing, pp. 307–318.
[33] IFRC. *Op. cit.*
[34] *Ibid.*

essence, the program provided the Kitui people with the opportunity to attain financial self-sufficiency via zakat, and in this way, it transformed them from zakat recipients into zakat payers.[35]

11.5.3 UNHCR Refugee Zakat Fund[36]

The United Nations High Commission for Refugees (UNHCR) is an agency of the United Nations (UN) that is responsible for refugees globally. As of mid-2022, there are over 32.5 million refugees for the agency to aid and protect under its mandate.[37] Muslims constitute a sizable portion of this number of refugees today.[38] For this purpose, the UNHCR sought and obtained *fatwa*, a Shariah legal clarification, as an enabler for it to get involved as an intermediary for zakat collection and distribution in a Shariah-compliant manner. UNHCR obtained several fatwas in this regard from different Islamic scholarly organizations in different countries.[39] One fatwa was issued by Tabah Foundation (UAE) in accordance with Hanafi jurisprudence which suits the context and mandate of the agency in relation to zakat: to collect zakat as an international agent and distribute the same to eligible asnaf. Another fatwa, on different issues of zakat administration, was issued by a fatwa body: the Fatwa Council of Tareem (Yemen).

Fatwas were also given by individual Shariah scholars like Sheikh Dr Ali Gomaa. The fatwas addressed Shariah issues on conveying zakat

---

[35] IFRC (2018b). Your Duty for Their Dignity: The Transformative Power of International Zakat Financing. Available at http://rfisummit.org/wp-content/uploads/2018/08/IFRC.pdf. Accessed November 22, 2022.

[36] Mahmood, H. & Muneeza. *Op. cit.*; Furber, M. (2017). UNHCR Zakat Collection and Distribution. Available https://reliefweb.int/sites/reliefweb.int/files/resources/TR-1-UNHCR-Zakat-Collection-And-Distribution-English.pdf.

[37] UNHCR (2022). Refugee Data Finder. Available at https://www.unhcr.org/refugee-statistics/. Accessed October 20, 2022; UN (2022). Office of the United Nations High Commissioner for Refugees. Available at https://www.un.org/youthenvoy/2013/09/office-of-the-united-nations-high-commissioner-for-refugees/. Accessed October 20, 2022.

[38] UNHCR (2022). Refugee Data Finder: UNHCR's Refugee Population Statistics Database. Available at https://www.unhcr.org/refugee-statistics/. Accessed October 20, 2022.

[39] UNHCR (2022). Refugee Zakat Fund – UNHCR. Available at https://zakat.unhcr.org/en. Accessed October 20, 2022.

outside its locality (internationalization), giving zakat to non-Muslim victims in emergency, and use of non-state agent intermediary to collect/distribute zakat, among other issues on which the Islamic *mazahib* (schools of jurisprudence) share different viewpoints. In general, however, the fatwas have all sanctioned three essential points: UNHCR can distribute zakat funds, one must give the zakat to the categories of recipients mentioned in Quran 9:60, and zakat must not be used to cover expenses or wages for the agency. On the basis of the said fatwas, the UNHCR Refugee Zakat Fund was established in 2019 as a source of funds for refugee aid and management.

Zakat is paid via UNHCR's web-based payment gateway/application. Also, an application called GiveZakat has been launched through which payers of zakat around the world can dedicate their zakat to refugees using mobile phones in a simple and easy way. All the application enables tracking of funds until it reaches eligible recipients.[40] In accordance with its fatwa, the UNHCR procedures are simple: it collects zakat in cash and distributes in-kind rather than cash. UNHCR ensures due process in its purchase/procurement of goods and related expenses with all standards of accountability. Accordingly, UNHCR periodically publishes reports detailing the amount it collected and distributed and the impact of the disbursed funds.[41]

The impact of the UNHCR Refugee Zakat Fund has been motivating and instilling hope in the lives of thousands of refugees. By the first half of 2022 alone, the Refugee Zakat Fund received more than $18.6 million in zakat funds. This is being currently distributed in a Shariah-compliant manner in accordance with the UNHCR distribution policy sanctioned by the fatwas received by the agency over the past years. These zakat funds help more than 645,000 refugees in 15 countries, namely Afghanistan, Bangladesh, Iraq, Yemen, Lebanon, Jordan, Algeria, Egypt, Tunisia, Iran, India, Nigeria, Somalia, Mauritania, and Malaysia.[42]

---

[40] UNHCR (2021). What you may not know about Refugee Zakat Fund App. Available at https://zakat.unhcr.org/blog/en/refugee-zakat-fund/about-refugee-zakat-fund-app.

[41] Furber, M. (2020). *UNHCR Zakat Collection and Distribution Tabah Report, No. 1* (May). Available at https://zakat.unhcr.org/wp-content/uploads/2020/05/UNHCR-Zakat-Distribution-English.pdf. Accessed October 20, 2022.

[42] UNHCR. (2022). *Islamic Philanthrophy Mid-Year Report 2022*. Available at https://giving.unhcr.org/wp-content/uploads/2022/11/ISLAMIC-PHILANTROPY-Mid-Year-Report-2022-311022.pdf, pp. 3–4. Accessed November 20, 2022.

On administration of the fund, UNHCR has declared to have good governance measures in place that guarantee transparency of the fund in every process of collection and distribution of zakat to eligible recipients. The involvement of UNHCR as an intermediary for zakat management running cross-border zakat program has given prominence to the relevance of zakat in international development agenda. The initiative has internationalized zakat and promotes its impact globally. The program has been attracting more Islamic scholars' approval, public confidence, and trust since its inception. Despite this prospect however, the practice of internationalizing zakat through the UNHCR program has been opposed by some Islamic scholars and organizations including the World Zakat and Waqf Forum (WZWF) on the basis of traditional zakat administration in Islam. According to Prof. Zainulbahar, the Secretary-General of WZWF, the UNHCR is not eligible to collect and distribute zakat "since the United Nations itself is not a zakat organization." Also, arguing further, the professor stressed that "zakat collected is for funding assistance for refugees forcedly evicted from their country for some reason. One who has the right to do so is the zakat organization from each country and in reality it has been done that way so far. Moreover, the UNHCR Zakat Refugee Fund is an unsupervised activity with a huge possibility for irregularities in the use of the funds."[43]

---

[43] BAZNAS PUSKAS. (2022). *Zainulbahar Noor Reject UNHCR Zakat Collection.* Available at https://puskasbaznas.com/news/1704-zainulbahar-noor-reject-unhcr-zakat-collection. Accessed November 20, 2022.

Self-Assessment Quiz (MCQs)

Question 1: Zakat management programs can enable asnaf, through a series of interventions including relief, business training, and funding to attain the following except …………..
(a) Prudence in zakat use
(b) Management of zakat grant
(c) Squander zakat
(d) Zakat utilization strategy

Question 2: Asnaf can have a deeper appreciation of zakat, its objectives, philosophy, and working principles through one of the following:
(a) Regular zakat statistics
(b) Impressive zakat use
(c) Zakat needy resettlement
(d) Zakat management programs

Question 3: Zakat programs can be run within one country or state only by a public or across borders through collaboration with multilateral humanitarian agencies leading to …………..
(a) Proper asnaf identification
(b) Greater spread of zakat
(c) Internationalization of zakat
(d) Proper identification of zakat payers

Question 4: One of the following is the primary objective of zakat that prompts the development and execution of zakat programs:
(a) Need to empower asnaf to self-sufficiency
(b) Identification of zakat recipients' family
(c) Need for solicitation among zakat payers
(d) None of the above

Question 5: Zakat management programs can have all the following impacts on asnaf except:
(a) Prudence in using zakat
(b) Acquisition of life-transforming skills
(c) Become zakat administrators
(d) Become eventual zakat payers

Question 6: Which of the following practice of agencies/bodies run a zakat management program that can be described as statewide?
(a) MAIPS-IFRC
(b) Lembaga Zakat Selangor (LZS)
(c) UNHCR
(d) None of the above

Question 7: All the following are factors to be considered when establishing a zakat management program except ……….
(a) Annual return from program
(b) Resources and personnel expertise
(c) Scope and relevance to asnaf's needs
(d) Value to impart in asnaf lives

Question 8: From 2013 to July 2022, Asnaf Entrepreneurial Program (AEP) of Lembaga Zakat Selangor has produced a total of ………… entrepreneurs who are now zakat givers.
(a) 2,570 asnaf
(b) 1,340 asnaf
(c) 1,230 asnaf
(d) 1,228 asnaf

Question 9: MAIPS-IFRC zakat program is an example of a public initiative for zakat program in collaboration with an international agency in ……….. that targeted recipients afflicted by ………
(a) Kenya …….. earthquake
(b) Kenya ……… drought
(c) Congo ……….. armed conflict
(d) Pakistan ……….. flood

Question 10: UNHCR Refugee Zakat program has been welcomed as a step toward internalizing zakat and its impact but one reason it is opposed is because ………..
(a) The United Nations is not a zakat organization
(b) The United Nations cannot deliver zakat value
(c) The United Nations has no zakat expertise
(d) The United Nations is not an Islamic agency

Self-Assessment/Recall Questions

Question 1: Explain what is a zakat management program and why such a program is needed today.

Question 2: Enumerate and discuss the impact of zakat management programs on asnaf.

Question 3: Critically evaluate the factors to consider in formulating zakat management programs.

Question 4: Highlight the practice of zakat management programs across the world.

Question 5: Select and explain one case study of zakat management programs.

Answers to Self-Assessment Quiz (MCQs)

1. c
2. d
3. c
4. a
5. c
6. b
7. a
8. d
9. b
10. a

Chapter 12

Contemporary Issues and Challenges in Zakat Administration

Learning Outcomes

At the end of this chapter, students should be able to know

- issues and challenges in collecting zakat,
- issues and challenges in managing zakat fund,
- issues and challenges in disbursement,
- selected case studies.

There are issues and challenges associated with contemporary practice of zakat administration.[1] Each aspect of zakat administration, for instance, the identification of eligible zakat recipients and the collection and distribution of zakat, has some challenges associated with them. Such issues and challenges have constrained the realization of the full potential of zakat in several ways. The following is an elucidation of these issues and challenges.

---

[1] Owoyemi, M. Y. (2020). Zakat management: The crisis of confidence in zakat agencies and the legality of giving zakat directly to the poor. *Journal of Islamic Accounting and Business Research*, Vol. 11, No. 2, pp. 498–510.

12.1 Issues and Challenges in Collecting Zakat

12.1.1 Lack of credible zakat-collecting institutions

Collecting of zakat is an important function of every Muslim states' zakat administration in accordance with the ideals of zakat since its enshrinement as an obligation. However, for the fact that Muslims today largely live under secular governments, the task of zakat collection being an Islamic religious duty has been relegated to private volunteer individuals and organizations. As such, payment of zakat becomes a volition out of self-sacrifice. That being the case, the question of whom to trust with one's zakat becomes an issue among zakat givers. The situation has prompted direct payment of zakat by payers to people whom they are able to understand as asnaf in their immediate community. The question of trust is important even in regulated zakat jurisdiction where zakat is collected by government agencies tainted with credibility and integrity issues toward the function.[2]

As a public institution, a zakat collecting agency needs to be professional with integrity and credibility. Integrity and professionalism in zakat assessment and collection are as important for zakat institutions as it is for a financial institution. Thus, instances of corruption, fraud, and embezzlement of public and/or zakat funds among state institutions' administration and personnel have undermined the confidence/trust of zakat payers in such institutions.[3] Lack of credibility and integrity compromises accountability in zakat collection by the institution. This discourages zakat payers to commit zakat payments to the institutions which results in under-collection.[4]

---

[2] Muhammad, S. A. & Saad, R. A. J. (2016). The impact of public governance quality, accountability and effectiveness on intention to pay zakat: Moderating effect of trust on zakat institution. *International Journal of Management Research and Reviews*, Vol. 6, No. 1, pp. 1–3.

[3] Sawmar, A. A. & Mohammed, M. O. (2021). Enhancing zakat compliance through good governance: A conceptual framework. *ISRA International Journal of Islamic Finance*, Vol. 13, No. 1, pp. 136–154.

[4] Oladimeji Abioye Mustafa, M., Har Sani Mohamad, M., & Akhyar Adnan, M. (2013). Antecedents of zakat payers' trust in an emerging zakat sector: An exploratory study. *Journal of Islamic Accounting and Business Research*, Vol. 4, No. 1, pp. 4–25.

12.1.2 Absence of institutional governance framework for zakat collection

Zakat collection needs to be guided by and in conformity with a framework for the governance of the zakat institution in relation to the zakat it collects. The institutional framework for this purpose comprises the systems of laws and regulations and the procedures informed by these regulations and informal norms that determine and regulate the scope and extent of the zakat collecting institution's function. This is necessary in order to ensure proper institutional governance whereby all structures of the zakat institution are designated and their internal and external relationships defined in accordance with a comprehensive governance code and its institutional mandate. The absence of an institutional governance framework for zakat collection institutions can lead to a loss of vision and the inability to effectively steer clear of its mission, resulting in potential inefficiencies and shortcomings in fulfilling their zakat collection responsibilities.[5]

12.1.3 Inability to identify zakat payers

Zakat collection needs to be well organized through a robust system that identifies zakat payers and facilitates reaching out to them with updates. This presupposes that the zakat collection system is integrated into the economy via a record system in a regulated zakat jurisdiction. Identifying zakat payers from potential stage to actual eligible zakat payers is important to designing policies on zakat collection. Inability to identify zakat payers and/or reach out to them with update for zakat collection is a challenge particularly where an institution exists for the function but lacks a suitable system for that purpose. A good system for this purpose encompasses adequate and qualified human resources/personnel needed for the management of a zakat institution or an Islamic not-for-profit and charity-based organization.[6] The ability to identify zakat payers via a record system from public and private sectors, individuals, and entities helps in

---

[5] Wahab, N. A. & Rahim Abdul Rahman, A. (2011). A framework to analyse the efficiency and governance of zakat institutions. *Journal of Islamic Accounting and Business Research*, Vol. 2, No. 1, pp. 43–62.

[6] Hasan, A. *et al.* (2019). A proposed human resource management model for zakat institutions in Malaysia. *ISRA International Journal of Islamic Finance*, Vol. 11, No. 1, pp. 98–109.

projection for the floating of a zakat program. It also facilitates understanding of the prospect and sustainability of such a zakat program.[7]

12.2 Issues and Challenges in Managing Zakat Fund

As jurisdictions differ in their approach to managing zakat fund, so also the issues and challenges associated therewith. Generally, however, both in regulated and unregulated zakat jurisdictions, challenges and issues in managing zakat funds include the following:

12.2.1 Lack of transparency in administering zakat funds

Transparency in administration encompasses operating in such a way that other people can easily see and understand all actions being performed. In other words, transparency is an ethic that implies openness, accountability, and communication of decisions and actions to all interested in such decisions and actions.[8] Transparency in managing zakat fund is very crucial for the success of zakat to achieve its goals. In this regard, transparency can be ensured through public reporting of what is collected and distributed of zakat, an elaborate disclosure system for monitoring and evaluating administrators' performance in their various roles.[9] Lack of transparency in managing zakat funds through public disclosure downgrades the prospect of sustainable zakat programs, vitiates effectiveness and efficiency within the zakat institutions, and, accordingly, erodes the trust of stakeholders in the zakat management system.[10] Lack of transparency in managing zakat funds has largely affected the potential of zakat payment which culminates in low zakat payment and collection in some countries.[11]

---

[7] Muhammad & Saad. *Op. cit.*
[8] Ball, C. (2019). What is transparency? *Public Integrity*, Vol. 11, No. 4, pp. 293–308.
[9] Farouk, A. U., Idris, K., & Saad, R. A. J. (2017). The challenges of zakat management: A case of Kano state, Nigeria. *Asian Journal of Multidisciplinary Studies*, Vol. 5, No. 7, pp. 142–147.
[10] Taha, R., Adam, F., Ali, N. N. M., & Ariff, A. M. (2017). Religiosity and transparency in the management of zakat institutions. *Journal of Legal, Ethical and Regulatory Issues*, Vol. 20, No. 1, pp. 1–9.
[11] Amilahaq, F. & Kiryanto, K. (2022, February 4). Enhancing accountability and transparency of zakat management organization. *Proceedings of Indonesian Conference of Zakat*, pp. 357–368. DOI: 10.37706/iconz.2021.343.

12.2.2 Corruption, misappropriation, and embezzlement

Indiscipline, greed, and selfishness have, often time, led zakat administrators and CEOs to get involved in the unwholesome attitude of bribery, misappropriation, and embezzlement of zakat funds among other mismanagement and corrupt practices.[12] Although in principles it is generally understood that strict adherence to Islamic good governance and work ethics can prevent these unwholesome practices, in reality, they are largely attributed to weak governance practices and absence of dedicated governance code for zakat institutions.[13] Several cases, comprising of different scandals, from bribery to misappropriation and embezzlement have been observed in zakat institutions.[14] Such cases and scandals devalue the estimation of the institutions rather than the person behind them which affects zakat payers and all stakeholders' trust and confidence in them.[15]

12.2.3 Imprudent zakat program affects zakat funds

Formulating zakat management program requires prudence and foresight so that the goals of the program can be sustainably achieved.[16] Often time, poor management of zakat funds emanates from imprudence and lack of foresight in formulating a zakat management program from the onset. This is because either the program lacks clear and attainable vision or it is led and steered by incompetent personnel, resulting in waste of resources so much so that the programs end up failing without desired impact in asnaf. Moreover, in such circumstances, zakat collection would become passive, and sustainability of zakat funds becomes unattainable. Therefore,

---

[12] Islam, M. K., Mitu, S. T., Munshi, R., & Khanam, R. (2022). Perceptions about the common malpractice of Zakat paying in Bangladesh during Covid-19 pandemic: Evidence from the supply side. *Journal of Islamic Accounting and Business Research* (ahead-of-print). DOI: 10.1108/JIABR-09-2021-0253.

[13] Wahyuni-TD, I. S., Haron, H., & Fernando, Y. (2021). The effects of good governance and fraud prevention on performance of the zakat institutions in Indonesia: A Sharī'ah forensic accounting perspective. *International Journal of Islamic and Middle Eastern Finance and Management*, Vol. 14, No. 4, p. 699.

[14] Hassan, R. & Muneeza, A. (2022). The need to eliminate mismanagement and corruption in Islamic social finance institutions. *IIUM Law Journal*, Vol. 30, No. S2, pp. 423–444.

[15] Wahyuni-TD, H. & Fernando. *Op. cit.*, p. 207

[16] Essof, M. H. (2020). Prudence in Zakat Management. Available at https://www.youtube.com/watch?v=I3aA8m08RFI. Accessed November 25, 2022.

the inability to ensure prudent zakat funds' management mostly transcends to inability to establish sustainable zakat funds and eventually the failure of a zakat program.[17]

12.3 Issues and Challenges in Disbursement

12.3.1 *Insufficient data on asnaf leads to their exclusion in zakat disbursement*

Generally, asnaf are to be identified and selected in accordance with divinely established criteria which provide for their conditions and status in life to determine eligibility. This is not an easy task. A major problem in this regard is however people are often unaware of officially authorized zakat institutions to present themselves. They are accustomed to seeing zakat funds directly and informally distributed to the recipient in mosques through clerics.[18] In contemporary practice, it is common for zakat administrators to establish and operate a database for this purpose. However, an ineffective asnaf identification and registration system leads to insufficient data about asnaf. The ineffectiveness is mostly the result of incompetence on part of personnel responsible for the identification and registration. This ultimately affects eligibility and eventual selection of true asnaf for zakat award.[19] Accordingly, deserving asnaf might be left out of the system and consequently out of a zakat program. Without identifying and selecting eligible asnaf, disbursement zakat is likely to be made to underserved persons at the expense of asnaf. Leaving deserving asnaf out of zakat program due to ineptitude of personnel or system failure is a disservice to the asnaf and affects integrity of a zakat management program.[20]

---

[17] Abd Wahab, N., Alam, M. M., Al Haq, A., Hashim, S., & Zainol, Z. (2020). Towards empowering zakat recipients: Assessing effectiveness of zakat institutions from the zakat recipients' perspective. *Journal of Critical Reviews*, Vol. 7, No. 8, pp. 1586–1597.

[18] Wahyuni-TD, Haron & Fernando. *Op. cit.*

[19] Che Mohamed Arif, A. S., Ta'a, A., Shaari, M. S., & Ahmad, J. (2019, 1–2 December). JCA: An application model for asnaf identification and reporting. In *Proceedings: International Conference on Zakat, Tax, Waqf and Economic Development (ZAWED)*, Adya Hotel Langkawi, Malaysia, pp. 45–62.

[20] Ramli, R. M., Ahmad, S., Wahid, H., & Harun, F. M. (2011, July). Understanding asnaf attitude: Malaysia's experience in quest for an effective zakat distribution programme.

12.3.2 Poor disbursement organization leading to tragedies

Ineffective disbursement mechanism — use of zakat funds mostly for consumption — has led to inability of zakat institutions to establish effective empowerment initiatives, thus unable for zakat to achieve its major object, i.e., empowering asnaf to the capacity of zakat payers in time. Also, disbursement of zakat needs to be orderly and properly organized. Regrettably, however, lack of regard for this fundamental ethic of zakat disbursement has often resulted in very rowdy and disorderly encounters during zakat disbursement. Unfortunately, several such encounters have resulted in tragedies that lead to serious injuries and death of asnaf due to stampede in uncontrolled crowds of people.[21]

12.3.3 Strict localization of zakat disbursement

While the prospect for expanding zakat impact through its internalization has been growing, strict localization of zakat persists. Localization of zakat renders the potential of zakat to be very limited which hampers internalization drive.[22] The internationalization of zakat has expanded the reach and impact of zakat as demonstrated by UNHCR Refugee Zakat Fund. The involvement of UNHCR as an intermediary for zakat management to run cross-border zakat program for refugees and displaced persons has given prominence to the relevance of zakat in international development agenda. The program has made zakat a global development instrument and promotes its impact accordingly. With strict localization of zakat, this prospect of zakat development would not be realized.

In *Proceedings: International Conference on Sustainable Zakat Development in the Poverty Alleviation and Improvement of Welfare of the Ummah*, UKM, Bangi, Malaysia, p. 13. Available at http://www.ukm.my/hairun/kertas%20kerja/Paper%20Raudha%20et%20al.pdf. Accessed November 28, 2022.

[21] See for instance Khokon, S. H. (2015). 10 women die in Chattogram, Bangladesh during zakat relief distribution. Available at https://www.indiatoday.in/amp/india/story/10-women-died-in-chattogram-bangladesh-during-zakat-relief-distribution-1233884-2018-05-14. Accessed November 28, 2022.

[22] Wahid, H. & Kader, R. A. (2010). Localization of Malaysian zakat distribution: Perceptions of *amil* and zakat recipients. In *Proceedings: Seventh International Conference on Tawhidi Epistemology: Zakat and Waqf Economy*, pp. 461–484. Available at https://www.ukm.my/hadhari/wp-content/uploads/2014/09/proceedings-seminar-waqf-tawhidi.pdf#page=462. Accessed November 28, 2022.

Where the need arises for cross-border zakat, strict adherence to localization would only impede an aspect of maqasid al-Shariah.

12.4 Selected Case Studies

12.4.1 Death of asnaf from zakat disbursement uproar, Bangladesh

Death of asnaf (and other people) due to commotion from rowdy zakat disbursement sessions is one unfortunate contemporary issue associated with zakat that recurs too often in Bangladesh, which is foremost in these tragedies. One incident occurred on 10 July 2015, in the district of Mymensingh, from which a spate of tragic death of 27 people (women and children) was reported. This followed a stampede of thousands of people who gathered at the residence of a wealthy Muslim to collect zakat. The stampede occurred in the frantic efforts of the people to get the zakat items (clothing) as they ran, pushed, and shoved each other in the process.[23] This was obviously due to the fact that the number of clothes to be distributed was by far less than the number of people that gathered to collect them, hence the rush and ensuing pandemonium. These unfortunate tragedies are yearly experience in Bangladesh and happen mainly because of 1. misconceptions and ostentations about the methods of zakat disbursement, 2. unethicality and egoism by some uninformed rich Muslims who demonstrate wealth and power via religious piety, and 3. extreme and overwhelming poverty among the people.[24]

12.4.2 Alleged corruption scandal in Zakat Pulau Penang (ZPP), Malaysia

It is alleged that the chief executive officer of Zakat Penang, the government agency charged with the responsibility of zakat administration in

---

[23] Hashmi, T. (2015). "Zakat-Deaths" in Bangladesh: An old story of piety and power. *The Daily Star,* 17 July. Available at https://www.thedailystar.net/op-ed/%E2%80%9Czakat-deaths%E2%80%9D-bangladesh-old-story-piety-and-power-113527. Accessed November 28, 2022.

[24] Islam, M. S. (2016). Towards an establishment of zakat institution in Bangladesh based on Malaysian experience: A juristic and analytical study. In Fuadah & Asma (Eds.) *Proceedings of the Muktamar Waqf Iqlimi III (IQLIMI2016),* Ban Nua Mosque, Songkla, Thailand, 13–14 October, pp. 109–126.

Penang, Malaysia, was charged in court with two counts of corruption. The first charge bordered on accepting a bribe for himself to the tune of RM5,000 from the proprietor of one company that had business dealings with the ZPP. The second charge was also against a bribe to the tune of RM4,000 from the CEO of a company that ZPP dealt with.[25] Previously, he had been charged, alongside other officers of the ZPP, state zakat agency, with accepting valuable items, cheques, and cash from some contractors as incentives to award them contract by the agency. In addition, he was charged for embezzling zakat funds by helping himself to education aid and scholarships for his child without having recourse to or going through the Penang Islamic Affairs Department.[26] The charges were brought by Malaysian Anti-Corruption Commission (MACC) under Sections 17(a), 17(b), and 23 of the MACC Act 2009.

12.4.3 *Alleged mismanagement of zakat funds, Singapore*

Islamic Religious Council of Singapore or Majlis Ugama Islam Singapura (MUIS) is the state agency responsible for the management of zakat as well as all other Islamic affairs in Singapore. Based on filings and audit reports at Singapore's Auditor General Office from 2018/2019, repeated irregularities in the MUIS zakat finances were severally noted.[27] The irregularities pointed at financial and operational irregularities that bordered on improper procurement procedures and poor financial procedures in managing zakat funds. This led to serious allegations of financial misconduct against MUIS.[28] A basis for the allegations stems from the fact

---

[25] Malaymail. (2017). Penang zakat CEO faces more corruption charges. *Malaymail*, 29 November. Available at https://www.malaymail.com/news/malaysia/2017/11/29/penang-zakat-ceo-faces-more-corruption-charges/1521147. Accessed November 28, 2022.

[26] Bashir, M. (2017). Zakat Penang Corruption Scandal: MACC releases six on bail. *New Straits Time*, 14 May. Available at https://www.nst.com.my/news/nation/2017/05/239179/zakat-penang-corruption-scandal-macc-releases-six-bail. Accessed November 28, 2022.

[27] Hunter, M. (2021). Singapore: Alleged Financial and Operational Irregularities at MUIS – Analysis. *Eurasia Review*, 16 June. Available at https://www.eurasiareview.com/16062021-malaysia-alleged-financial-and-operational-irregularities-at-muis-analysis/. Accessed November 28, 2022.

[28] Hunter, M. (2021). Singapore's Islamic Council Faces Potential Corruption Charges. *Asia Sentinel*, 15 June. Available at https://www.asiasentinel.com/p/singapores-islamic-council-faces. Accessed November 28, 2022.

that MUIS officers, irrespective of designated responsibility and grade level at work, can have access to accounts and can effect changes to information about them, a pointer to the risk of performing unauthorized activities on the zakat system.[29]

12.4.4 Poor zakat management wanes confidence and raises doubts, Brunei

Brunei Islamic Religious Council or Majlis Ugama Islam Brunei (MUIB) is the state agency responsible for the management of zakat and all other Islamic affairs in Brunei. MUIB runs and manages zakat programs to render assistance to and empower the poor using zakat. This includes the collection and disbursement of zakat. However, realizing MUIB's level of poor management of zakat has raised doubt in the confidence of the Brunei ruler over that assistance. According to report, sometime in 2020 amidst the COVID-19 pandemic, His Majesty Sultan Haji Hassanal Bolkiah questioned the commitment of MUIB in helping the underprivileged through zakat program; he was assertive of the persistence of poor zakat management by MUIB, indicative of the doubts over MUIB's proactiveness to help the poor in that regard. Citing instances of passivity, His Majesty raised concerns about zakat applicants and recipients being unable to settle pressing matters despite repeated visits to MUIB office. The office has been likewise very difficult to reach via telephone by the applicants and recipients as well as members of the public.[30]

---

[29] *Ibid.*
[30] Abu Bakar, R. H. (2020). HM Raises Concerns of Poor Zakat Management. *The Scoop*, 16 September. Available at https://thescoop.co/2020/09/16/hm-raises-concerns-of-poor-zakat-management/. Accessed November 29, 2022.

Self-Assessment Quiz (MCQs)

Question 1: Contemporary issues and challenges of zakat administration have been generally acknowledged to include the following except ………..
(a) Ability to disburse zakat
(b) Lack of credible zakat collecting institutions
(c) Absence of institutional governance framework for zakat collection
(d) All of the above

Question 2: As a public institution, zakat collecting agency needs to be professional and act with credibility and …………..
(a) Self-service
(b) Integrity
(c) Pride
(d) Indiscipline

Question 3: A zakat collecting institution needs adequate and qualified human resources/personnel with background in the management of a zakat institution or ……………
(a) Corporate governance
(b) Business discipline
(c) An Islamic not-for-profit/charity-based organization
(d) Banking institution

Question 4: Zakat can be disbursed locally but its scope and objectives are capable of addressing cross-border expansion which idealizes ……………. of zakat
(a) Intellectuality
(b) Investments
(c) Internationalization
(d) Entrepreneurship

Question 5: Contemporary issues and challenges in managing zakat funds generally comprise all the following except ……………
(a) Misappropriation and embezzlement
(b) Lack of transparency
(c) Exceptional transparency
(d) Imprudence

Question 6: Contemporary issues and challenges in disbursement of zakat funds generally comprise all the following except ....
(a) Inadvertent asnaf exclusion
(b) Entrepreneurial asnaf
(c) Avoidable tragedies
(d) Strict localization

Question 7: Strict localization of zakat has limited the territorial scope of zakat, which in turn hampers the .... of zakat's impact.
(a) Juristic consensus
(b) Reputation of Islamic charity
(c) Islamic philanthropy
(d) Internationalization

Question 8: Death of asnaf (and other people) due to commotion from rowdy zakat disbursement sessions is a contemporary challenge to zakat distribution frequently reported in which country?
(a) Saudi Arabia
(b) Bangladesh
(c) Singapore
(d) All of the above

Question 9: Corruption scandal in zakat management is considered a serious challenge to zakat program because it is an unwholesome practice that causes …………………..
(a) Building confidence in zakat
(b) Lack of trust in zakat program
(c) Appreciating maqasid al-Shariah
(d) Attainment of SDGs

Question 10: UNHCR obtained ………….. that provided requisite Shariah backing for it to partake in zakat program for collection and distribution of zakat for refugees.
(a) Advice
(b) Injunction
(c) Fatwa
(d) Order

Self-Assessment/Recall Questions

Question 1: Explain the contemporary issues and challenges associated with collection of zakat.

Question 2: Discuss the contemporary issues and challenges in the management of zakat funds.

Question 3: Examine how the issues of insufficient data on asnaf and poor disbursement process undermine the prospect of zakat.

Question 4: Highlight how corruption scandal in zakat administration undermines public confidence and trust in zakat program. Discuss.

Question 5: Evaluate how passivity of Majlis Ugama Islam Brunei (MUIB) raised doubts about its proactiveness to assist the poor through zakat funds.

Answers to Self-Assessment Quiz (MCQs)

1. a
2. b
3. c
4. c
5. c
6. b
7. d
8. b
9. b
10. c

Index

A
Accounting and Auditing Organization for Islamic Financial Institutions (AAOIFI), 84, 139
adjusted growth method, 138, 142, 144
adjusted working capital, 138
adjusted working capital method, 142–143
administration, 153
affordable and clean energy, 173
affordable housing, 29
Africa, 26
agency, 85
agricultural produce, 137
agricultural product, 4, 99
ahlul bait, 126
Al-Gharimin/debtor, 2, 24
'alihah, 2
al-infaaq, 56
alleviating poverty, 26
al-*nisab*, 22
Al-Rahma City, 39
al-Sunnah, 11
alternative financial tools, 10
amanah, 161

amil, 97, 100, 106–108, 119
'amileen, 2, 119
amilin alayha, 153
animal products, 78
animals, 36, 75
annual basis, 22
anti-money laundering, 201
anti-poverty program, 41
app, *see also* BAZNAS, 101
aqidah support, 122
arbitrary estimation, 135
artificial intelligence, 184
asnaf, 207, 224, 226
Asnaf Entrepreneurial Program, 208
Asnaf Personal Financing, 29
assessment of zakat, 139
assets, 4, 13, 98
atheist, 128
audit, 142
Azerbaijan, 157

B
Badan *Amil* Zakat Nasional (BAZNAS), 29, 101–102
Bahrain, 88, 139, 156

balance sheet, 146
Bangladesh, 88, 159, 226
banking, 202
banking services, 101
Bank Islam, 29
Bank Negara Malaysia, 139
basic necessities, 23, 118
basic needs, 23, 51, 68, 203
BAZNAS Welfare Index, 36
beneficiaries, 28, 153, 207
Bitcoin, 193
blockchain, 184
blockchain technology, 84
Blossom Finance Indonesia, 193
bonds, 83, 99
book value, 142
borrow, 23
Brazil, 171
Brunei, 155
Brunei Islamic Religious Council, 228
buried treasures, 78
business, 79
business revenues, 4

C

calculation, 135, 139
capacity building, 120
captives, 7
cash, 23
   allocation, 202
   assistance, 38
   grants, 202
   waqf, 60
cassava, 38
centralized, 155
centralized body, 26
centralized zakat administration system, 191
challenges, 219

charity, 2
Chatbot, 189
check and balance system, 160
child abuse, 123
clean water/sanitation, 173
climate change, 174
clothes, 118
collection and distribution, 22
collection and distribution of zakat, 219
commercial/business inventory, 79
commodities, 178
common shares, 84
community, 104
compensation, 153
computation, 138
conditions, 97
contemporary examples, 98
contemporary issues, 219
conventional tax, 5
converts, 121
corruption, 10, 220, 223
cost, 38
COVID-19 pandemic, 35, 59
crops, 37, 74
cross-border zakat program, 214
cryptocurrencies, 84
cryptography, 185
crypto zakat, 192
currency, 138
cyberspace, 191

D

data, 205
da'wah, 121
debt, 11, 99, 123, 145
debtors, 8, 123
decentralization, 185
decentralized, 155
decent work, 173
deduction, 84

default debtors, 11
delegated, 155
Department of Awqaf, Zakat, and Hajj, 161
disaster management, 178
disbursement, 224
disobedience, 124
distributed, 155
distributed ledger technology, 184
distribution, 172
Diwan al Zakat, 88
Djibouti, 37
Dompet Dhuafa, 124
donation, 2, 176

E
economic
  activity, 104
  growth, 173
  impact, 115–116
  program, 31
  role, 154
  tool, 172
education, 123
'Eid al-Fitr, 69
eight categories, 2
eight recipients, 22
eligible Muslims, 12
eligible recipients, 162
embezzlement, 220, 223
emergency relief, 38
empowerment, 202
ending hunger, 173
enforcement actions, 202
enhance zakat administration, 183, 190
enhancing agriculture, 38
eradicate poverty, 25, 51
eradicating poverty, 11, 21
Eritrea, 37
essential needs, 11

ethical economy, 67
ethical society, 13
Ethiopia, 37–38
external borrowing, 125
e-Zakat Pay, 186

F
families, 128
faqir/poor, 22, 116
farmers, 37
Federal Islamic Religious Council, 27
fertilizer, 138
fi ar-Riqab/the captives, 2, 24
Financial Accounting Standard, 139
financial
  institution, 23
  literacy, 124
  services, 183
  statement, 143
fintech, 184
Fiqh scholars, 121
fisabilillah, 2, 125, 128
fisabilillah causes, 24
fishing industry, 78
fixed capital, 80
food, 37, 51, 118
forecast-based financing approach, 211
formula, 137, 143
for the sake of Allah, 8
fraud, 220
fruits, 99
fulfilling one's basic needs, 81
full possession, 81
full potential of zakat, 219
fuqara, 2, 116

G
gari, 38
Ghana, 38
gharim, 123

global partnerships, 174
Global Sadaqah Malaysia, 194
gold, 4, 73, 99, 136
good governance, 214
goods, 138
goods and services, 54
governance, 120, 159
governance framework, 221
government, 22
gross annual rent, 80
gross domestic product (GDP), 11
growth, 52
GSM, 184
guarantee, 123
guardianship, 122

H
had al-kifayah, 161
halal, 2
halal income, 79
haul, 99, 136
haul/lapse of a full year, 81
hawl, 136
healthy life, 173
hijrah, 74
Hijra year, 2, 75
honey, 75
Horn of Africa, 37
human capital, 175
human development, 117
humanitarian assistance, 38
humanitarian support, 206
hunger, 202

I
Ibnu Sabil, 2, 25, 125
identification of eligible zakat recipients, 219
ihsani behavioral norms, 104
inclusive and quality education, 173
income, 23, 120
income generating, 80

Income Tax Act 1967, 82, 145
index, 122
India, 159
Indonesia, 26, 29, 119, 156
inefficient zakat administration, 88
information technology, 120
innovative ways, 146
institution of zakat, 8
insufficient data, 224
integrity, 220
interest, 10
internal control, 120
International Federation of Red Cross and Red Crescent Societies, 38, 186, 209
Internet-of-Things, 184, 187
Iran, 158
Iris ATM, 189
irrigation, 138
Islam, 1
Islamic economics, 67
Islamic social finance, 57, 59
isolated, 155

J
Jabatan Wakaf, Zakat dan Haji (JAWHAR), 139
Jamam Ghana Village, 38
jewellery, 118
jihad, 125
Johor Islamic Religious Council, 29
joint venture, 29
Jordan, 88
judiciary system, 51
just distribution, 22

K
kafir dzimmi, 128
kafir harbi, 128
Kedah State of Zakat Authority, 29
Kelantan, 27
Kenya, 38, 209

Kenya Red Cross, 38
khatib of zakat, 100
khilafah/viceregency, 52
Kitui, 212
Kuwait, 88, 156, 158
Kuwait Finance House, 147

L
law enforcement, 51
lawful earnings, 120
legal recipients, 115
Lembaga Zakat Negeri Kedah, 28
Lembaga Zakat Selangor, 208
less fortunate, 104
liabilities, 145
liberating prisoners, 24
liberating slaves, 7
Libya, 158
line chat application, 101
livelihoods support, 38
livestock, 75
livestock breeding, 35
loan, 30, 145
localization, 225
localized community, 157
lunar year, 101, 137

M
maal, 58
Madinah, 74
Majelis Ulama Indonesia, 85
Majlis Agama Islam Perlis, 38
Majlis Ugama Islam Brunei, 228
Malaysia, 26, 119, 140, 156, 158, 226
Malaysian Accounting Standards Board (MASB), 139–141
Malaysian Islamic Development Department (JAKIM), 141
Malaysia Tax Law, 82
Mali, 159

management, 153
management of zakat, 115
management programs, 203
maqasid al-shariah, 172, 175
maqasid shariah, 28
marine life/ecosystem, 174
masaakin, 118
Metaverse, 103
middle class people, 41
Middle Eastern countries, 158
minerals, 78
minimum threshold amount, 3
Ministry of Islamic Affairs and Awqaf, 88
Ministry of Justice and Islamic Affairs, 88
misappropriation, 223
miskins, 2, 118
Mobile USSD/WAP/apps/digital wallets, 186
monthly salary, 80–81
moral economy, 3, 104
Morocco, 155
mosque, 2
Mozambique, 157
muallafat-ul-qulub, 2
Muallaf/revert, 120–121
mujahid, 125
multilateral agencies, 201
multilateral development agencies, 201
Muslim, 115, 145
  countries, 26
  majority, 201
  societies, 10, 21
  wealth, 50
  Ummah, 25
mustahik, 32, 106–107, 109, 117
muzaki, 99, 106, 108
muzaki/zakat, 102
muzaki/zakat giver, 97

N

National Amil Zakat Agency, 29
national defense, 51
National Zakat Foundation Worldwide (NZFW), 139–141, 146
natural springs, 138
needs, 126
needy, 2, 7, 23, 127
Negeri Sembilan, 28
net asset method, 138, 142–143
net invested funds, 138
net invested funds method, 142
Nigeria, 38–39, 157, 159
nisab, 2, 24, 52, 99, 105, 116, 138
nisab level, 144
non-Muslims, 97
non-trading investments, 143
not-for-profit, 139

O

obligation, 1
obligatory financial duty, 105
Oman, 88
one year, 99
orphanage, 39

P

Pakistan, 155, 158
peace and justice in societies, 173
penalties, 202
Penang, 27
perfect ownership, 98
Perlis Islamic Religious Council and Malay Customs, 209
plants, 99
poor, 2, 7, 52, 68, 105, 115, 127
poverty, 10, 115, 117, 172, 201
poverty alleviation program, 107
poverty eradication, 174
precious metals, 138

prisoner, 123
procedure, 97
productive programs, 27
profit, 38
prosperity, 9
punishment, 77
Pusat Pungutan Zakat, 147

Q

Qatar, 156
quality of life, 27

R

rain, 138
Ramadhan, 100
rate, 137
real estate, 80
receiver, 10
recipients, 10
redistribution of wealth, 22, 172
reducing inequality, 173
reducing poverty, 13
refugee, 176
registration, 205
regulators, 139
relatives, 127
religious, 21
religious philanthropy, 173
rent, 80
rented buildings, 80
resilient industry and infrastructures, 173
responsible consumption, 173
revenue, 50
reverting to Islam, *see also* muallafat-ul-qulub, 7
riba/interest, 10, 21–23, 39, 122–123
rice ATM, 188
rich, 115
rich people, 41
rikaz, 78
Rio de Janeiro, 171

riqab, 122
Robo officer/Chatbot, 188
Rumah Sehat Terpadu Dompet Dhuafa, 31
rural mustahic entrepreneurship, 119

S
sadaqat, 6, 49, 55
salah, 103
Salam Tani, 37
salary deduction, 41
sale, 79
Saudi Arabia, 155, 158
savings, 100
scholarship, 34
SDG strategies, 178
security risk, 192
self-independent institutions, 157
shares, 83
Shariah, 101
Shariah governance, 191
Shariah p2p fintech, 177
silver, 4, 73, 136
Singapore, 227
slaves, 122
SME projects, 40
social and economic investments, 173
social justice, 115
social obligations, 21
social service, 4
society, 153
socio-financial products, 22, 115–116, 119, 125
socio-financial tools, 21, 50
solvent, 145
Somalia, 37–38
Somaliland, 39
South Africa, 158
spiritual and material purification, 21
spiritual purification, 21
standards and guiding principles, 139
staple food, 38, 70

State Islamic Religious Councils (SIRCs), 162
State Islamic Religious Council of Perlis, 85
statistical data, 88
stock, 84, 99
Sudan, 158
sukuk, 83
supervision, 153
supply of goods, 54
Supporting education, 34
Surabaya, 35
Surah al-Taubah, 8
sustainable cities/human communities, 173
sustainable development goals (SDGs), 171
Sustainable Livelihood Impact Assessment, 36

T
tax, 9, 49, 68, 145, 202
taxation, 145
tax system, 50
tazkiyah, 103
technical assistance, 178
technological advancement, 82
technology, 183
technology-driven innovations, 183
terrestrial life/ecosystem, 174
the Wayfarer, 8
third pillar, 1
trade, 79
transparency, 222
travelers, 126

U
UAE, 88, 156
unfair distribution of wealth, 173
UNHCR Refugee Zakat Fund, 212
UNHCR's Refugee Zakat, 38, 176
United Nations, 171

Universiti Utara Malaysia, 28
Universiti Teknologi Malaysia, 29
untapped potential, 172

V
victims, 123
virtual assistants, 100
voluntary, 86
volunteers, 128, 201

W
waqf, 49, 60, 137, 158
wealth, 1, 22, 56, 100, 104, 115, 118, 135, 172
wealth redistribution, 4
web-based applications, 186
web-based payment, 213
welfare, 115
welfare of poor, 33
West Sumatra, 118
women, 38
World Bank, 40
worship, 97, 103

Y
Yemen, 156, 158

Z
zakat, 1, 21, 49, 55, 75, 67, 97, 153, 171–172, 221
zakatability, 84
zakatable assets, 52, 80, 99
zakatable wealth, 12, 22, 26, 67, 72, 74, 88, 135–136
zakat
　administration, 153, 156–157, 162, 183, 219
　administrative services, 156
　administrator, 159
　agencies, 159
　agent, 26

al-fitr, 4, 67–68
al-mal, 136
assets, 123
base, 138, 143, 145
calculation, 82, 142, 146
calculator, 100
campaign, 103
collecting institutions, 220
collection, 88
counter, 102
distribution, 109, 162, 205
Zakat Distribution Management Manual, 161
zakat due, 144
zakat fitrah, 58
Zakat Foundation of America, 147
zakat fund, 22, 28, 88, 117, 120, 122, 201, 222
zakat giver, 98, 101–102, 117, 127
zakat grants, 203
Zakat Law, 82
zakat
　management, 22, 50, 115, 199
　management administration, 204
　management programs, 199
　managers, 7, 23
　obligation, 102
　on wealth, 68
　organizations, 100, 106–107, 153, 160
　payers, 9, 163, 221
　payment, 105
　portion, 13
　programs, 118, 122, 200, 202, 205
　rate, 138
　receiver, 9, 117
　recipients, 23, 86, 108, 165
　system, 153
　ul-Fitr, 100
　year, 137

Printed in the USA
CPSIA information can be obtained
at www.ICGtesting.com
LVHW050710010324
773095LV00001B/1